D1637284

# THE

# MYSTERY

## OF THE

# CHRISTOS

## By CORINNE HELINE

NEW AGE PRESS, INC.
3912 Wilshire Blvd.
Los Angeles, CA 90010

*Grateful acknowledgement is hereby extended to
Elizabeth Hill and Ann Barkhurst
for invaluable editorial and proofreading assistance
in the preparation of this publication;
also to Frances Paelian
for her illustrative art work.*

IN

# DEDICATION

TO THOSE WHO HAVE GLIMPSED
THAT CROSS OF LIGHT WHEREBY
THE BLOOD ESSENCE IS TRANS~
FORMED INTO A FRAGRANCE AS
OF FLOWERS
AND THE
VIA
DOLOROSA
BECOMES
THE
HIGHWAY
OF THE
KING

MY YOKE IS EASY AND MY BURDEN IS LIGHT

This volume, which may be considered the seventh in the series on New Age Bible Interpretations, together with the six volumes previously published, are humbly and gratefully dedicated first and foremost to

My Reverend Teacher and Beloved Friend
MAX HEINDEL

whose encouragement in undertaking this work and whose inspiration and assistance in pursuing it have been incalculable.

# TABLE OF CONTENTS

## PART I

### THE HOLY CHRISTMAS MYSTERIES

**CHAPTER I**

**CHAPTER II**

**CHAPTER III**

# PART II

## THE HOLY EASTER MYSTERIES

# PART III

## THE PATH OF HOLINESS or THE WAY TO CHRIST

# PART IV

## FURTHER ELUCIDATION OF THE MYSTERY OF THE CHRISTOS

### CHRIST IN THE OLD TESTAMENT

### THE CHRIST IN HIS SEVERAL ASPECTS
#### COSMIC—PLANETARY—HISTORICAL—MYSTICAL

### CHAPTER XXXIX
#### SEVEN KEYS TO THE CHRIST MYSTERY

# PART V

## THE CYCLE OF THE YEAR WITH CHRIST

### CHAPTER XL

*The story of the Sun God and the story of the Son of God are one and the same.*

—Lyman E. Stowe

# PREFATORY NOTE

It has been stated repeatedly throughout the *New Age Bible Interpretation* series that the principal events in the life of Christ do not refer exclusively to His personal experiences. They also represent certain initiatory steps taken by every aspirant at some time during the course of his becoming Christed.

It is the intent of this volume to deal with the Christ in His several aspects: cosmic, planetary, historical, and mystical. In these various treatments references are made to the foremost events between the Annunciation and the Ascension, since each one has a specific meaning relative to progressive attainment in these different phases of spiritual unfoldment. Recurrent interpretations of these events are not repetitions of what has gone before. Instead, they are elucidations from the various points of view and in connection with different contexts.

When man walks the highway of spiritual unfoldment he arrives ultimately to a state of divine atonement; that is to say, he becomes a Christed individual. Such is the exalted destiny in store for humanity as a whole.

# The Holy Family
# A Cosmic Glyph

FRANCES PAELIAN

# MYSTERY OF THE CHRISTOS

# The Christmas Story

And there were in the same country shepherds abiding in the field, keeping watch over their flock by night,

And Lo, the angel of the Lord came upon them, and the glory of the Lord shone round about them and they were sore afraid.

And the angel said unto them, Fear not for behold, I bring you good tidings of great joy, which shall be to all people,

For unto you is born this day in the city of David a Saviour, which is Christ the Lord.

And this shall be a sign unto you; ye shall find the babe wrapped in swaddling clothes, lying in a manger.

And suddenly there was with the angel a multitude of the heavenly host praising God, and saying:

Glory to God in the highest, and on earth peace, goodwill toward men.

*Luke 2:8-14*

# PART I

# The Holy Christmas Mysteries

## CHAPTER I

### SPIRITUAL SIGNIFICANCE OF THE ADVENT SEASON

Advent Season is known as the time of purification and preparation. It is the season when an aspirant seeks to attune himself more fully to the joys of the coming Christmastide. If he knows something of the significance of the mystic Christian Initiation he enters with much deeper understanding into the disciplines of the Advent Season.

Early disciples of the Lord Christ observed this as a period for receiving fresh revelation from on high, and as especially favoring their own spiritual development. Definite preparation was made for what they hoped to receive when Advent reached its climaxing hour on Holy Night.

In harmony with zodiacal influences, Advent occurs when the Sun is passing through the sign Sagittarius. This is the sign of true soul ecstasy and seership. Early mystic devotees frequently referred to the Sagittarian period as the Feast of Light, as it is the time when the radiance of the Christ light most completely permeates the earth.

1

Advent usually begins with the last Sunday in November and culminates in the golden glory of the Winter Solstice. For an esoteric Christian it embraces three steps or Degrees which reach their fruition at midnight on Holy Night. This period of preparation and advancement refers not only to the four weeks of Advent, but also to definite stages of spiritual unfoldment correlated to those four weeks.

During the week following the first Sunday of Advent the work is that of the First or Preparatory Degree. This is also designated as the Degree of the Annunciation. The Blessed Virgin Mary was the first of our humanity to attain the power invested by this Degree in any who merit it—a fact understood by those of the early Christian Church, which is one reason why Mary occupies such an important place in meditations and ceremonials related to Advent.

The Degree of Annunciation is related primarily to the cultivation of purity. Average students have but slight realization of the significance of this quality as one of the most important aspects of spiritual development. They do not recognize that purity, far from being a static condition, is a dynamic power in the life of an aspirant. The Lord Christ made this emphatically clear when He said "Blessed are the pure in heart: for they shall see God." Initiates of the ancient Mystery Schools were given long probationary periods in which to cultivate purity of mind, soul and body—for it must condition the whole of man's being, embracing his every thought, word and deed.

The foregoing explains why the Degree of Annunciation is likewise termed the Degree of Purity.

One of the initial steps in the purification of man's physical and desire bodies has to do with food. No sincere aspirant can condone the sacrifice of younger brothers of the animal kingdom to gratify his bodily appetites and comfort. With the elimination of flesh food comes sensitization of the physical vehicle. This results in greater receptivity to soul impressions and spiritual ideation. Hence there comes a time when aspirants on the Path will nourish their bodies on the fruits of the earth only, such as nature has provided in abundance.

As progress is made toward attaining the Degree of Purity or Annunciation, an aspirant discovers within himself increasing power to overcome negative and destructive thoughts and emotions; and as these are mastered, his consciousness becomes centered on the good, the true and the beautiful. This Degree found perfect expression in the Divine Mary. Her life was as pure and fragrant as a lily. Contemplation of her life, therefore, is of primary value in the cultivation of purity, the first step on the Path of Attainment.

The important place held by Mary in connection with Advent disciplines does not cease with the first week. It continues with ever deepening significance throughout the rest of the period.

With the development of purity the higher faculties of other centers are gradually unfolded. As these come into activity they give ability to perceive celestial realms and their glorious Beings. It was after Mary had developed powers belonging to the Degree of Annunciation that she became aware of the ever present companionship of Angels. So very close was her association with those of the angelic kingdom that she was known to early Christians as the Queen of Angels and of Men.

The Second Degree is, of course, assigned to the second week of Advent. This is the Degree of the Immaculate Conception. Here again the Virgin Mary emerges as the supreme embodiment of this sublime attainment. It is during this period that Mary, attended by hosts of Angels, comes close to earth to bestow her blessing upon all mankind. Her chant to the world, "I am the Immaculate Conception," carries the promise of an attainment that all aspirants one day will acquire. When the Second Degree is passed, disease is no more and mortal man puts on immortality. While passing through this Degree Mary became the preeminent type-pattern for the Immaculate Conception. Herein is found the reason why one branch of the Christian Church declares that even the physical body of Mary was translated to celestial realms in all the beauty and purity to which she had attained while in her earthly state. When humanity as a whole reaches this exalted level of development, there will be no more disease, deformities and maladjustments so common to the race today; and man will realize that he was, in very truth, created in the image and likeness of God. Mary read the record of what was to come in future ages and realized that she herself was to serve as the type-pattern of that Immaculate Conception which all mankind was to demonstrate eventually— when, in her own words, all the world would rise up and call her blessed.

The Third Degree, assigned to the final two weeks of Advent, is the Degree of the Holy Birth. Herein we approach the very heart of the Christian Mysteries. The Lord Christ came as the Supreme Way-shower. That to which He attained must someday be attained by all humanity. As Angelus Silesius, the German mystic, ex-pressed it: "Though Christ in Bethlehem a thousand times be born, and not within thyself, thy soul will be forlorn."

As previously observed, the Christ Child was born in a manger, where beasts feed, because there was no room in the inn. This fact conceals one of the innermost secrets of the Christian Mysteries. The crib scene of the Nativity symbolizes the birth of the Christ in man. It is not until after the Degree of Purification that the Holy Babe can be lifted from the manger (lower nature) to find his rightful place in the inn (head center or higher nature). The alchemical action of this process consists in raising the spinal spirit fire from the base of the spine upward to the heart (Jerusalem, the city of peace), and from there to the head (Bethlehem, the house of bread). In the crib scene Mary and Joseph are usually represented as kneeling in adoration on either side of an Angel. They thus typify the awakened and illumined masculine and feminine forces in harmonious interaction. As these forces are interwoven they vivify the head centers situated in the positively charged pineal gland and the femininely charged pituitary body. The result of this interaction is spiritual illumination. The third ventricle in the brain, which connects the two glands, then becomes the manger in which the Christ Child is born and now rests. Room has been made for Him in the inn. His aura so fills the entire body that it becomes a veritable temple of light. This Christing of an aspirant is the triumphant consummation of the quest and the culmination of the evolutionary process belonging to the present Earth Period.

The shepherds in the field and the Wise Men who came to worship the Christ Child are an important part of the spiritual processes portrayed in the Advent Season. The Bible relates that the shepherds were watching their flocks by night when Angels appeared and directed them to follow the Star that would lead them to Bethlehem. The shepherds are the aspirants or neophytes who have passed the Degree of Purification, and so have come into communion with Beings of celestial realms who tell them to follow the Star, their own higher selves, to the place of the Holy Birth.

The Wise Men from the East also followed the Star, bringing with them rare and precious gifts to lay at the feet of the Christ Child. These Wise Men represent disciples who have passed both the First and Second Degrees of the Christ Mysteries. They come, therefore, with their shining gifts, symbolical of the sublimated essence of the physical body which, added to the spiritualized forces of the etheric sheath, the purified desire body, and the spiritualized mind, creates their radiant body light. This is the ''golden wedding garment'' with which each disciple must be clothed before he can enter into the presence of the Christ. The golden vase of perfume which Mary Magdalene laid at the Master's feet has a like meaning.

Every aspirant who treads the Path of the Christian Mysteries learns to follow the glorious star of his own higher nature, which ever guides him along the way that leads to Jerusalem and then on to Bethlehem.

As already said, Advent Season reaches its climax on Holy Night of the Winter Solstice. A seed thought for meditation at that time is the ideal of emulating the Wise Men who followed the Star that leads to the Christ Child.

# CHAPTER II

## THE COSMIC NATIVITY SONG

The Earth Initiation whereby man learns the supreme Rite of Purification, or the conquest of spirit over matter, constitutes a part of the mystic ceremonial of the Winter Solstice season. For the Initiate, the Nativity means the overcoming of the last enemy, death, and birth into the glory of immortal life.

Those who attain to this sublime experience are eligible to take part with others of like Illumination in spiritualizing the atoms of this earth planet. This work also constitutes a part of the Winter Solstice ceremonial.

This spiritualizing process is accomplished largely by means of sound. The Christ Himself through His mighty intonation gives the keynote of the Great Work. This intonation corresponds to the *Word* of St. John's Gospel by which all things were made. In other words, it was the initial musical tone sounded forth by the great Sun Spirit, the Christ, that built all the worlds of the solar system to which this earth planet belongs. Thus He becomes truly the Lord and Saviour of this earth before whom every knee must bow. His keynote it was that fashioned our planetary scheme, so consequently our evolutionary life is attuned to His Being in the most intimate sense. In Him we literally live and move and have our being.

The four Sacred Seasons accentuate this planetary song. The tones of the Spring Equinox and the Summer Solstice are outbreathing in their action; they are radiating and building in quality. The tones of the Autumn Equinox and the Winter Solstice are inbreathing in this action; they are sustaining and enfolding. It is from the very innermost heart of the earth that the Christ note emanates the holy season of the Winter Solstice.

The powerful intonation or Word sounded cosmically at this season lifts and harmonizes every atom of the planet and is accompanied by such a mightly outburst of light that all the world is enfolded in a divine radiance such as never yet lay on land or sea.

Multitudinous Hosts of higher Celestials unite with resplendent arrays of Angels and Archangels in this majestic chorus with our Lord until every animate thing, every tree of the forests and every minute growing plant sways and bends with the high ecstasy of music and light. Numerous and exquisite legends abound relative to the influence of the spiritual forces on the animal kingdom during this most gracious time. These legends all have their basis in fact, as animals are extremely sensitive to inner plane activities.

It is during the Winter Solstice season that down through the ages, the Temple doors swing wide and those who aspire to come into atonement with the Great Light of the world enter therein. To focus consciousness so completely in life that there can be no negative reaction, and to so harmonize every body-atom with the rhythms of the Christ Song so that the spirit responds only to the high, the beautiful and the true is the requirement essential for this entrance.

As the victorious one becomes increasingly absorbed in the Light Eternal, he begins to discern something of the words of the planetary song and listens to the supreme musical mantram to which this earth planet is attuned. This song is translated for human hearing in the words: "I am the way, the truth, and the life."

During the Christmas Season this supreme chant is lifted up into the starry spaces by innumerable Hosts where their triumphant choral is augmented by the voices of those belonging to our human life-wave who have attained unto this exalted state of consciousness.

The last enemy to be overcome is death. This has always been a Temple teaching and is the goal of man's highest quest in the Initiation of the Winter Solstice. From the aureole of His transcendant glory, the Master, who is our divine life pattern, bends low above us in this hallowed time and beckons us forward upon that illumined way, as all the earth becomes resonant with the vast re-echoing music of His words that we shall hear when we have made this high attainment our own: "Well done, thou good and faithful servant . . . enter thou into the joy of the Lord."

# CHAPTER III

## THE TWELVE HOLY DAYS

### *Foreword*

A belief commonly prevails that December 25th, celebrated as Christmas, brings to a close the spiritual festival of the mid-winter solstitial season. This is not true. It only marks the beginning or the entrance upon a period of deep significance. That period is the twelve-day interval between Christmas and Twelfth Night, days which embrace the spiritual heart of the year to follow. These twelve days have been very aptly termed the year's Holy of Holies.

This work is designed for serious students of the Christian Mysteries, to assist them in placing themselves in more complete attunement with the twelve zodiacal forces released upon the earth during this time.

Everyone of the twelve Holy Days is under the direct supervision of one of the twelve zodiacal Hierarchies, each one of which projects over the planet a cosmic pattern of the world as it will be when the combined work of the Hierarchies has been completed. Also, the twelve Disciples are correlated with these twelve Holy Days, as are the twelve spiritual centers through which the twelve forces operate in man's body-temple.

Every earnest student will, therefore, make use of this sacred period for visualizing the perfected work of the Hierarchies, in meditation upon the life and work of the Disciples, and in directing the spiritual radiations from the Hierarchies through the inner centers in his body to which they are attuned. If he is faithful and persists year after year in this high endeavor, he cannot fail to receive compensation in the form of great spiritual unfoldment.

From the time of the Winter Solstice when the Christ light enters the heart of earth, the planet is swept by powerful solstitial radiations which continue, though somewhat abated, throughout the twelve Holy Days. Many and wondrous are the inner plane activities during this time. The early Christian Church concluded its esoteric ministry on the mystical Twelfth Night with the Rite of Baptism, one of its highest Initiations. Modern neophytes who have earned illumination know that it is then possible to enter into communion with divine Beings and the Lord of Light. It was such an experience that inspired St. John's Gospel, frequently designated the "Gospel of Love."

In the outer darkness of the present historical era man has largely lost contact with the Christ light and these days of spirit-renewing. By the travail of soul through which he is now passing, he is destined to find them again and to make them a vital part of his daily life and his yearly consecration. May this work serve him to that end.

### ARIES

On December 26th dedication is made to the Hierarchy of Aries, the Hierarchy which sets the cosmic pattern for life during the month that the Sun is transiting the sign Aries. From March 20th to April 21st Aries holds the archetypal pattern of a perfected earth above the world. This is the new heaven and the new earth envisioned by St. John and recorded in his sublime *Revelation*.

According to all sacred calendars Aries introduces the solar New Year. Therefore it is termed the sign of resurrected consciousness. One who has attained this consciousness sees and knows only the divine in all persons, things, circumstances, conditions and events. *Seeing the Godward side* is the motif of dedication throughout the Aries period.

The Disciple correlated with Aries is James, brother of John. He was the first to answer the call of discipleship and the first to walk the path of martyrdom, a true spiritual pioneer. During the month of Aries an aspirant should study the life of James and endeavor to emulate his virtues.

The body center related to Aries is the head, and the Hierarchy projects the pattern of the human head in all its divine and wondrous perfection. A student is urged to visualize the head with its spiritual organs awakened and illumined, and all its functions in full maturity.

The biblical seed thought for meditation on both December 26 and during the solar month of April (March 20th to April 21st) is the quotation:

*Behold, I make all things new. —Rev.* 21:5

Aspirants are admonished to meditate upon the inner meanings of the above passage while the vibratory rhythms of Aries are permeating the earth.

### Taurus

Dedication for December 27th and through the solar month of May, April 21st to May 22nd, is to the Hierarchy of Taurus. This is the Hierarchy presiding over the realm of cosmic archetypes and the pattern it holds above the earth is that of perfected forms. Love and harmony are the forces that it continually pours out upon our planet.

The Disciple correlating with Taurus is Andrew, whose distinguishing characteristic is humility. This is one of the most important attributes to be cultivated by every aspirant. When developed to a certain high degree it becomes a tremendous soul power.

The throat is the body center ruled by Taurus. In New Age bodies the throat will be a luminous center from which the divine Creative Word is sent forth.

Dedication for December 27th and the solar month of May consists in making oneself a more perfect channel for the reception and dissemination of love and harmony in all the varied experiences of life, be they joyful or sorrowful, exalting or depressing.

The biblical seed thought for meditation on the second of the Twelve Holy Days and its correlated month is:

*He that dwelleth in love dwelleth in God.*
                                              —I John 4:16

Aspirants are urged to meditate upon the deep significance of the above passage during the entire period that the vibratory rhythms of Taurus are permeating the earth sphere.

## GEMINI

The dedication for December 28th and through the solar month of June is to the Hierarchy of Gemini. The cosmic pattern held by this Hierarchy for the earth is that of great peace, the peace which passeth all understanding and which will be the heritage of the coming Christed race.

Characteristics to be cultivated during the Gemini period are such peace and poise as St. Paul had attained that enabled him to say, "None of these things [of the outer world] move me." And thus sings the psalmist of the highest Gemini attributes: "He maketh me to lie down in green pastures: he leadeth me beside the still waters."

Gemini rules the hands. These are to be visualized as flower centers, fragrant, luminous and endowed with the precious gifts of healing and of bestowing benediction.

The Disciple correlated with Gemini is Thomas. So intimately did he become identified with the Christ that his doubts, natural to the mortal mind, were transcended by a dynamic realization of the Christed powers previously latent within himself. Many and wondrous were the miracles he performed following this transformation.

The biblical seed thought for meditation on December 28th and during the solar month of June, May 22nd the June 22nd, is:

*Be still, and know that I am God.* —Psalm 46:10

Aspirants are instructed to meditate upon the deepest meanings of this passage during the whole period that the vibratory rhythms of Gemini permeate the earth planet.

## CANCER

December 29th and the solar month of July, June 22nd–July 23rd, are dedicated to the Hierarchy of Cancer, which holds for earth the cosmic pattern of exaltation of the divine feminine principle in all creations. This sign is the home of the glorious World Mother, a high Initiate of the Cancer Hierarchy. This Being, and the principle for which she stands, are recognized and defied in all great world religions.

Aries deals with *life;* Taurus with *form;* Gemini with *mind;* Cancer with *soul*—soul as the revealer of truth. Consequently, dedication for the Cancer month is devotion to a quest for the light never yet seen on land or sea.

Nathaniel is the Disciple correlated with Cancer. He is a mystic in whom there is no guile.

The body center governed by Cancer is the solar plexus, sometimes referred to as "the sun of the stomach." In pre-Christian days this center was considered a most important one in relation to initiatory development. And in the new Christed race the solar plexus will again be linked with spirit, for the sympathetic nervous system will be transformed into the feminine column of the human body-temple.

For December 29th and during the solar month of July this is the biblical seed thought assigned for meditation:

> *But if we walk in the light, as he is in the light, we have fellowship one with another.* — I John 1:7

Aspirants who faithfully meditate upon the real significance of this passage while the vibratory rhythms of Cancer pervade our sphere will be rewarded by knowing such fellowship.

## LEO

December 30th and the solar month of August, July 23rd–August 24th, are dedicated to the Hierarchy of Leo. The cosmic pattern held by this host of celestial Beings is that the earth will be permeated by the power of love, even as divine wisdom is interwoven into the entire fabric of nature, while this Hierarchy holds sway above our planet. All activities should be motivated by this power. Every thought should be radiant with love; every word vibrant with love; every deed embellished by love.

Judas is the Disciple correlated with Leo. Herein is indicated the great transforming power of love.

An intimate relationship exists between Judas and John. Judas typifies personality; John, the spirit. A deep significance is attached to the fact that Judas, after betraying the Christ, took his own life. Personality must always wane that spirit may wax strong. St. Paul admonishes aspirants to the Christed Way to put off the old man and put on the new.

As personality becomes subordinated to the spirit, man's lower love nature—concerned entirely with the personal life that is transient and must, therefore, die as did Judas—is superseded by that higher love nature evidenced by John the Beloved, the Disciple who never knew death and who was closest of the Immortal Twelve to the heart of the Master.

The body center correlated with Leo is the heart. As this center unfolds its divine latencies it will become more and more powerful and luminous, until its radiance is that of "the day star which shines unto the perfect day."

And love is the subject of the biblical seed thought for meditation on December 30th and all through the solar month of August:

*Love is the fulfilling of the law.*—Romans 13:10

Every aspirant should concentrate on the innermost import of this passage while the vibratory rhythms of Leo are permeating the earth.

### VIRGO

Dedication for December 31st and the solar month of September, August 24th–September 23rd, is to the Hierarchy of Virgo. Leo's *love* leads to Virgo's *service*.

That divine Being whom we know as the World Mother is the prototype for the Madonnas of all great religions; she is the teacher of these high feminine Initiates at certain stages of their development.

During the time that Virgo's ray permeates our sphere this Hierarchy holds high above the planet the cosmic pattern of a cleansed and rejuvenated earth. At a certain point in human attainment purity becomes a tremendous soul power—a verity stressed by the Lord Christ when He said, "The pure in heart shall see God."

The Disciple who correlates with the sign Virgo is James the Just, brother of Jude and Simon. For many years he was revered as the head of the early Church in Jerusalem, and was well known for his purity of character and consecration to selfless service.

The intestinal tract is the physical center of man's body-temple correlating with Virgo. Let the aspirant visualize that tract as manifesting perfection in its every function.

From the Gospel of Matthew—Chapter 23, Verse 11—comes the biblical seed thought for December 31st and the solar month of Virgo:

*But he that is greatest among you shall be your servant.*

Those aspiring to spiritual unfoldment are urged to meditate upon the deep significance of this magnificent passage so long as the vibratory rhythms of the Virgo Hierarchy are permeating this planet.


LIBRA

Dedication for January 1st and the solar month of October, September 23rd–October 24th, is to the Hierarchy of Libra. The cosmic pattern held by this Hierarchy is *the world beautiful*. Its imprint is to be seen in every landscape, every tree, shrub and plant, every form in the various kingdoms of nature. Beauty and harmony are Libra's signatures. Hence, whatsoever comes under the influence of this celestial sign will express these divine attributes. When humanity receives more fully its influence, poverty, disease, discord and pain will be abolished.

The Disciple correlating with Libra is Jude. This disciple was a minister of the beautiful. Many and far-reaching in results were the works he performed as its devotee.

The human body center correlating with Libra is to be found in the adrenal glands. These glands, when functioning properly, create absolute physical and psychological balance through each organ and its processes.

Meditation for the first of January and the solar month of October is on the biblical seed thought of John 8: 32:
*Ye shall know the truth, and the truth shall make you free.*

Great are the inner meanings of this passage. An aspirant should meditate upon them on January 1st and every day that the vibratory rhythms of Libra are focused upon the earth.

### SCORPIO

For January 2nd and the solar month of November, October 24th–November 23rd, dedication is to the Hierarchy of Scorpio. The cosmic pattern which this Hierarchy is working to establish on earth is *attainment through transmutation of matter into spirit.* By this process the sublimated essences of mind and body become

John the Beloved is the Disciple who correlates with Scorpio. Transmutation was the keynote of his life. He progressed so far in the divine science of transmuting matter into spirit that he never knew death.

The physical center correlating with Scorpio is the generative system. In an earnest aspirant this becomes the center of transmutation. As previously mentioned, there is a close relationship between Judas (personality) and John (spirit). Judas must die that John may reign supreme.

There is also a strong connection between the heart (Leo) and the generative system (Scorpio). So long as personality dominates, the former is under the control of the latter. When personality has been exalted into spiritualized individuality it is the heart that rules. In the body of Christed man human passion has been transmuted into divine love.

*Blessed are the pure in heart: for they shall see God.* —Matt. 5: 8

This is the biblical seed thought for meditation on January 2nd and during the solar month of November. It is urged that the aspirant concentrate upon its deep significance on the second day of each new year and while the vibratory rhythms of Scorpio flood the earth.

## SAGITTARIUS

Dedication on January 3rd and during the solar month of December, November 23rd–December 22nd, is to the Hierarchy of Sagittarius, the Lords of Mind. The cosmic pattern held by these glorious Beings is of earth as a vast altar-piece made radiant by the golden aura of the supreme Light of the World.

The Disciple Philip correlates to Sagittarius. Before he found the Lord he had no concept of what a spiritualized, or Christed mind would mean in his life. He was essentially a mentalist. But after the Christ light was shed upon him he became worthy to be numbered among the Immortal Twelve.

Sagittarius operates through the sacral plexus, the body center located at the base of the spine. The spinal cord, which connects the sacral plexus with the brain, has been termed "the Path of Discipleship." When an aspirant lives a life motivated solely by pure and holy aspiration, the spinal spirit-fire coiled within the sacral plexus awakens and then ascends through the spinal cord to the two spiritual organs located in the head, the pineal gland and the pituitary body. It is by this process that a man's mind becomes Christed. Hence, Sagittarius is always symbolized by light, the light of spiritualized mind.

When rightly appropriated and transmuted into soul values, the experiences of daily life become stepping-stones by which an aspirant attains to atonement with the universal Divine Light, the Light that lighteth every man who cometh into the world. It was to such that the Master was speaking when He said:

*Ye are the light of the world.* —Matt. 5: 14

This is the biblical seed thought for January 3rd and throughout the time that the Hierarchy of Sagittarius pours its vibratory rhythms upon the earth. Untold blessings await those who meditate upon its promise.

## CAPRICORN

Dedication for January 4th and the solar month of January, December 22nd–January 20th, is to the Hierarchy of Capricorn. These are the archangelic Beings of whom Christ is the head, and from them comes the wondrous power whereby mortal man can be lifted into His likeness. It is also the sign of world Avatars.

The cosmic pattern held by the Hierarchy of Capricorn envisions the magnificent scope of life when the Christ spirit manifests in all mankind. Then it is that our planet will respond to its own musical keynote, first sounded by Angels and Archangels on that long ago Holy Night when they sang "On earth peace, good will toward men."

The Disciple correlating with Capricorn is Simon, brother of James and Jude. Although Simon was close to his Lord by family ties, he was most reluctant about accepting the divinity of the Master. But when he was finally awakened by the Christ his dedication was complete. His one desire was to serve the Lord, and neither life nor death had any meaning for him apart from this ideal.

The dual body center correlating with the sign Capricorn is located in the knees. In Christed man these points will become glorious whirling vortices of light.

Galatians 4:19 gives the biblical seed thought for meditation on January 4th and during the solar month of January:

*Let the Christ be formed in you.*

Aspirants should meditate upon the above passage until its inner purport falls into harmony with the vibratory rhythms to which the Hierarchy of Capricorn is attuning the earth.

### AQUARIUS

Dedication on January 5th and throughout the solar month of February, January 20th–February 19th, is upon the Hierarchy of Aquarius. During these two periods this Hierarchy holds above the earth a cosmic pattern embodying the ideals of the Fatherhood of God and the brotherhood of man, the foundation for a type of friendship that is destined to expand until it becomes all inclusive and world embracing. This ideal should be held in the soul's Holy of Holies and never marred or desecrated by an unworthy thought, word or deed. Working to bring it into manifestation is the mission of Aquarius, the divine water-bearer of the skies.

Through the benign influence of the Aquarian Hierarchy love

will become the motivating force in all that lives. In that glad day an emancipated humanity will show forth, as St. Paul prophesied, love as the fulfilling of the law. In other words, every law will be founded upon love and love, in turn, will bring the fulfillment of every law.

Aquarius is the home of Angels, and the above aptly describes the joyous life of these celestial Beings.

The Disciple correlating with Aquarius is Matthew, the rich publican and sinner who, when he heard the voice of the Lord, left all and followed Him gladly. He renounced all worldly possessions for which he later received rare compensation in the form of a spiritual realization which found expression in the immortal Gospel bearing his name—a priceless heritage to all mankind.

The two lower limbs form the dual body organs correlating with Aquarius. They are the two columns of man's body temple and should be visualized as coordinated in motion and symmetrical in form.

The biblical seed thought for meditation on January 5th and during the solar month of February is John 15:4.

*Ye are my friends.*

If an aspirant will concentrate upon the subtle meanings hidden in these four short words, and keep them alive in consciousness while the Aquarian rhythms vibrate above and through earth, great will be his illumination.

PISCES

The dedication for January 6th and the solar month of March, February 19th–March 20th, is to the Hierarchy of Pisces. This Hierarchy works to bring into manifestation the principle of unification throughout all creation. Ralph Waldo Emerson gave a perfect Piscean inscription: "The Imperfect adores my own Perfect. Life is no longer a thing of shreds and patches, but a glorious divine unity."

Pisces is the last sign before the birth of the spiritual new year, a period of recapitulation and self-examination. It marks the sunset of a past life and the sunrise of a new life.

The cosmic pattern held above the earth by this Hierarchy is one of perfected man, created in the image and likeness of God and manifesting the divine within himself. *Godlike Man* is the keynote of Pisces, as it is also the cosmic pattern of Aries. In fact, the perfecting of man is and has been the divine labor of all twelve creative Hierarchies since the beginning of human evolution. When it comes to its ultimate completion it will be under the ministry of the Piscean Hierarchy.

Peter is the Disciple who correlates with Pisces—Peter the unstable, the "wave" man who, after he had awakened the Christ principle within himself through his faith, became the Rock of Initiation on which the church was founded.

The dual body center correlating with Pisces is the feet, and in the human race at large this center is yet to be awakened. In the vision of Fatima the children described particularly the beautiful roses blooming upon the hands and feet of the Blessed Lady.

This body made in the image and likeness of God will be luminous with scintillating stars, or flowers, awakened within its vital centers. This glorified body is the golden wedding garment described by St. Paul as the glorified celestial body. It was his vision of this luminous vehicle in the Memory of Nature which inspired him to declare in exaltation: that man is "little lower than the angels"; and it doth not yet appear what he shall be.

For meditation on January 6th while the vibratory rhythms of Pisces pervade the earth, and during the solar month of March, the following biblical seed thought is assigned:

*So God created man in his own image.* Gen. 1:27.

During the twelve Holy Days between Christmas and Twelfth Night the earth is enveloped by the light of the archangelic Christ. The fragrance of His transcendent aura permeates the planet with a rare perfume, like an intermingling of the breath of fairest roses and purest lilies. But the radiant light and healing fragrance are gradually absorbed by the earth during this sacred interval, making it an ideal time for soul dedication to the Path of Holiness.

# CHAPTER IV

The Feast of Epiphany marks the culmination of the twelve Holy Days. It is observed on the final day, January 6th, and commemorates the coming of the Three Wise Men to lay their three gifts at the feet of the Christ Child.

The events in the life of the Christ represent successive steps on the Way of Attainment for a Christian disciple. The Three Wise Men typify body, soul and spirit; their gifts, supreme dedication to the Master. Myrrh stands for the bitterness of pain and sorrow before the lower nature of the aspirant has been transformed; frankincense, the way of transmutation; gold, the spirit which refines the lower nature and eventually brings it into subjection.

Epiphany is a Greek word meaning *to manifest, to show forth*. The Feast of Epiphany is a preparation for the manifestation or showing forth of Christed man. It is of such spiritual potency that its influence extends over a period of four weeks.

## *First Week—Prayer and Meditation*

The first week is given entirely to preparation for disciplines to follow. Its keynotes are *prayer* and *meditation,* and the work extends from January 6th through January 12th. St. Paul admonished his disciples to pray without ceasing. Many modern disciples are well aware that it is possible to maintain a consciousness of prayer though engaged in activities of the outer world.

Each evening an earnest candidate engages in the exercise of retrospection, reviewing the events of the day and rededicating himself to a better, more noble performance in the future. He also reviews the events of the year just terminated, recognizing his weaknesses and failures and planning how he can use them as stepping stones in the year ahead.

## Second Week—Purity and Transmutation

The second week begins on January 13th and runs through January 19th, and has as its keynotes *purity* and *transmutation*. This work is done upon the desire nature, for a true Christian aspirant disciplines his desire nature by these two measures.

It is the fad of various modern schools to deride the ideals of purity and chastity. Some go so far as to maintain they were not taught by the Lord Christ, and this despite the fact that He told His Disciples it was the pure in heart who would see God.

Purity was the prime requisite of the Grail Knights; only as they developed this virtue into a power were they found worthy to stand in the presence of the Holy Cup.

## Third Week—Awaken and Spiritualize the Mind

Disciplinary exercises are now centered upon the mind, the mental body, from January 20th through January 26th. The keynotes for this period are *wakefulness* and *spiritualization* on the mental level.

The seeker's mind must be kept always alert and active. The old saying that "Idle hands are the devil's workshop" is equally true of an idle mind, for it easily becomes an open door to admit discarnate entities. Many and tragic are the consequences which may ensue.

Aspirants must practice discernment and discrimination in their thinking, thus learning to differentiate between the everlasting and the evanescent. They should seek to choose enduring values in music, literature, drama, and every other form of culture, relaxation, or diversion. Certain it is that a person's persisting thoughts give evidence of what he is or what he will become.

*Finally, brethren, whatsoever things are true, whatsoever things are honest, whatsoever things are just, whatsoever things are pure, whatsoever things are lovely, whatsoever things are of good report; if there be any virtue, and if there be any praise, think on these things.*—Philippians 4:8

## Fourth Week—Sublimation and Unification

Work for the fourth week is from January 27th through the early days of February. Its keynotes are *sublimation* and *unification*. The goal of this final week is to sublimate qualities of the lower nature and thus lift them into unison with those of the spirit.

It is literally possible to develop purity to such a degree that it becomes a spiritual power. Parsifal possessed this power of purity. It enabled him to dissolve into dust the magnificent castle of Klingsor and so abolish all its sensuous pleasures. When a modern disciple realizes the nothingness of worldly illusions he possesses the power to banish them from his life forever. As he lifts his thoughts higher and higher, they become Christed with each thought and its resultant deed centered in the Christ. Such a one will be worthy to serve with the Blessed Lord when He comes again.

*      *      *

The foregoing merely outlines disciplines with which to start each New Year and then continue throughout that year, the next, and all the years of a lifetime—and maybe, of many earthly life spans.

If putting the quest for things of the spirit first seems to make life vague and uninteresting to anyone, he has never truly experienced spiritual hunger—hunger of an intensity that far exceeds any physical craving and ultimately brings an aspirant to a clear understanding of the Master's statement "I have meat to eat that ye know not of."

As a candidate goes forth upon this glorious quest for the eternal and develops within himself increasing powers belonging to spiritualized consciousness, he realizes more fully the divine law underlying the words of the Lord Christ when He said,

*Seek ye first the kingdom of God and his righteousness; and all these things shall be added unto you.*

# CHAPTER V

## THE ETERNAL MADONNA

The *Madonna and Child* theme is ageless. It holds for mankind the supreme ideal of perfected motherhood as embodied in the Blessed Mary, immaculate mother of Jesus who was the bearer of the Christ.

In the earliest days of human civilization the first Mystery Temples were instituted in the land of Lemuria. To them were taken pioneers of the next race that they might be trained to serve as leaders and teachers of their fellow men. Among the first pictures given to these pioneers to study and interpret was that of the Mother and Child.

Ages passed. Lemuria disappeared and Atlantis rose above the waves. Pioneers of a new race were taken into Mystery Temples to be given teachings and training that they might qualify as leaders and teachers of those less evolved than themselves. Repeating the Lemurian practice, as eternal scrolls containing the Memory of Nature were unrolled before them, one of the first pictures they were called upon to study and interpret was that of the Madonna and Child.

Then came the birth of our present Fifth Root Race. During its development the guardians of humanity have given each rising civilization a religion perfectly suited to the development of the people, and to the performance of their task as a factor in human evolution. Each and every one of these world religions has been blessed by a high feminine Initiate, one whose privilege it has been to be the immaculate mother of that enlightened Being who came to the race as a way-shower. The last of these religions, the culmination of them all, arose with the coming of the Christ. To this religion we owe the incarnation of that most glorious Master Initiate who ever came to earth in a feminine body, the adored Mary of Bethlehem, mother of the Christed Jesus.

It was this same eternal Madonna *impress* upon the Akashic Records that St. John saw in his sublime vision, and which he described as the woman clothed with the Sun, her feet upon the Moon, and crowned with the glory of twelve stars—indicative of conscious communion with the twelve zodiacal Hierarchies: Pisces, home of earth's Masters who now return as Lords of Compassion that they may minister to, and uplift, mankind; Aquarius, home of the Angels; Capricorn, home of the Archangels; Sagittarius, the Lords of Mind; Scorpio, Lords of Form; Libra, Lords of Individuality; Virgo, Lords of Wisdom; and Leo, Lords of Flame (light and love). This enumerates eight of the twelve Hierarchies. During the season of the Winter Solstice, the Christmas Season, these Hierarchies flood the earth with harmonies of celestial choirs. The four remaining Hierarchies are so high that their music can be heard only by earth's Masters. They are Cancer, home of the Cherubim; Gemini, home of the Seraphim; Taurus and Aries, both so exalted that their names are far removed from the cognition of humanity. It is known, however, that Taurus holds the cosmic pattern of all earthly form while Aries, a Fire Hierarchy, holds the secret of life itself. All religions retain at least a fragment of this truth, hence fire is symbolic of Deity in all world faiths. The Old Testament taught its people to journey toward the Promised Land under the guidance of a *pillar of cloud* by day and a *pillar of fire* by night. In the New Testament the Lord Christ, the supreme World Teacher, came declaring "I am the light of the world."

There is a most profound significance to the fact that the ageless theme of the *Madonna and Child* has paralleled the entire evolutionary span of the human race. Together, they are the archetypal image of mankind's future spiritual unfoldment, for they symbolize the birth of the Christ consciousness within man himself. The feminine typifies an awakened and illumined soul; and the Christ consciousness can be born only in one of such soul attainments.

For modern man, therefore, the true significance of the Christmas Season lies in the birth of the Christ consciousness within himself. This is God's great gift to humanity at this time. And so on holy Christmas Night the aspirant reconsecrates himself that he may love and serve in fuller measure all those whom he meets in daily life, for in this way he receives increasingly the Christ light within himself. Until this birth has occurred within him he can never know the deep joys of a truly spiritual Christmas.

We have said that in initiatory Temples of both Lemuria and Atlantis candidates were lifted in consciousness to study Akashic Records, and there they saw the glorious mission of the Mother and Child. In those early days healing formed a prominent part of the religion of the people; their science and their art were religious science and religious art. Each Temple had its own healing sanctuary. Here patients were taught to project their consciousness unto the Memory of Nature and thereby receive the healing forces emanating from the holy figure of the Divine Mother.

We have also said that after the passing of these prehistoric continents, and the differentiation of humanity into races and nations, to these nations was sent periodically a high Initiate in feminine form, one who was to become the mother of a Master Teacher of the age. In every instance this has been a holy birth preceded by an angelic annunciation and an immaculate conception (not a miraculous conception, be it noted). The feminine Master for Egypt bore the name Isis—she who gave birth on the 25th of December, culmination of the Solstice interval, to the Holy Babe Horus. The Winter Solstice was celebrated in Egypt with stately processions and vivid pageantry, elaborate homage being rendered to the Divine Mother Isis and her new-born son, Horus. The *mystae* emerged from an inner shrine chanting: "The Virgin has brought forth. The Light is waxing."

Rama of India, one of the first Avatar messengers to mankind, received his illumination on the night of the Winter Solstice, and through its power he healed all who came to him. He created sacred ceremonials in commemoration of this hallowed period which he called "Holy Night." The date of Rama's incarnation is lost in the mists of civilization's dawning. Krishna, often referred to as the Christ of India, was, like Jesus, born in crudely humble surroundings. His birth occurred while his mother and foster father were on a mystic journey into the hills. It is interesting to note that, instead of shepherds, it was cowherds who came to the cave to adore the child. This religion was inaugurated when the Sun by precession was in Taurus, sign of the bull. So cows were regarded as sacred animals at that time, and this has been carried over in India even to this day.

Holy Night in Greece was hailed by singing to the accompaniment of flutes. When the cock crowed, neophytes descended with lighted torches to an underground chapel where they paid reverence to the image of a babe bearing on its brow, hands, knees and feet a shining cross of gold. The babe was then carried in processional seven times around the inner Temple, then back to its underground sanctuary to the accompaniment of a triumphant chorus: "At this hour today Kore (the Virgin) bore Aeon (the new age or year)."

The Winter Solstice was observed in Rome as the Feast of Saturnalia (Saturn, whose influence predominates when the Sun passes through Capricorn). This festival commemorated the marriage of Cybele (earth) and Attis (Sun). Their ceremonial emergence from the bridal chamber represented the new birth (Initiation) of the mystic from the cave sanctuary of the Mother Goddess. It took place amid the rejoicing of friends and companions, those who had passed through a similar experience.

When the Holy Birth occurred in Palestine the Sun had passed by precession from Taurus into Aries, sign of the lamb. Hence it was shepherds that came to adore the infant Jesus. Again it is interesting to note that while the Sun was by precession in Taurus, a feminine sign, the worship of a goddess was paramount. When the Sun preceded into Aries, a masculine sign, worship of a masculine deity prevailed. (Students will bear in mind that what is meant by this is the Sun's position in the spring, when it crosses the celestial equator. This crossing point, the Vernal Equinox, seems to go backward through the constellations at the rate of about one degree in seventy-two years. The same thing is true of the other points of the Sun's circuit, the Summer Solstice, Autumn

Equinox and Winter Solstice. At the Equinoxes the Sun crosses the celestial equator, but at the Solstices it seems to stand still for a time before turning northward or southward in its course, as the case may be).

In the coming Aquarian Age, when the Vernal Equinox will occur in Aquarius, neither the masculine nor the feminine will dominate. They will receive equal recognition, both in material and in spiritual affairs.

Mithras, the holy one of Persia, was also born on the 25th of December. He too received the homage and gifts of the Wise Men who foretold his glorious destiny in service to his people.

The Scandinavians had a beautiful ceremonial in worship of the Sun God, Baldur, whose mother was the Virgin Frigga or Freya. This Holy Birth occurred at the culmination of the Winter Solstice.

In Mexico and the Americas the great God Quetzalcoatl was born of an Initiate Virgin who was called the Queen of Heaven. Both an annunciation by Angels and an immaculate conception figure in her history.

This supreme Mother-Goddess, adored throughout the universe, is the great and illustrious Being who heads the Hierarchy of Virgo, the Lords of Wisdom. Under the supervision of this celestial Mother all Initiate Madonnas have their training and preparation. To Palestine came the most exalted of them all, Mary of Bethlehem, mother of our Lord Jesus. She was more than any earthly mother has ever been. She was, and is, a great spiritual teacher who bequeathed to her son the riches of her profound wisdom.

The Christ Mass of early Christians was celebrated on Holy Night of the Winter Solstice when Jesus, Lord of Love, descended to earth that He might bring to man the new Christ Mystery, wherein he is taught how to develop within himself this living Tree of Light. He learns to impress upon his own body, through love and service, the golden symbols of the Holy Babe. St. Paul, an early aspirant who followed in the Master's steps, proclaimed this truth to his own disciples when he asserted: ''I bear in my body the marks of the Lord Jesus.'' Paul was not referring here to bruises and stripes inflicted upon his physical body by his persecutors, as orthodox friends interpret his words; rather, he meant the glories of the fiery Christ Star that flamed up within himself and shone forth with such effulgence that for a time he was blinded by its shining. It was this Christ Star, brought forth within him by the Risen Christ as he was on the way to Damascus, that he later described as the "body celestial." It is always this Star-Body, this celestial body, that bears the marks of the Christ, though sometimes they are superimposed upon a "terrestrial body" in a stigmatization visible to all.

Paracelsus states that every constellation of the heavens is within man. "The Sun is in the heart," he writes, "and the other planets of the solar system are within the brain."

On Holy Night Temple doors are open, altar lights are agleam, and the Hymn of Capricorn may be heard amid the chime of Christmas bells ringing from the realm of peace. Then the neophyte who is esteemed "worthy and well-qualified" by reason of the Christ birth within himself, learns the true significance of the Christ Mass, the Feast of Light.

For the sensitive the Christmas Season is marked by a profound inner stillness as though the whole world was wrapped in the white light of a great benediction. And this is what really occurs at this, the year's most blessed season. The desire currents of earth are largely stilled and the spiritual forces become paramount. Heaven, as it were, bends low and earth is lifted up; a pathway of light connects the two over which Angels and Archangels in gleaming array pass in luminous splendor, chanting in joyous tones "On earth peace, goodwill toward men."

As these celestial forces sweep toward the earth, they assume long swirling lines of symmetrical beauty which take on the likeness of the Woman and Child. Throughout the etheric realms in the Memory of Nature is stamped this earth's most holy signature, the golden Star and the Mother and Child.

Some centuries after Christ, master artists came to earth to perpetuate the meaning and purpose of the Madonna ideal, as envisioned on inner planes during the period between incarnations.

One such was Coreggio, whose studio was a sanctuary and who declared that when working on a canvas of a madonna he was actually, as well as figuratively, on his knees. So holy was the atmosphere of his studio that it has been poetically described as filled with the purity of little children at prayer.

Fra Angelico was another of these divinely illumined painters. He is said to have lived half in the world of Angels and half in the world of men. Legends have it that Angels often posed for his pictures. The exquisite supernatural quality of his Madonnas and Angels would seem to verify this statement. His figures are more etheric than physical, more divine than human.

But it was left to Raphael to project in highest perfection and spiritual power the glorious Madonna ideal. Raphael was an emissary of a great Mystic Brotherhood and created his work according to what he saw in the Akashic Records. His famous Sistine Madonna, which many critics have considered the world's greatest painting, has been used for meditative purposes in schools of esoteric Christianity. In this masterpiece of spiritual art Raphael has transmitted far more than mere beauty of form. The eminent occultist, Dr. Rudolf Steiner, recommended that his pupils meditate on this famous picture, declaring that it exercised a curative effect upon its beholder and was actually a medium for spiritual healing. He said also that when the picture is viewed and studied in such a way, it has an after-effect upon the human soul. Then this soul can dream during sleep about the Madonna image and receive from it even today a true healing power.

"In Christ Jesus," writes Dr. Steiner, "we have the great Prototype of that which should be born out of the human soul. This human soul, fecundated from without of the Spiritual Universe, is symbolically set forth in the Madonna." Further, it is "an image of the human soul born out of the Spiritual Universe which can bestow the inner power of vision and bring about a spiritual birth, the birth of the higher man within the earthy man." We are told that in it we can behold "the world's creative activity produced anew."

Another appraisal of the spiritual significance imparted by

Raphael to his Sistine Madonna appeared in an article by Violet
Plincke, published in the Anthroposophical Quarterly for Christmas of 1929. In it she writes:

    "The mystery of Mary, bearer of all that the soul, undefiled
and unbounded, can be, and the Jesus-Babe, vessel of the Sun-
power of Christ, and archetype of man's eternal child within—the
Ego—is revealed in this picture and sealed withal so that each
man's heart has to forge a new key to unlock Raphael's heritage to
humanity. A little book has recently been published, tracing the
influence of the Sistine Madonna through the ages and relating one
by one the experiences of men as they stood before the picture and
realized how the contemplation of it marked a turning point in their
lives. . . . Maria-Sophia, clad with the blue mantle of surrender
and the red robe of love, desires to be reborn in the seeking man of
today. And in her arms she holds the radiating Child 'I AM'—the
Ruler within us. And so we can apprehend the meaning of Rudolf
Steiner's words when he said that in very truth the mightiest
problem of humanity confronts us in the form of the Madonna.''

    The Archangel Gabriel and his ministering Hosts are the
guardians of all mothers, prospective mothers, and the newly born
in both the human and animal kingdoms. He was the companion
and teacher of the Blessed Mary throughout the years of her life on
this planet. It is eminently fitting, therefore, that Gabriel should be
the guardian of the forces of Nature during the interval from
December 21st to March 21st, for this is the period when new-
birth currents become active and flood inner planes with their
vibrancy and power. Toward the latter part of this interval they
come into manifestation on the physical plane in a floodtide of
beauty that man calls *spring*.

    Each year at the Christmas Season hosts of Angels and Ar-
changels under the leadership of Gabriel set upon the world the
impress of the Eternal Madonna. Humanity is intuitively conscious
of the power that radiates from this impress, so the chief theme of
its devotion at Christmastime is the Mother and Child. The most
beautiful Christmas music centers in the Madonna and the Holy
Babe.

This is the most propitious time of the year to pass through the portals of Initiation, when one can rise to higher planes to the accompaniment of celestial choirs. And fortunate is he whose star-call then announces that his earthly pilgrimage is ended and he is free to pass into a larger life through what is called *death*. Then he too makes his ascent to the harmonies of transcendent chorusing. There is a close affinity between Initiation and death, the principal difference being that in death one lays aside his physical vehicle permanently, whereas in Initiation it is laid aside temporarily during inner plane work only. When this is finished the earthly garment must be donned again so that the duties of every day living may be resumed.

St. Paul tells us that the last enemy to be overcome is death. Initiation holds the key to his statement, for death is "overcome" by the development of Initiate consciousness. Initiation is the key to eternal life. And it is through Initiation that man comes to know the wonder and the glory of the Eternal Madonna.

# CHAPTER VI

## CHRISTMAS MAGIC

Christmas is the magic time of the year. It is the most enchanting of all seasons. The very air seems to tingle and sparkle with happiness and anticipation.

One who has learned by means of deep inner communion to contact the hidden realms of nature recognizes that the sacred festivals of the year are observed on the inner plane whence they set their impress upon the outer physical world. This is particularly true at the Christmas Season. The joyous festivities, the color, music and rejoicing which take place in the outer world are but pale reflections of the corresponding observances in the spiritual realm. When the Lord Christ passes into the heart of the earth at this most blessed season the brilliance of His vast emanation floods the entire planet with splendor.

This radiance penetrates even the outer physical world, but material denseness blinds most persons to its effulgence. Many sensitives, however, feel the outgoing light. While they do not see it, yet they are conscious of high exaltation and rich inspiration which sets the Christmas Season apart from the rest of the year.

The tremendous love light with which the Christ floods the planet each year at Christmas time is gradually changing the atomic vibration of the earth and it is this great outpouring of love-light each year which is the real Christmas gift of Christ to the world. By it the planet is becoming etherealized and sensitized to the point where it is responsive to new and higher vibrational rhythms. Gradually, then, the Christ rhythm, throbbing in the earth, will become so powerful that all unlike vibrations are eliminated; the terrible blight of war now separating man from man and nation from nation will no longer be possible. Disease, poverty, and finally even death itself will be overcome. Every atom of the

32

globe responds to the divine inflow with a vast rhythmic pulsation like music to one who can hear it. It is echoed in the joyous chiming of Christmas bells, for at no time in the year do the bells chime as joyously as during the magic time of Christmas.

The Angels, too, must love this season with a special love, for then they draw closest to earth and sing their most blissful songs. Day and night multitudes of them hover over the earth pouring their blessing upon everything that lives, a blessing which again has its physical counterpart in the incense which perfumes many places of worship at this holy time. The early Christian Initiates contacted at will the observances of the higher planes and many of the ceremonials they established in the Church reflect the initiatory rituals of the inner planes. Master musicians have caught strains of angelic music and brought them down to earth in the inspired Christmas carols which will endure as long as the earth stands. "Joy to the world, the Lord is come" is an angelic song, giving utterance to a cosmic mystery which belongs to Angels as well as men. Amid the angelic bands that sing above the earth at Christmas time is one whose auric light extends into vast spaces, "The Queen of Angels and of men," who adds her song to that of the celestials as she pours out her blessing, particularly upon mothers and their babes; for she bears in her sacred memories, and she realizes more deeply than any other the profound sacrifice of this holy time. Her musical keynote sounds forth in the *Ave Maria*, and all who hear it are touched, consciously or unconsciously, by her benediction.

In each of the four Sacred Festivals celestial Beings flood the etheric realms with a divine radiance. Each of these seasons possesses its own characteristic color, as well as its own musical keynote, which have been used in the ceremonials in Temples of Initiation for ages past.

Everyone is familiar with the red and green of the Christmas Season as celebrated in western countries. Green is the color of new life. It is generally associated with spring, when the new plant life makes itself visible in the northern hemisphere. However, it is at Christmas time that this new life first stirs within the planet, and that is why the wise seers of old used it as a decorative motif for their midwinter festival. Red is the color of Mars. It is also the color of activity which surges through the planet when the Christ Ray is "reborn" within it. Mars is exalted in Capricorn, and the Christmas festivities are observed when the Sun enters the sign of Capricorn December 21st. The place of a planet's exaltation is where spiritual forces are concentrated. The red which belongs to Christmas is not a murky crimson but the pure, clear color produced by the transmutation of the heavy red of passion into the brighter tone of compassion. This comes with the change from the personal to the impersonal, from the individual to the universal.

The magic of Christmas is characterized by a spirit of universal good will. People generally are animated by friendly and generous impulses. Few there are who are too self-centered to give something of themselves and of their substance to others. Communities, large and small, carry out various projects in service to the needy, the sick and the unfortunate. Hospitals and orphanages are alight and festive with good cheer and loving, tender thought and care. It is the common aim of people everywhere to brighten at least some corner and to bring some fresh hope and joy to the less fortunate. This feeling of universal friendship finds its most joyful symbol in Santa Claus. He it is who makes his annual visit to the rooftops of the world on Christmas night distributing gifts and good cheer for everyone. He is known by many names in many different lands, but his spirit is always the same for he is the personification of the universal goodwill which the Lord Christ brings each year to earth, and which is becoming an ever more powerful and moving force in human consciousness throughout the world.

Underneath the beauty, color and rejoicing which animates the magic of Christmas, beneath all activity, bustle and confusion, there sounds an intonation more tender and beautiful than the singing of Angels and Archangels—the voice of the Christ Himself who reiterates His assurance that whatsoever is done to ease the burden, to heal the hurts, to relieve the suffering or to brighten the days of a fellow human being, or any living creature, is an act done as even unto Him. As He Himself expressed it, "For I was hungered, and ye gave me meat: I was thirsty, and ye gave me drink; I was a stranger, and ye took me in: naked, and ye clothed me: I was sick, and ye visited me: I was in prison, and ye came unto me."

## The Magic Star

As music produces exquisite geometric patterns in the ethers so also do particular modes of meditation. In the Christian Mystery Temples the basic pattern is the Star. It is by means of prolonged and devout meditation that this Star appears in the aura of the devotee, and at its appearance a Teacher appears, even as did the Magi at the Nativity of the Christ Child. The Star is never over-looked by the Great Ones from the inner planes, as it always signals the Holy Birth of one who has begun to walk the Christ way. Their loving response is inevitably eager and immediate.

The magic of Christmas is intimately connected with the Star. The golden Star that shone in the sky above Bethlehem on that holiest of all nights was the radiant body of the glorious Ar-changel, the Christ, who was pouring out His blessing upon the body of the perfect Child Jesus, later to become the vehicle for the indwelling Christ during the three years of His sublime ministry on Earth.

The Star is the soul signature of Christ. The Cross is His earth signature. From Christmas to Easter the Path leads from the Star to the Cross. In the course of the forty-day interval from Easter to the Ascension, the Path ascends from the Cross to the Star.

As previously noted, above the entrance to a Grecian Mystery Temple was inscribed the words, "Man, know thyself and thou shalt know all the mysteries of the universe." And so it is that we find both the mysteries of the Star and the Cross inscribed upon the body of man. When the arms are outstretched and the feet held together, the human body forms a cross. When the arms are outstretched and the legs spread apart, the body assumes the form of a five-pointed star.

The Cross represents the early years of probationship, the time of testing and of trial. The Master's admonition to disciples of all ages has ever been: If you would be my disciple you must take up your cross and follow me.

The Star represents the culmination of discipleship when the spirit is no longer bound to the prison house of the body but passes at will to the freedom of larger and wider spheres, using the physical form only as a channel for service within the physical realms. The five sacred wounds in the body of the crucified Christ mark the signature of this liberation. His last words from the cross also refer to this supreme event when He cried, "My God, how Thou hast glorified me."

In the transmutation of the lower nature into the higher, the Body-Cross becomes the Body-Star. This intermingling of the forces of the Star and the Cross holds profound mystic meaning for the disciple's meditation during these holy seasons.

### The Christmas Tree

While the Christmas Rite belongs to times immemorial, the Feast of the Christmastide had its first observance at the beginning of the Aryan civilization. The prototype of the Christmas tree was the "Celestial Sun Tree" of the earliest Aryans.

It was in the pure and rarified atmosphere of Aryana that the Sun first rose so clear man was able to perceive the tremendous downpouring of light with which transcendent Ones were suffusing earth. People likened these shafts of light to a mighty tree with outspreading branches. There is still a tradition in India—the Aryans of India were the first race of the Aryan Epoch—that in the "center of the earth stands the Tree of the Sun, which at sunrise shoots forth from the earth, and as the Sun ascends towards the zenith grows up into the air until its topmost branches reach the Sun when at noonday it stands high in the heavens, diminishes with declining day, and at the set of the sun sinks back into the earth." In one form or another, various legends relative to the World Tree are found in almost every country and its origin is always placed in this mystic light tree.

Mystics are well aware that a peculiar sympathy exists between the tree kingdom and the human kingdom. The most primitive altars are usually a stone with a fruit tree growing beside it, and these primitive altars are most often associated with a Mother

Goddess to whom it is held sacred. Archeologists digging in the area of the Temple of Diana at Ephesus found the ruins of one Temple over another, in descending strata, and in the lowest stratum they found only a stone altar and the clear suggestion of a sacred tree associated with it.

In the brilliance of the Rainbow Age, the dark, vital, powerful evergreen trees of Lemuria and Atlantis yielded place to the airy and bright food-bearing and flower-ornamented trees of Aryana.

While this evolutionary change took place, man still had a vestige of the old negative clairvoyance, and he could still commune with the nature spirits even though he had by this time lost touch with the great angelic and archangelic Hierarchies occupying areas of spiritual consciousness which he could no longer reach.

Far into the Aryan Epoch, even into our own Piscean Age, many races still knew the fairy-peoples of the fields and waters, the awe-inspiring sylphs of the crags and mountains and the gentle spirits of the friendly breeze. And among all these, they felt most deeply their kinship with the dryads, the spirits of the trees. Groves were invested with a haunting presence which impelled them sometimes to fear and somtimes to worship.

For tree consciousness is a very definite thing, and its varying moods may be easily sensed by the mystic. Trees, like humans, feel both joy and sadness. Sometimes a tree's great trunk will shiver, its drooping leaves quiver, and it appears to evidence almost a glint of tears. Again, an entire tree structure will become luminous with ecstasy. This ecstatic gladness of woodlands reaches its climax in the glory of the Resurrection or Easter Morn.

Sensitives have often heard heart-rending cries issuing from their trunks on the eve of their destruction. In one instance the cry was so persistent that inquiry revealed that the tree was to be destroyed the following day. Then efforts were made to save it but to no avail. The tree spirit, knowing this, was bemoaning its untimely destruction.

Every tree is presided over by a Deva or Angel. This Angel is literally the guardian of the tree and is ofttimes referred to as the *spirit* of the tree. It supervises all life processes which take place within its charge, including the work of the nature spirits in and through the tree's organism.

When the great Christ Ray descends to earth in the autumn, the plant kingdom readily absorbs its radiance. Forests appear crowned with a golden halo as this luminous Ray penetrates more into the earth and its light descends through tree branches. As the mystic hour of Holy Night approaches the golden stream has penetrated to the very depths of their trunks, where it gleams like an altar flame. At Christmas time every tree is a herald proclaiming the annual return of the cosmic Lord of Love and Light.

There is a lovely old legend which relates that in the hush of that holy time, while Angels carol of the Christ Child, beasts kneel in their stalls and bow their heads. Then it is that the little nature folk cease their activities and, forming into a joyous processional, pay homage before the altar light flaming within the tree which is their home. Thus does nature and all living things honor the birth of the new-born King.

There are some who think that the most beautiful, and certainly the most profound of all symbols connected with Holy Night is the Christmas tree. The golden star which usually adorns its crest typifies the Star of the East that calls all men to worship Him Whom the mystic greets at the midnight hour as *the newborn Sun.* Lights and colors upon the festive tree represent emanations from the aura of this new-born Sun, which permeate and illumine the realms of earth, both inner and outer.

A tree so adorned year after year to honor Him gradually comes to send forth a blessing and a benediction, not only at Christmas time, but every day of the year. This is easily discernible to the sensitive who approaches its environs. In this lies the importance of using live Christmas trees instead of imitations.

Every man is a Christ in the making. Therefore, all Christmas symbols signify varying degrees of spiritual development. In the human body, man's temple of the spirit, are many latent centers awaiting awakening and vitalization. When this occurs he himself will be a veritable Christmas tree, radiant, illumined, walking ''in the light as he is in the light.'' An illumined mystic sensing this truth has written that *"the body is filled with candles all in place, just waiting to be lighted by the flaming torch of Love."*

### The Ministry of Angels at Christmas Time

The modern world is turning each year with renewed reverence and understanding to the revivification of the feasts and ceremonials belonging to the early Christians. The Feast of Advent has perhaps never since the time of its inauguration in the first century been so emphasized as of recent years.

It is in harmony with cosmic law that Advent occurs when the Hierarchy of Sagittarius is sending its radiations upon earth, since these foster high idealism and a strengthening of spiritual aspirations. The colorful lights seen everywhere and the joyous music heard on every side combine on this outer plane to reflect and re-echo the sublime beauty, the intense activity and the glory of color and music which flood the inner worlds. It is then that the Angels come closer to Earth than at any other time of the year.

During this interval the earnest aspirant devotes as much time as possible to purifying and preparing himself by means of fasting and prayer to come more completely into attunement with the Feast of Christmas. This preparatory work actually began with the Autumn Equinox when the regency of earth was taken over by the Archangel Michael, who presides over the processes of purification and regeneration for all of Earth's progeny. From the time of the Autumn Equinox until the Winter Solstice, Michael and his ministering Hosts are engaged in cleansing the desire and mental envelopes of the Earth. If it were not for such cleansing activities carried out by great celestial Beings, the murky psychic atmosphere generated by man's evil thoughts, emotions, and deeds would become so dense that humanity would be hopelessly submerged in it, and cut off from the vivifying forces of the spirit. That cannot be, for it is the supreme redemptive work of the Christ to do battle with the forces of evil and darkness, symbolically portrayed in Michael's slaying the dragon, Michael being next to Christ in the Hierarchy of Light. The conquest of light over darkness takes place each year when the Sun passes through Libra, Scorpio and Sagittarius. The mystic Christian understands this, and he knows how to attune himself to the influences of Michael and his ministering Hosts. He is thus aided tremendously in his own personal conquest of darkness by the never-failing light that is in him.

At the time of the Winter Solstice, Michael's work for the year having been accomplished, he returns the regency of the earth over to Gabriel, the Archangel of tenderness and love. Gabriel is the glorious Being who typifies the spirit of motherhood, for he is the angelic guardian of mothers and children. The vast array of nature Angels work under his guidance during this season.

Beginning with the time of the Autumn Equinox, the golden radiation of the Christ, which is then being poured upon earth, gradually penetrates its atmospheric layers and then the earth globe itself, until at the Winter Solstice it has entered into its very heart. Then the great miracle of nature occurs. There is a white magic, a breathless hush and a tender reverence permeating the atmosphere on Holy Night as the nature Angels, together with loftier celestial Beings, combine their forces and reverse the cosmic currents. For the past six months they had been moving on the descending arc; for the next six months, culminating at the Summer Solstice, they will move upward on the ascending arc. The mighty surge of this cosmic power propels all life upward; and the same rising tide of spiritual force lifts the spinal spirit fire in the body of man; so in those who have made sufficient preparation this fire may be lifted to the head and effect a state of true illumination.

This cosmic process is accomplished through the power of musical harmony and rhythm. It is an action of the Creative Word, the Word which St. John declares to have been from the beginning and by which all created things came into being.

The musical keynote of this planet is attuned to the song of Angels: ''Glory to God in the highest on earth, peace, good will toward men.'' It is the harmonious, rhythmic enunciation of this planetary Word, resounding again and again through all the earth, that accomplishes the miracle of Holy Night.

The vast celestial forces that play between heaven and earth in this blessed season sound forth with an unsurpassable beauty. Some faint echoing of this celestial harmony was captured by Franz Schubert and transcribed for human hearing in the exquisite strains of his *Ave Maria*. This composition may be regarded in a way as the musical keynote of the Christmas Season. Its music carries a tremendous spiritual power, particularly during this time of the year when it re-echoes, as it were, the celestial rhythms brought down from cosmic spaces.

At this enchanted time there occurs a threefold birth: first, the *cosmic birth* of the Christ Spirit after the manner previously indicated, quickening all nature into new life; second, the *historical birth* of great World Teachers who choose this time to incarnate, as did the Master Jesus who became the bearer of the Christ light, Teacher of Angels and men; and third, the metaphysical birth of the Christ within the disciple in a state of illumination.

The disciple now understands why heretofore there was no room in the inn and why the Christ must be born in a manger where beasts feed. He knows now that the supreme work of his life has been to open the door of the inn, to make room for the Christ, and to transform the manger into a cradle of light. He knows that this "cradle" is the third ventrical of the head where it is surrounded by the radiant forces of the awakened pituitary and pineal glands, symbolically figured in Mary and Joseph respectively. Becoming illumined, he is a Christed one, and the glory of his new birth is hailed by the multitudes of Angels on high.

All three births are accompanied by the jubilant chorusing of celestial Beings, who proclaim these several transforming events to the musical keynote of the Christian Dispensation: "Glory to God in the highest, on earth, peace, good will toward men."

On December 21st, the planetary keynote changes from Sagittarius to Capricorn. The key of Sagittarius is divine ecstasy, expressed in the joyous fellowship and in the riot of bright colors and tunefulness of Advent Season. The keynote of Capricorn is divine consummation. The earth is submerged in the white light of consecreation as the planetary life currents are reversed and the Cosmic Christ force turns upward with the Sun. These forces increase from December 21st until they reach their maximum on midnight of the 24th; but they do not decline all at once. The powerful solstitial radiations of spiritual force envelop the earth until the twelfth night thereafter, an interval held sacred by the early Christians and destined for revival today.

The song of the Angels when the Sun moves southward is set to minors. At midnight of December 24th, Holy Night, their chorusing changes to majors as they chant joyously the musical keynote of the earth: "Glory to God in the highest, on earth, peace, good will toward men."

# CHAPTER VII

## THE HOLY FAMILY—A COSMIC GLYPH

The Christmas story is familiar in history and song throughout the world. The mystic Christian, while accepting the literal version as told in the Gospels, also finds deeper meanings concealed therein. He accepts Mary of Bethlehem as one of the most illustrious Master Teachers who has ever come to earth. He also knows Joseph to be one of the first Initiate Teachers of the Temple Mysteries and the child Jesus as the most advanced ego who has ever taken embodiment on the earth plane. The child Jesus, with the assistance of the Divine Mary, fashioned the most perfect physical body ever brought to earth for he came as the supreme type pattern for the emulation of all mankind.

The mystic Christian, while accepting these spiritual truths, also realizes that every man is a Christ-in-the-making. He therefore understands that every character in the Christmas story represents a certain phase of his own inner development and that every experience of these persons will sometimes form a part of his own spiritual experience as he learns to ascend ever higher on the Path of Holiness.

It is this understanding of the Christmas story that inclines the earnest aspirant to return year after year with ever deeper enthusiasm and ever deeper reverence to study and meditate upon these profound inner truths. That there is a lofty goal possible of attainment the Master Himself indicated when He said in effect, not only the things that I do shall ye do, but greater things shall ye do.

Inscribed above the portals of an ancient Greek Mystery Temple were the words, "Man, know thyself and thou shalt know all the mysteries of the universe." It is in the light of this profound esoteric truth that we shall study the inspiring Christmas story and the life and experiences of the Holy Family as described therein.

THE FOURTEEN STEPS IN INITIATORY DEVELOPMENT

In every human body-temple there are two currents of mag-
netic force, the one a positive or masculine potency, the other a
negative or feminine. They are sometimes referred to as the two
poles of the body. In mystic language, they are often spoken of as
the elements of Fire and Water, and are represented by two
columns, the one crowned with the Sun and the other with the
Moon. In the average person these two currents do not function in
a harmonious relationship; there is an imbalance that gives rise to
discord and maladjustment in the body. The work of the initiatory
Path is to bring these two currents into harmonious interaction, one
with the other. The various steps on this Path are outlined in the
most important events in the life of the supreme Way-shower, the
Lord Christ.

### Annunciation

The negative or feminine potency is centered in the heart, the
seat of intuition; the positive or masculine potency is centered in
the head, the seat of the intellect. The illumination attained with
the Annunciation Degree gives the ability to see the perfected body
that will result from the balancing of the masculine and feminine
forces. Not until this is achieved will man externalize a body in
accordance with the divine archetype as it exists eternally in the
heavens. It is the vision of this glorified body-temple built in the
image and likeness of God which gives the spiritual keynote of this
attainment: "Let it be according to thy word."

### Immaculate Conception

As the Degree of the Annunciation brings about a glorified
vision, so the Degree of Immaculate Conception impresses this
vision upon the body. The vibration of every atom is raised under
the new surge of spiritual power. The entire organism is lifted into
closer attunement with the archetype. The body-temple is literally

made new and becomes a holier abiding place for the spirit in which to live and work. The spiritual keynote of this Degree is voiced in Mary's prophetic words, "All generations shall call me blessed."

### The Holy Birth

In this Degree a new light burns in the heart and a new radiance emanates from the mind. Hosts of angelic ministers, together with the Great Compassionate Ones upon the inner planes who are ever scanning the world for the appearance of this new light within the mind and heart of man, greet the discovery with celestial chants of great rejoicing. Those among men who give birth to this new light now come under the close and tender guidance of spiritual Beings. In consequence of this development and expression life takes on new and deeper meanings. Mary is symbolic of the feminine current which has its seat in the heart and Joseph is representative of the masculine current which has its seat in the head. On whatever plane these two currents of force unite harmoniously a new element is brought into manifestation. This third element constitutes a holy birth or the awakening of a new power, the power of will. This spiritualized creative will power is the magic White Stone, since by means of its further development man becomes superman, a son or daughter of the King. At the time of this birth, ministering Angels encircle the Earth, chanting, "Glory to God in the highest, on earth, peace, good will toward men." That is, peace within man's body-temple, and good will, for he could then truly come to know that great peace and that joyous fellowship with Angels and men that passeth understanding. When this becomes the spiritual attainment of all men, love, goodness and tranquility will reign supreme upon earth.

### Presentation in the Temple

A temple is a place of dedication and it is here that the aspirant who endeavors to walk the Path of Holiness comes for meditation and prayer. Such must necessarily live according to standards and disciplines far more exacting than for those who are still content with the world as it is. Thoughts must be guarded to admit no destructive or negative influences. Words must be watched so as never to hurt. Deeds must be measured for their constructive and helpful values. Such a watch over thoughts, words and deeds cannot be successfully maintained except after long periods of strict discipline and much prayer and meditation. Often the aspirant must repair to a place of dedication for renewal of purpose and restoration of inner strength. If his efforts are earnest and sincere, the time will come eventually when he, like the child Jesus, will receive the blessing of both the High Priest and the High Priestess (the masculine and feminine forces), and upon him will also be bestowed a new soul name which will attune him with his own spiritual powers and provide him with a magic key by which he can summon guidance and protection from those on high.

### The Flight into Egypt and the Return

In the early stages of spiritual development the aspirant will often experience a "flight into Egypt," or slipping away into darkness. The inner life will be temporarily veiled. He will feel that he has been left without spiritual guidance. This will bring a sense of desperate loneliness and despair from which he will cry out in an agony of spirit, as did the psalmist at this same place upon the Path. But if he persists in his efforts to regain the light he will again tread the Path as it was taken by the Holy Family who, though they fled to Egypt, the symbolical land of darkness, they returned in gladness, accompanied by the hosannas of an angelic chorus. This is a difficult place upon the Path. Many stumble here and turn back to the allurements of the world. The Rosicrucian mystic, Max Heindel, gave the encouraging admonition that when meeting with such difficulties "the only failure is in ceasing to try." This truth is of like import to the biblical statement that "the wind is tempered to the shorn lamb."

## *The Teaching in the Temple*

The masses of people are divided into two classes, those who follow the heart path and those who follow the way of the head. Aspirants who are centered largely in the heart are more easily swayed by their emotions. Unless balanced and steadied by the powers of mind, theirs is literally a house built on sand which winds and floods destroy. Those predominantly mental, with power centered in reason, build their houses on the rocks which also are subject to destruction by tempestuous winds. Through Temple teachings the aspirant learns how to blend the powers of mind and heart, of reason and intuition, of the masculine and feminine forces within himself. When this has been accomplished emotion becomes winged with reason and the mind illumined with the light of the spirit. With this comes a degree of perfection, new-found power, and an expanding consciousness that henceforth leads to a consecration of the whole of life to the service of the kingdom of God on earth. Another interest that might temporarily inject itself would meet the same response that the child Jesus made when His parents found him in the Temple giving of his wisdom even to his elders, the Priests: "Wist ye not that I must be about my Father's business?"

## *The Baptism*

The Baptism was a formula of Initiation and represented a most illustrious event of Holy Week. The Blessed Virgin and the other women disciples were always important participants in this sacred rite. For those who were able to partake of this ceremonial, the heavens were open to their enraptured vision, and many were the transcendent activites that then became both audible and visible to them.

In all ancient Mysteries the rite of Baptism was symbolic of "bringing to sight." It is at this place that the candidate develops a greater degree of equilibrium between the masculine and feminine forces in his body-temple; the Mary and Joseph principles are brought into a more harmonious interaction. The aspirant now acquires the capacity to think with his heart and love with his mind. It is necessary that this development should take place at this particular time, for with the expansion of sight he is able to look into the inner realms and contact the higher Beings that inhabit them. In order to function safely when thus contacting the inner world, it is all-important that a firmly balanced relationship has been established between the positive and negative forces of one's being. At this stage of development Max Heindel's admonition to his disciples was that they keep their head in the stars and their feet on the ground. If this advice were followed many of the psychic tragedies which beset the aspirant at this point on the Path would be avoided.

Pictorial symbolism showing the candidate standing between two columns at the entrance of a Mystery Temple, sometimes alone and in other instances beside a teacher, refers to this particular place on the Path. Here it is that he, too, will hear the voice that was heard by Jesus on the day of His Baptism; for it is a Temple benediction bestowed on all worthy participants in this sacred rite: "This is my beloved Son, in whom I am well pleased."

The Baptism forms the connecting link between the Water Mysteries of Christmas and the Fire Mysteries of Easter. Herein is to be found the meaning of that cryptic statement in an early secret legend, namely that when Jesus stepped down into the River Jordan, great balls of fire appeared on the surface of the water.

Whenever an aspirant experiences a high state of exaltation it is always followed by subtle temptation. Temptation, therefore, usually constitutes the opposite of Baptism. After the baptism of Christ Jesus, a sublime occasion of dedication and consecration, came His temptation in the wilderness; and after the glory of His transfiguration there followed the agony of Gethsemane. This sequence has constituted the Path of Discipleship in all ages so that a disciple might fully comprehend the power of discrimination; that is, ability to distinguish the true from the false, the real from the unreal.

The fall of the Angels is recounted in the description of the war in heaven. The fall of humanity is recorded in the biblical version of the expulsion of Adam and Eve from the Garden of Eden. The Archangels have never "fallen." Although they possess desire bodies, they have transmuted desire into a spiritual power and the body of desire into a body of light. It was necessary, therefore, that the Saviour of Angels and men should come from the archangelic Hierarchy. The Lucifer Spirits understood this well and were in great distress over the coming to earth of the Archangel Christ. Saint Mark, in his Gospel, refers to the evil spirit that called out to the Christ, "I know thee who thou art, the Holy One of God" (Mark 1:24)

Immediately after His baptism the Lord Christ retired into the wilderness for forty days. He needed to familiarize Himself with the use of a physical body, and to learn how to function in it without its being shattered by the powerful radiations of His exalted spirit. It was at this time that Lucifer approached and tempted Him, hoping that His incarnation in a physical body would render Him vulnerable.

Lucifer's temptation was threefold; physical, mental and spiritual. He offered the Christ all the kingdoms of this world, probably the most subtle of all enticements. More persons have been turned from the Path by reason of wealth, fame, prestige and worldly power than for any other seductions, as symbolized by Christ's parable of the rich young man.

Again, Lucifer tested the Master by the promise of magic power for turning stones into bread. Countless thousands are now using their powers of mind to attract worldly possessions to themselves, all unmindful of, or willfully indifferent to, the fact that by so doing they place themselves increasingly under Luciferic influence.

Finally, Lucifer took the Lord Christ to the pinnacle of the Temple and bade Him cast Himself down after first commanding the protection of Angels. When one begins to awaken inherent powers of the spirit, many and subtle are the temptations to use these powers for personal benefit. But the Christ declared, "I can of mine own self do nothing" (John 5:30). In that illuminated manual on discipleship, *Light on the Path* by Mabel Collins, aspirants are admonished to kill out all personal ambition and yet to work as do those who are ambitious. Verily, "Strait is the gate, and narrow is the way, . . . and few there be that find it" (Matt. 7:14). Complete personal detachment is the keynote to the true Path of Discipleship.

## The Transfiguration

When the candidate reaches this place of holiness, equilibrium between the opposite polarities has been established. With this step comes the full flowering of the two spiritual organs in the head, the pituitary and the pineal glands. These two organs are now the lighted lamps of the body-temple. The pineal gland crowns the masculine or fire column, the column of Joseph, and the pituitary gland crowns the feminine or water column, the column of Mary. As the light emanating from these two glands unites through the third ventricle which lies between the two, this point in the head is transformed into a veritable manger of light and the focal point for the activity of the Christ principle in the life of the candidate. The earliest manifestation of this principle occurred, as previously noted, in the Degree of the Holy Birth. In the Degree of Transfiguration this divine creative Christ principle is increased in potency a thousandfold. The expanding light which then extends beyond the periphery of the head forms the radiant halo of the saints. Gradually this halo is extended until it envelops the entire body in what is described as the golden wedding garment. The creation of this luminous soul body is a requisite for entrance into the still higher Degrees of the Mysteries.

One of the evidences of advanced discipleship is ability for instantaneous contact with the Master regardless of time or space. Mary's communion with her Blessed Lord was of this nature. Her white soul bore the instant impress of His every thought and emotion.

During the Transfiguration the Master appeared in all the resplendent glory of His archangelic body to those disciples who were able to raise their consciousness high enough to behold Him.

Mary, though not physically present, experienced all the ecstatic joy of this sublime event.

## The Triumphal Entry

In the Triumphal Entry the Lord Christ came riding upon an ass and was greeted by the plaudits of His followers, who waved palm branches, scattered flowers along the way and shouted hosannas to Him who came in the name of the Lord (spiritual law). This processional is symbolic. It represents the Path of the candidate who has been victorious in the Degree of Transfiguration. He rides upon an ass, symbolizing the attainment of soul wisdom, and receives the acclamation of those who have previously attained to this Degree, and also those of lesser development who are striving to achieve it. It was St. John, the beloved Disciple, who experienced the exaltation of this Degree on the Saturday night preceding the Triumphal Entry into Jerusalem. John was the first Disciple to receive the deeper Christian Mysteries brought to earth by the Lord Christ, and it was in celebration of this far-reaching event that the first Triumphal Entry was inaugurated.

Mary and the other women disciples of the Master were among those who lined that sacred way and watched the glorious procession as it passed into the city of Jerusalem. They felt the great overwhelming surge of enthusiasm which animated the throngs and reveled in the waves of adulation and devotion which encircled their beloved Teacher at this time of the Triumphal Entry. They understood well both the inner and outer significance of the occasion. They grasped the opportunity it gave to those who had benefited by His loving ministry to show Him homage and reverence. They realized also the deeper meaning of the day. They knew that the life of Christ outlined the Path of Initiation for man and that the Triumphal Entry marked the consummation of the Great Work, namely, the entrance into the Temple of Light.

## The Feast in the Upper Room

The Feast of the Eucharist is called esoterically the Feast of Polarity. This aspect of the Feast was referred to by Christ at the time of breaking the bread (the feminine or water potency) when He said "This is my body, broken for you." Then taking the wine (the masculine or fire potency) he said, "This is my blood shed for you." Only those who attained to this Degree of Initiation were eligible to commune with the Christ around that sacred table and to receive from Him the deep Mysteries which He then imparted to them. As previously stated, the blending of the opposites brings equilibrium and equality. This refers not only to a perfect balance between the masculine and feminine principles within the body, but also to equality between man and woman in their personal relationships in the outer world. Before such equality can be fully realized in the world without, it must first have become universally achieved in the inner natures of all individuals comprising the social body of mankind. Such was the attainment of those who met with the Christ in the upper room on the eve of His sacrifice on Golgotha. This company included both men and women.

### The Garden of Gethsemane

The candidate who ascends to the topmost vision, there to receive a divine outpouring from above, must also descend into the world's garden of sorrow to share with the less fortunate something of the blessing which comes from on high. The keynotes of Gethsemane are *sacrifice* and *selflessness*. Before these have been attained, the candidate must return again and again to this garden until he can say as did Christ "Not my will, but thine, be done." Only when this surrender has been complete and its imprint placed permanently upon the soul will Gethsemane cease to be the familiar place it now is to mankind.

In all biblical symbology there is no more arresting instance of this attainment than that of Abraham when called upon to sacrifice his best beloved son, Isaac. When Abraham (the candidate) consented to obey the divine command, and had made his surrender to what was understood to be the will of God, the inner work it was designed to accomplish was done, and consequently the actual sacrifice was not required. The lamb caught in the thicket which took the place of Isaac as a sacrificial offering typifies the power gained through the sublimation of the animalistic forces into spiritual power through sacrifice. This story typifies a crucial place on the Path of Holiness and is one of the most generally misunderstood of all biblical stories. In this respect it is like the story of Jonah and the whale, which also has to do with processes connected with Initiation.

The Blessed Mary was in such complete attunement with the Christ that she was one with His every joy and with His every sorrow. Although she was not physically present in the Garden of Gethsemane, the agony of the Master set its impress upon her heart and she, too, spent that lonely interval in prayer and supplication, that His burden and the sorrow which weighed on His heart and that the weakness and ignorance of mankind might be assuaged.

While His travail in the Garden pierced her heart with agony and grief, our blessed Lord in turn was conscious of her love and the supplication which encircled Him with all the sweetness and power of an angelic benediction.

### *The Trial*

The Trial marks a critical place upon the Path. The candidate has by this time developed powers ranging far beyond those of the average individual. The temptation that now confronts him is whether he will use these powers for the gratification of personal ambition or for the benefit and blessing of his fellow men. The Lord Christ came as the supreme Way-shower for all the world. He experienced each step or Degree through which the candidate must pass upon the Christ Way. How did the Lord Christ meet this test? When on trial before Pilate and surrounded by an angry multitude shouting hateful epithets and clamoring for His crucifixion, He had it within His power to summon legions of Angels for His safe removal, but of this power He made no use. He came not to save Himself but to offer Himself as a living sacrifice for all the world. Few even now understand that sacrifice in its universal and cosmic significance. Even His Disciples at this time had little concept of the vast mission He came to perform. They thought He was to set up a throne in Jerusalem to make Himself king of the earth. They did not understand that He was to become the indwelling Regent of this earth and that His reign could not come into full manifestation until a large part of the world had come to live in accordance with the idea He embodied and the precepts He annunciated. At the heart of this ideal and these teaching lies sacrificial service based on a selfless love for one and all. Contrary to certain current popular teachings, the Path to true spiritual attainment does not lie in attracting to oneself the maximum of worldly goods but in a realization of the truth that a "loving, self-forgetting service is the shortest, the safest, and the most joyful road to God."

The Blessed Lady, accompanied by others of the Master's feminine disciples, mingled with the excited and turbulent throngs which accompanied the Master during the so-called trials that were but a travesty in the name of justice. Outwardly these holy women appeared calm and composed in marked contrast to the distraught mobs mingling around them. Inwardly they were engaged in the work which they knew would best please the Master, and were sending forth great streams of love to soothe and calm the tumultuous and angry throngs, together with fervent prayers that their ignorance and blindness might be forgiven them.

There is profound inner significance in the statement that on the way to Golgotha the Lord Christ met his mother and the other holy women. This refers to the fact that the women were inwardly torn with anguish for the inhuman indignities and tortures inflicted upon the Blessed Master. Knowing this, the Christ poured out upon them His divine compassion and enfolded them in the loving tenderness of His great heart. Thus they were strengthened and fortified so that they were able to bear up under the ordeal to the end.

## The Crucifixion

Christ, the Supreme Initiator, declared "If ye would be my disciple, ye must take up the cross and follow me." There is no other way. Here indeed the Path becomes narrow and the candidate finds that he has no other support than to cling to the cross. Not a few there are who, on reaching this place on the Path of Holiness, turn back through inability to meet the severity of this final test. To be first nailed to the cross and then to be elevated on it before a scorning multitude requires the renunciation of every personal tie that would in any way hinder a complete harmonization with the divine will. Translated into terms familiar in experience to the disciple, the Crucifixion Rite calls for the ability to meet unflinchingly misunderstandings, ridicule and persecution, not only from people generally, but particularly from those nearest and dearest. It means the ability to renounce position, fortune and prestige. It means the renunciation, if necessary, of possessions, friends, reputation and life itself. All things must go until only spiritual realization remains. The candidate here comes to understand what the Master meant when He said that He who would be His disciple must take up the cross and follow Him. St. Francis of Assisi had come to this place upon the Path when he was inspired to give utterance to that sublime prayer that has never ceased to be used by countless souls aspiring to live more fully after the manner of the world's supreme exemplar, the Christ:

> *Divine Master, grant that I may seek,*
> *Not so much to be consoled as to console,*
> *To be understood as to understand,*
> *To be loved as to love.*
> *For it is by giving that we receive,*
> *By pardoning that we are pardoned,*
> *And by dying to self that we are born into eternal life.*

The Blessed Virgin walked with the Christ to the very end of the Path and stood beside the cross to the last. This means that she had trod every step of the Path of Initiation and was awaiting the great liberation with her Lord. Many of the disciples followed the way of the cross but only part of the way; some did not venture it at all, and Peter, one of the foremost of the Disciples, actually denied his Lord and followed Him from ''afar off.'' The Blessed Mary was faithful to the end. It was she who became the most advanced feminine disciple of the Lord Christ and so was made the teacher and leader of them all. It was in her loving arms that the mangled body found its haven on its descent from the cross. For her fortitude and faithfulness, her sublime courage and divine love, hers is the brightest crown bestowed by the angelic Host.

### The Resurrection

The Christian Mystery School teaches that the last enemy to be overcome is death, and that through the final Resurrection Degree the candidate steps forth a son of conscious immortality. As the Christ passed from the Crucifixion Degree into that of the Resurrection, He exclaimed, "My God, My God, how hast thou glorified me," for so reads the correct translation. The Resurrection is truly the Glory Degree. At this stage the candidate passes into the realization of a love that is all-encompassing and a light that is immortal. Though as a server he may yet experience more lives on earth, he will never again know an interruption of consciousness between the activities on the outer plane and those on the inner. Death as it is now understood will exist for him no more. When the Christ went through this Degree for the sake of all mankind, He triumphantly intoned the words, "I am the resurrection and the life." Each candidate who becomes a "son of immortality" by attaining to this high place of consciousness is surrounded by Hosts of Angels echoing these same words of the Christ, "I am the resurrection and the life."

In accordance with biblical records, the Lord Christ made His first appearance to Mary Magdalene in the mystic dawn of that first Easter Day. But secret records inform us that the Lord Christ showed Himself first to the enraptured eyes of the Blessed Mary. So high and so sacred was this divine reunion of soul with soul and heart with heart that it could never be described by mere words. It is only as the modern aspirant learns to walk this same Path that he also comes to know how to ascend sufficiently in consciousness to contact something of the wonder of that first Easter Day, that he may touch something of its divine rapture and of its enduring beauty.

It is only as the modern aspirant endeavors to walk this same Path that he acquires the ability to contact something of the magic of the Easter Dawn with the divine rapture and transcendent glory experienced by Mary on that sublimest of all days.

In his occult novel *Zanoni,* Sir Bulwer Lytton gives the following inspired description of the soul's transit from this side of life to the other:

"All space seemed suffused in eternal sunshine," he writes. "Up from the earth he rose . . . . a thing not of matter—an idea of joy and light! Behind, heaven opened, deep after deep, and the hosts of beauty were seen rank upon rank afar and "Welcome' in a myriad melodies broke from the choral multitude, Ye people of the Skies.

"Welcome! Earth purified by sacrifice immortal only through the grave—This it is to die, and radiant amidst the radiant, the Image stretched forth its arms and murmured, 'Companion of Eternity! This it is to die.' "

## The Fourteen Stations of the Cross

The fourteen Degrees of the Christian Mysteries from the Annunciation to the Resurrection form the basis for the teachings given in the Fourteen Stations of the Cross. In the early Christian Mystery Schools these stations marked the definite steps of initiatory progression and were not merely sumbolical in character as they are generally regarded today. The original seven steps of the ancient Mystery Schools were expanded into fourteen by the Christian mystics. Each candidate entered into the particular Degree for which he had been prepared. Only the two most advanced Disciples of the Christ were qualified to pass through the entire fourteen Degrees. These two were Mary of Bethlehem, the Blessed Virgin, and St. John, the Divine, the best beloved of the Disciples. These two, therefore, were looked upon by the early Christian Initiates and their followers as personifying the two columns before the Temple. They became, as it were, the two enduring pillars of the initiatory Temple and a perfect outward manifestation of the inner development within the body-temple of man. To attain to this state constitutes the prime purpose of the work to be done on the Path that leads to holiness.

The Christmas and Easter Mysteries are intimately connected. The first seven Degrees from the Annunciation through to the Baptism correlate to the feminine or Water element whereas the last seven Degrees from the Transfiguration through the Resurrection correlate to the masculine or Fire element. Polarity or equilibrium is the basic work of the Christian Mysteries. This being so, it follows naturally that Christmas and Easter are the two most important festivals of the Christian Dispensation.

# THE TRANSFIGURATION
## The Transfiguration Event Linking in the Christmas and the Easter Mysteries

The Transfiguration marks the beginning of the glorious Fire Mysteries belonging to Easter which find their culmination in glorious radiance of Resurrection morn.

Christ is not only Lord of the Earth but also the spiritual Ruler of the Sun and the great Hierophant of the Christian or Sun Mysteries. These Mysteries comprised the secret teachings of the early Christian Church. Mankind is just beginning to realize something of the tremendous power emanating through the radiation of the physical Sun and how the earth can be transformed by means of energy. It will be the new Aquarian Race man who will receive and transmit the *spiritual* radiations of the Sun.

At the time of the Transfiguration the Lord Christ appeared before three of His most advanced Disciples clothed in the radiant splendor of His shimmering Sun body, and this marked a definite point in His three-year ministry. From then on the most important events in His life assumed a cosmic rather than a personality aspect. He was preparing Himself to become the world Regent and Savior of the entire planet. At the raising of Lazarus He was initiating John, His most advanced Disciple whose initiatory name was Lazarus, into the new Sun Mysteries. At the Last Supper He was instructing His Disciples in fundamentals which are to become the religion of the new Aquarian Age.

In the Garden of Gethsemane the Lord Christ engaged in the difficult process of bringing Himself into complete attunement with the vibratory rhythms of earth as preparation for his more far-reaching service to the entire planet.

From the cross on Golgotha He passed into the heart of the earth, there to become its indwelling Planetary Spirit and Lord of all created beings, both within and without the earthly sphere.

At the time of His Resurrection He gave to mankind the most glorious of all Easter messages: the demonstrable fact that death is but transition and will eventually have no part in man's planetary experiences. Joyously did He proclaim for all the world that most transcendent of all resurrection themes: Life is eternal and love immortal.

# THE EASTER STORY

*Now upon the first day of the week, very early in the morning, they came unto the sepulchre, bringing the spices which they had prepared, and certain others with them.*

*And they found the stone rolled away from the sepulchre.*

*And they entered in and found not the body of the Lord Jesus.*

*And it came to pass, as they were much perplexed thereabout, behold, two men stood by them in shining garments:*

*And as they were afraid, and bowed down their faces to the earth, they said unto them, Why seek ye the living among the dead?*

*He is not here, but is risen; remember how he spake unto you while he was yet in Galilee,*

*Saying, The Son of man must be delivered into the hands of sinful men, and be crucified, and the third day rise again.*

*And they remembered his words,*

*And returned from the sepulchre, and told all these things unto the eleven, and to all the rest.*

*Luke* 24:1-9

# PART II

# The Holy Easter Mysteries

## CHAPTER VIII

The Lenten Season is a time of soul work preparatory to receiving the inflow of the Easter Mysteries, just as the Advent Season is a preparatory time for the reception of the Christmas Mysteries. The Lenten Season is a period of forty days preceding Easter. While this is according to the calendar, the mystic Christian understands that there is a deeper significance in the numerical value of this period. The number 40 represents a time preparatory to the culmination of some high spiritual endeavor. The Israelites, for example, wandered forty years in the wilderness, symbolical of a goal that was being sought but not yet found, before they were qualified and worthy to enter into the Promised Land; or in other words, to serve as pioneers of a new race and a new age. What this preparatory period actually accomplishes depends upon the effort put forth by the ego. In rare instances this might be completed in forty days. It could occupy forty years and in some instances even forty incarnations.

To the first Initiates of the Christian Mysteries the Lenten Season was not a mere forty-day period of partial fasting and

Holyday prayers as observed in the Church today. It was an extended interval of probation commencing with the Sun's entrance into Capricorn at Christmas and continuing through the succeeding months as the Sun passed through Aquarius and Pisces, and then entered into Aries, the sign of new beginnings, when life mounts to the heights in the miracle of resurrection.

During this period there was a deep searching of heart; events of the past year were recapitulated and the essence of the experiences appropriated by the soul. This process of inner self-examination finds ceremonial expression in the rituals of Ash Wednesday, the first day of Lent, when the palms which waved with rejoicing on the previous Palm Sunday are burned and their ashes poured over the heads of the penitents. Thus is symbolized the failures in the course of the year past to live true to the high ideals to which the soul was awakened on Palm Sunday.

On Saturday, when Saturn the Teacher presides, the "Scrutinies" were observed. That is, the teacher then scrutinized the inner bodies of the disciples in order to ascertain the effects of the disciplines they were undergoing.

The principal subjects for study and meditation during this preliminary period were the books of Job and Jonah. Neither of these two books can ever be understood in their true light until they come to be studied as manuals of Initiation dealing with certain definite processes of development which were further amplified by the Christ during the period of His three-year ministry.

The principal events in the life of the Lord Christ Jesus from the Annunciation to the Ascension outline the initiatory Path which has been given all people and all races through the various religions of the world. This is why many occultists declare that the story of Christ as told in the Gospels is a myth to be read allegorically, and that it is not historic but symbolic of that path of perfection which eventually all mankind will follow. This interpretation leaves out the supreme light of esoteric Christianity, namely, the glorious archangelic Being, the Lord Christ, who even in that remote eonic past which comprised the second great Creative Day, in occult terminology designated as the Sun Period, dedicated

Himself to the guardianship of our earth planet; and in the fullness of time descended into our planetary sphere to take upon Himself a human form in the person of the Master Jesus, the incarnation occurring at the time of the baptism of Jesus by John when the Voice from on high declared, "This is my beloved Son, in whom I am well pleased."

In the Christmas and Easter Mysteries we endeavor to follow the Path of Holiness which the Christ traverses annually in His ministry to this world and its humanity. As we have shown, all nature, which in its totality constitutes the body of this earth, moves in harmonious unison with the ascent and the descent of the Lord Christ, and the path of spiritual progression or Initiation for man follows the same course. Hence when we learn to place ourselves into an ever closer and even more intimate relation with the Lord Christ, we find ourselves correspondingly in closer attunement with the inner spirit of the changing seasons, and with the particular work best accomplished in each of the four seasons of the year.

While the life of the Christ duplicates the experiences of earlier World Teachers and the initiatory steps as taken in the Ancient Mysteries, He not only adds a deeper and more profound significance to all that went before, but enacts it on the plane of history for the world to see and contemplate. Thus the Christed Mysteries are the supreme attainment awaiting the future development of mankind.

As the sum of work accomplished during the Advent Season consisted of three Degrees, the Annunciation, the Immaculate Conception and the Holy Birth, so the sum of the work accomplished during the Lenten Season also consists of three Degrees, namely those of Gethsemane, the Trial and the Crucifixion. The three Degrees which prepared the candidate to take part in the Christmas Mysteries are beautiful and tender, for the work is centered in the love of the heart, and in them the candidate enters into the secret belonging to the feminine column of the Temple which is, symbolically, the Water element in nature.

In the three Degrees which prepare the candidate to enter the Easter Mysteries, the work is difficult and the self-discipline strenuous, for it calls for the development and expression of a firm and concentrated will. Here the candidate learns to unveil the secret belonging to the masculine column of the Temple which is, symbolically, the Fire element in nature. He, therefore, dedicates the powers of his will, and resolves to mobilize all the strength at his command to successfully accomplish the task that lies ahead. It is at this point that, in deed and in truth, he must learn what it means to "walk alone."

In the first or Gethsemane Degree, the Path narrows and becomes as steep as the church steeple with nothing in sight but the surmounting cross. All the purity, all the love and all the faith which have been incorporated into the soul body in preparation for the reception of the Christian Mysteries must now be brought into play, in addition to the strength and firmness of purpose which have been built into the soul during the preceding Lenten Season.

The purpose of the Christmas Mysteries is to guide man along the Path that leads to the Christed consciousness and the dedication of his life to the service of his fellow man. The purpose of the Easter Mysteries is to initiate man into the state of conscious immortality and enable him to gain liberation from the physical body, not only during hours of sleep and between earth lives, but at whatsoever time he may choose, that he may thus become a conscious Invisible Helper at any or all times as may be required, either on this plane or in the realms of the spirit. To attain this development entails a difficult and arduous preparation. The Rite of Gethsemane calls for a life of purity and selflessness. The ceremonial of Ash Wednesday which marks the beginning of Lent includes the placing of ashes of contrition upon the head of the kneeling penitent. The act is symbolic of supreme dedication and selflessness which are necessary before the candidate can pass into the Degree which is known as Gethsemane.

The Agony Rite in the Garden may well be termed the Rite of Transmutation. Christ's agony was caused by His effort to reduce His lofty celestial vibratory state to conform to the limiting conditions of the earth so that He might become its indwelling planetary spirit. When He opened Himself to the earth rhythm, all the powerful and sinister currents of evil that abound in our world swept over Him. He not only felt their crushing weight but saw, in kaleidoscopic vision, their origin and purpose. Humanity's weakness, failures and waywardness seared Him like flames while greed, selfishness and hatred bore down upon Him as leaden weights. The sorrow, anguish and suffering caused by man's wrong-doing wounded Him to the very depths of His loving and compassionate heart.

The limit of agony even an Archangel can know was brought about as pictures of the future passed before His vision and He saw how few of humanity's vast multitudes would recognize the meaning of His coming or the real goal at which he aimed. He watched with profoundest sorrow as the dark veil of materialism blinded the modern world, its consequent failure of discernment, its restlessness and fear. The blindness and ignorance of the masses as to His mission, the crystalization and ever narrowing concept of those avenues which were formerly dedicated channels to His service, brought His Agony Rite to its culmination in the prayer: "Let this cup pass from me, nevertheless not as I will."

Gethsemane was not on the Mount of Olives by chance. It was there because this Mount marks one of the most highly charged of earth's areas. What the Christ accomplished in that highly charged Garden He accomplished beneath the overshadowing wings of Angels. It was a time when the whole program of planetary evolution received a new and powerful impulse.

In the Degree of the Trial the tests encountered by the candidate are in accordance with his spiritual status. The farther one advances upon the Path, the more subtle and penetrating are its trials. None could compare in severity with those experienced by Christ Jesus, for no one possesses His spiritual strength and power.

Again, it is in the Degree of Trial that the candidate realizes the vast importance of his long training in selflessness. If the preparatory work has not been properly done, he will not succeed in passing through this very important Degree. Few there are who have been able to walk along its straight and narrow way. An illuminating manual dealing with this high work declares, "Before the ears can hear, they must have lost their sensitiveness. Before the tongue can speak in the presence of the Master, it must have lost its power to wound; before the feet can stand in the presence of the Master they must have been washed in the blood of the heart.''

The final or Third Degree which leads to liberation is that of the Crucifixion. In this Degree the candidate stands before one of the Holy Mysteries which must ever remain sealed to the profane. Its sacred meaning can only be touched upon briefly here; its true, inner purpose can only be revealed to those who seek and find the light within themselves, the flame of the great white love which passeth all understanding.

There have been some who have reached this high place on the Path and then turned back, not having the strength to walk farther with the Christ on the road that leads to Golgotha. Others have been "nailed" to the cross and then failed because they could not bear to have the cross elevated. Narrow is the Path and subtle are the testings to the very end.

The stigmata in hands, feet and head are in the same relative positions to each other as are the points of the five-pointed star. The five nails are the five senses which bind the spirit to the cross of the physical body. Plato declares: "Each pleasure and pain is a sort of nail which rivets soul to body." The spirit is bound most closely to form through the five senses and here the power of the spirit fire must be most potent. The "drawing of the nails" from these points results in the Five Sacred Wounds.

The scourging is caused by the creative fire mounting upward through the threefold spinal cord. After this has gone on for a time, Neptune lights the spinal spirit fire. This fire vibrates the pineal and pituitary glands in the head, and as the vibratory action strikes the frontal sinus, it awakens to life the cranial nerves or Crown of Thorns. Later the Crown of Thorns becomes a halo of light, and the scarlet robe is changed for one of royal purple.

As the Christ spirit was liberated from the body of Jesus and passed into the center of the earth, His great soul flooded the entire globe with a surpassing brilliance so intense that the sunlight itself seemed dark by comparison.

Every sacrifice bears its spiritual compensation. Every man who dies on the field of battle for something he counts to be greater than himself is reborn on a higher level of attainment. The evolutionary status of the ego is advanced when the blood, which is its direct vehicle, is cleansed of impurities through flowing from the body at death. Every ego, during its vast cycles of earth pilgrimage, knows at least one life where the spirit passes out as the blood flows. The Christ, by His sacrifice on the cross, was lifted into the great Initiations belonging to the kingdom of the Father.

The victorious candidate who follows the Christ to the end of the Way comes to the glory of the great Liberation. He is now free to pass at will from the physical plane into spiritual realms. The Crown of Thorns is transmuted into a halo of light, for he has earned the greatest of all life's gifts, which is conscious immortality. Passing triumphantly into the inner planes he joins the white multitudes that surround the Christ, who raise their voices in joyful chant which echoes the words uttered by the Master at the time of His great Liberation: "My God, my God, how hast thou glorified me!" (Modern translation).

The victorious one now knows the full glory of his own resurrection morning.

# CHAPTER IX

## THE ESOTERICISM OF EASTER

The profound spiritual radiations of the Easter Season bring a quickening of spiritual impulses to even the unthinking and unknowing, while those who understand something of its deep import give reverent obeisance in their very contemplation.

Upon looking at a calendar one notes a difference between the observance of Christmas and of Easter. The Christmas festival always occurs upon a fixed date, whereas Easter sometimes occurs as early as the middle of March, and sometimes even after the middle of April. The reason for the variation is that Easter Sunday must always fall on the first Sunday after the first Full Moon following the Spring Equinox. The procedure was introduced by persons who fully understood the profound esotericism of the Easter Season. The real Easter occurs at the Spring Equinox when the Sun passes from the southern to the northern latitude and the Christ is released from His travail. Then this radiant Being enters into earth's spiritual realms, there to work with celestial Hierarchies and with those members of humanity who have been translated by death into vaster spheres of activity.

During this high season the forces of Pisces (March) and Aries (April) are fused in a wondrous blending of Water (Pisces) and Fire (Aries) which, on every plane of being, holds the key to the Mystic Marriage. All nature knows the joy of this blending. By its magic it gives an added brilliance to flowers, a more exultant note to the songs of birds and the promise of more plenteous fruitage. These mighty fire impulses are under the supervision of the Hierarchies of Aries and Leo. They are, however, of too high a potency to be disseminated directly upon the earth; therefore they are passed down to the Hierarchy of Sagittarius which, in turn, distributes them to humanity. The great Waters of Life of this mystic union are under the guidance of the Hierarchy of Cancer, the Cherubim, and these forces are passed down to the Hierarchies of Scorpio and Pisces and then in turn distributed upon earth.

It was in this season of the Spring Equinox that the ancients who understood these inner world truths established elaborate rituals dealing with the blending of Fire and Water. Even today in this modern world which has lost the key to these sacred truths something of its form still remains and a part of the Easter celebration in the Church consists of the blending of holy water and the sacred new fire. It is in the ''proper'' union of these two forces that the key to transmutation is to be found. Transmutation is the great work in which the Lord Christ and celestial Beings on the inner planes, together with the most advanced of humanity both in and out of the body, are engaged during the interval that we know as the spring and summer seasons. Mystery Temple work upon the earth is also connected with this secret of transmutation. In the coming New Age this law of transmutation will be worked with as understandingly as are the laws governing electricity at the present time.

The magician Mephistopheles worked with this law when he transformed the tired old scholar, Faust, into the exuberant young man in the height and bloom of youth. It was the understanding of this magical secret of transmutation which St. John described in his vision of the New Day when he said that ''the former things are passed away.'' He was referring here to age, disease and death which, through the power of transmutation, can no longer obstruct the full expression of man's immortal spirit.

As stated previously, Easter Sunday can be rightly observed only after the Full Moon which follows the Spring Equinox. Easter is observed on Sunday since this is the Sun's day and the Sun is the home of the archangelic Christ. The focusing of the Sun's powerful spiritual rays upon the earth on Sunday brings to man a vibratory impulse greater than that of any other day.

According to annals of early Christian Mystery Schools their highest revelations and their most ecstatic visions were received on this day. The Hierarchies previously referred to who disseminate this powerful transmutative impulse upon the earth focus it on the

Sun under the guidance of the Sun Spirit, the Christ. This force, however, is not yet strong enough to make its full impress on humanity and so it is here that the Full Moon becomes the channel for its final dissemination. This is the reason that humanity as a whole is not conscious of this great inflow which we know as the celebration of Eastertide until the Full Moon occurs after the Spring Equinox. The masses of people still continue to respond to this inflow largely as an instinctive impulse or desire to take part in some spiritual meeting. Many say they attend church only once a year and that is at Easter. There is also the impulse to be arrayed in new apparel even like nature itself, and to be decked out in new clothes and colorful bonnets and take part in some kind of commemorative service or some fashion parade. Such is largely the modern world's concept of Easter. The Mighty Ones, however, are persistent and unfailing in their ministry to the earth planet, and year by year this powerful spiritual inflow lifts and spiritualizes by degrees the earth and all that lives thereon. Mankind will someday come to realize that, through the process of transmutation during the season of Eastertide, it will be possible not only to wear a new dress but, as Saint Paul expresses it, to put off the old man and to put on the new. This is the true and high meaning and purpose of the Easter Season, and year by year an increasing number of dedicated ones are learning to become more efficient servers of the Christ in His great work as He sings His triumphant Easter song, "I am the resurrection and the life."

# CHAPTER X

The Lenten Season having been spent in deep meditation upon the coming Mysteries of Easter, the candidate is now prepared to enter into the divine Mysteries themselves, as they are celebrated yearly on the inner planes at this holy time of the year when the Christ Archangel returns to His home in the spiritual Sun. To know these Mysteries is to penetrate to the core of the most illuminating of all spiritual revelations ever vouchsafed to man, the Christ Mystery. Something of the truth of Easter may be apprehended from a study of its external features, but only with the esoteric approach can its most transcendent significance be uncovered.

In the days of the early Church the Lenten Season was a time of deep and earnest preparation for meeting the tests and trials of Passion Week which, successfully passed, would lead to advancement in the ever-ascending degrees of illumination.

Orthodox Christianity, having lost the keys to Initiation, stresses the historical Easter; esoteric Christianity emphasizes its initiatory aspect in terms of individual spiritual unfoldment.

Orthodoxy centers upon the Passion of the Christ, while the esoteric Christian concentrates on the effect of the Passion within himself, recognizing that he, too, is a Christ-in-the-making. Hence the statement of Origen, the third century Alexandrian teacher of the Christian Mysteries, that "the happenings in Palestine are useless to us unless they occur within ourselves." And also the words of like import by the medieval saint, Angelus Silesius:

> *The cross on Golgotha thou lookest to in vain*
> *Unless within thyself it be set up again.*

In common with the Ancient Mysteries, the Greater Mysteries inaugurated by the Christ are divided into three principal steps or Degrees. The first is the Rite of Purification, which is concerned with the cleansing of the lower nature of the sense life. This leads to the beginning of what is commonly referred to as "living the life."

Every step on the Path carries with it a spiritual compensation. That of the First Degree is the ability to serve as a conscious Invisible Helper. Many instances of disciples who attained to this Degree, and its accompanying powers, are mentioned in the Book of Acts.

The Second Degree is the Rite of Illumination. This sets into motion certain currents in man's inner vehicles which awaken the power of positive clairvoyance and clairaudience. Numerous examples of this attainment are to be found in both the Gospels and the Acts.

The Third Degree is that of Mastership. With its attainment the Mystic Marriage between the personality and the spirit is consummated. The forces of the personal self have been so sublimated as to be able to enter into perfect union with the indwelling spirit. Heaven and earth unite to do obeisance to one who has attained, for he becomes in very truth the master of all he surveys.

The formula for this Degree is concealed in the story of the marriage at Cana in Galilee with which John opens his Gospel. This marriage, pertaining as it does to the Third Degree, is recorded as occurring on the "third day." The word Cana means "to heal" or "to forge," and the word Galilee signifies "the whiteness of snow." John begins his Gospel with the marriage feast, because it conveys to those who can discern its inner meaning the place on the Path to which he himself had arrived.

There are "keys" placed within the biblical records of the lives of the followers of the Christ which to the initiated reader indicate the specific Degree to which they had progressed and which, moreover, serve to outline the process of development for the esoteric aspirant who seeks to take the Way of the Cross and to follow the Path of Christian Discipleship.

The greater part of the Gospels is devoted to the work of the men and women disciples of the Christ and the efforts they put forth to attain to illumination in the Christian Mysteries during the Passiontide. These days have been termed the Great Week because of the tremendous significance of the events associated with it, and also Holy Week because of the deep sacredness of the Mysteries with which it deals.

Holy Week begins with the Triumphal Entry into Jerusalem and concludes with the glory of the Resurrection when death is truly swallowed up in life. Between these events are the Stations of the Cross making up the Via Dolorosa or the Sorrowful Way. They come after Palm Sunday and before Easter. They succeed the hosannas accompanying the Entry and precede the Resurrection when the Christ consciousness that was only awakening on Palm Sunday rises into the glory-tide of the illumined, resurrected life on Easter Morn. The ideal first visioned becomes the ideal made real.

### The Lazarus Initiation

The exalted initiatory work undertaken through the week of the Passion was inaugurated on the Saturday preceding the Triumphal Entry with the Initiation Rite of Lazarus. Due to the upward course of man's evolution, the ancient phases of Initiation, together with certain aspects of the Jehovistic religion, were passing away. The Christ came "to make all things new." The forces which He released with His coming were necessary to save humanity from losing its way in a materialism which was destined to become darker and denser for many centuries that lay ahead. But in the orderly processes of growth, the new takes over and incorporates the values that have been created in the old. Thus in the initiatory Rite of Lazarus both the processes that prevailed in the old rituals and those that were now being instigated in the new were combined, the result being the birth of the new Christian Mysteries. This event, therefore, marked the beginning of the Holy Easter Mysteries, or the deeper spiritual teachings upon which was founded the early Christian Church.

The great power possessed by the early Chirstian Church—
power to heal and to perform miracles—was derived from its
knowledge of these Mysteries. Later, as worldly interests encroached more and more upon the Church and materialistic thinking darkened its consciousness, the Church lost contact with its
original source of power and fell into relative impotency, a condition that has prevailed for centuries past and which continues into
our own time. Not until the truths of Initiation are recovered by the
Church can it again come into the power that will enable it to lead
mankind in effecting the regeneration required to qualify it for
establishing a Christed order on this earth. But some there have
been always, both in and out of the Church, who have retained the
inner light and conserved for humanity the wisdom of the initiatory
teachings. Such we know as the illustrious saints whose lives and
works have glorified the pages of history through the centuries past
and present.

In the three Degrees of the Christian Mysteries, the work of
the First Degree, as previously mentioned, is Purification. It is
related primarily to the desire body. The work of the Second
Degree is Enlightenment and pertains more specifically to the
etheric body. The work of the Third Degree is called the Rite of
the Master which unites the forces of the etheric and the desire
bodies in such a way as to create thereby a medium by which the
illumined spirit can contact the inner realm and enter into conscious communion with beings belonging to both the superhuman
and the subhuman kingdoms of life.

In the Rite of Purification, the neophyte is taught how to live
the chaste and the harmless life. If the aspirant remains true to the
principles set forth in this Degree, he experiences in time an
awakening of certain latent centers in the desire body. This accomplished, he henceforth comes into firsthand knowledge of the
facts belonging to planes of being that lie beyond the cognition of
the physical senses.

The next stage in esoteric development, that of the Second
Degree or Rite of Illumination, consists in causing the awakened
centers in the desire body to make their impress on corresponding
centers in the etheric body. To this end aspirant practices certain

exercises in concentration and meditation until clairvoyance and clairaudience are developed. This result was obtained quite differently in the pre-Christian Initiations. In the ancient rites of Egypt and Babylon, for example, rites derived originally from ancient Atlantis, the candidate for Initiation was taken out of his physical body by the supervising teacher and during a three and a half day period on the inner planes the active desire centers made their impress on the centers of the etheric body, these two vehicles having been withdrawn simultaneously for this purpose. Thus a supernormal condition directed by an Initiate Teacher was necessary to achieve this result. With the coming of the Christ, this condition was altered, making it possible for man to attain to a development in normal waking conditions which had hitherto been possible only under an abnormal state and especially supervised condition under higher guidance. Awakening from the trance state, the neophyte of the pre-Christian Initiations was hailed as one risen from the dead. He was truly "new born," having acquired supernormal faculties and powers of which he hitherto had no experience.

Materialistic thinking and sensual living tend to interlock the etheric and desire bodies so closely as to make Initiation extremely difficult, if not impossible. Such was the general condition of humanity at the time of the coming of Christ Jesus. His work was to set man free from this barrier to higher spiritual attainment. The beginnings of this accomplishment are produced by means of concentration and meditation to which is added the nightly exercise of retrospection, all of which formed a part of the teachings of the early Church. In concentration the masculine pole of spirit, or the will, is primarily active; in meditation, the feminine pole, or imagination, is the dominant factor. By means of such exercises the centers of the desire body can be impressed upon the etheric without disassociating the latter from the physical body. At the present time, due to the prevailing materiality, the difficulty in severing the two vehicles in the way of pre-Christian times is so great as to be likely to prove disastrous. Insanity, and even death, would too often be the result.

The most highly advanced of all the followers of Christ was

chosen to receive the new form of Christian Initiation. This was the disciple best beloved of the Master whose initiatory name was Lazarus. The name Lazarus means "whom God assists." It was the high status of his development that enabled him to respond to the initiatory summons: "Lazarus come forth," and later to receive his great Teacher's commendation in the words: "Lose him and let him go."

It was the bridging of the old and new that took place in the raising of Lazarus which brought such great rejoicing to the people when Christ Jesus made His Triumphal Entry into Jerusalem on Palm Sunday, the day following the Initiation of Lazarus.

### *The Triumphal Entry*

Every event in the life of Christ Jesus during the Passiontide represents some phase of Initiation into the Christian Mysteries. The Triumphal Entry typifies the joys of the Path as Calvary symbolizes its sorrows. To the masses who watched the Palm Sunday procession it was merely beautiful pageantry honoring the great Teacher who for the three years past had performed such wonders in their midst as causing the blind to see, the lame to walk and the sick to become whole. But to the esoteric Christians its significance was far greater. To them it was an outer manifestation of the holy joys that would be all mankind's when it shall have attained to the Christed consciousness now made possible through the newly instituted processes of Initiation into the Christian Mysteries.

The hosannas of the multitudes that lined the road along which the Master passed in His Triumphal Entry were reverberating echoes of the angelic song that greeted the birth of Jesus. Then they had sung, "Peace on Earth, good will toward men"; on the day of His entry into Jerusalem for the concluding acts of His earthly ministry they sang: "Blessed be the King that cometh in the name of the Lord: peace in heaven, and glory in the highest." Thus they heralded the dawning of the New Dispensation under which every man is destined to become a king in his own spiritual kingdom and to walk in the name of the Lord, or in the law of love and light and truth.

The scene of the Triumphal Entry was Jerusalem, the City of Peace, representing the heart or love center of the body wherein the Christ spirit first comes to life. The ass on which Jesus came riding symbolizes the Ancient Wisdom, and the palms strewn on His path represent victorious attainment. Thus the Christ enacted a scene in His processional entry which pointed to the glories of the New Age when the truths of the Christian Mysteries shall have become the universal religion of humanity.

The Master had sent two of His Disciples, Peter and John, to prepare the way for His entry, instructing them to go to the "village which is in front of us" where they would find a colt. This they were to bring to Him, and on this the Christ rode into Jerusalem.

The village "in front" is the Path which always looms before the aspirant, and the colt—symbol of Wisdom—that had never before been ridden upon, is the newly released spiritual impulse which gave birth to the Christian Mysteries. That His Disciples had become initiated into the Christian path of spiritual illumination is indicated by the fact that they knew the way to the village and promptly brought back the colt.

## The Master in Bethany

Each night of the Passover Week the Master spent in the well-beloved home of His most spiritually advanced follower, Lazarus, and his two sisters, Martha and Mary. Monday of Holy Week was devoted to instructing these disciples in the deeper phases of the initiatory work.

It is important to note that two of these three advanced disciples were women. This is the more remarkable when considering the low status to which women were then relegated, especially in Oriental countries. But in coming to elevate the whole of humanity, the Christ makes it plain that the two polarities, the masculine and the feminine, must be brought into equilibrium. He, therefore, extended a recognition to woman and to the high place which she should rightly occupy, a recognition foreshadowing the position she will assume in the world when the New Aquarian Age of equality and comradeship between the sexes shall have become fully manifest.

The two women disciples, Martha and Mary, typify the two Paths. Martha represents the mentality, the Path of works. Martha was always "busy about many things." Mary typifies the heart Path or way of devotion. She renounced all else to sit at her Teacher's feet. Of the two, the Master observed that she had chosen the better part.

As previously stated, the awakened sense centers in the desire body make an impress upon the corresponding centers in the etheric body according to certain definite processes that take place in the course of spiritual development. A body so prepared acquires a luminosity that becomes the most welcome of all gifts to the Christ, for it means a dedicated life qualified to serve on both the inner and the outer planes as both a visible and an Invisible Helper. Herein is to be found the true significance of Mary's breaking the alabaster vase at the Master's feet and anointing them with fragrant oil. In early Christian symbology a vase represents the soul. Something of the spiritual attainment of Mary is indicated by the statement that the perfume from her vase filled the house. Thus it was the fragrant soul body fashioned in the luminous whiteness of an alabaster vase that Mary dedicated to the service of her Lord.

### Monday—Tuesday—Wednesday of Passiontide

The Monday of Passion Week, as previously noted, was spent in Bethany with Lazarus, Martha and Mary. The deeper teachings given to the two sisters at this time are beautifully portrayed in the allegory of the supper which was made for Him in the house of Lazarus as described in the twelfth chapter of St. John's Gospel. Initiatory processes are ofttimes veiled in the description of a supper or feast, for to reach such exaltation of consciousness is truly a soul feast beyond compare.

Though Martha, the neophyte, was through her service preparing for spiritual promotion, the text makes it plain that she was not yet ready to partake of the initiatory repast. Lazarus, the recently "new-born," sat at the table with the Master, and partook with Him freely of the bread of heaven and the waters of eternal life.

Mary stood upon the very threshold of the Temple of Light as her dedicatory ceremony of anointing the feet of the Master during the course of the supper makes plain.

On Tuesday the Master commenced giving to other men and women disciples advanced work leading up to the glorious Resurrection Rite. The Book of Proverbs was the textbook used at this time because its mantramic values are such as to stimulate and lift certain vital body currents that must become active in the initiatory processes.

On Wednesday, Judas succumbed to the temptation of the high priests who typify human reason or the mortal mind unillumined by the power of the spirit. The thirty pieces of silver point numerically to the triad $(3+0)$ composed of the physical body, desire body and the lower or concrete mind. When these bodies or principles operate on the lower level as they did in Judas when making the great betrayal, they always destroy themselves as in the case of his self-destruction. This failure of Judas indicated that he had not succeeded in passing the First Degree, or Rite of Purification.

### Holy Thursday

In preparation for the Rite of the Eucharist which was celebrated on Holy Thursday, the Christ commissioned two of His Disciples to go into the city where they would meet a man bearing a pitcher of water. Him they were directed to follow into a house where a large "upper room" was to be ready for the coming of the Master and His Disciples. Together they were to eat there the Passover supper.

These instructions are really a cryptic anagram pertaining to the esoteric development of the aspirant. The man bearing a pitcher of water has reference to Aquarius, the sign of the water bearer, and ruler of the New Age when the spirit of true illumination will be poured out anew on all flesh and for which preparation was being made even then. The "upper room" is the head which, when "furnished and ready" through the quickening of the spiritual centers therein, gives insight into the inner and higher worlds. With the pineal gland and the pituitary body awakened and active, the veil before the Holy of Holies is lifted and man stands in the presence of his own higher self as created in the image and likeness of God, and is capable of manifesting the powers of a Christed one.

In the light of this symbolic reading may be deduced the spiritual status of Peter and John, the two Disciples sent ahead by the Master. They had already been found worthy to enter into the "upper room." Theirs was now the high privilege to prepare the way for whosoever would, in all time to come, follow in their footsteps.

## *The Footwashing*

Perhaps the most important lesson the candidate for Initiation has to learn is humility and the willingness and readiness to serve each and all. Not until this lesson has been mastered is man properly qualified to rule or to wield with safety the powers that Initiation bestows upon him. It is a fundamental law of evolution that the most advanced continue their further progress only as they stoop to serve the lowliest and to help them to rise to higher levels. Self-sacrifice lies at the heart of all true attainment. It was in obedience to this cosmic law that the footwashing preceded the most exalted teaching which the Master gave to His innermost circle in the whole of His earthly ministry. "If I wash thee not," said He when Peter protested that the Master should not so humble Himself, "thou hast no part with me." Humility and forgetfulness of self are passwords to the highest attainment. It is he who becomes as nothing who attains to all.

The Christ knew the high destiny awaiting Peter when his pride and impetuosity would be replaced by serene humility. Consequently Peter becomes the central figure in the footwashing scene in which all disciples of all time are given the supreme object lesson in humility as a prerequisite to true spiritual attainment.

It is from the old custom of washing the feet of the poor on this day as a fulfillment of the "new commandment" that the Church gave to this day the name Maundy Thursday, a term derived from the Latin, *mandatum,* meaning "to command."

## The Last Supper

"If thou wilt go up with Christ to celebrate the Passover, He will give to thee that bread of benediction, His own Body, and will vouchsafe to thee His own Blood," writes Origen, the early Christian mystic.

The Last Supper or Rite of the Eucharist has formed a part of every initiatory teaching that has ever been given to man. In Egypt the mystic bread and wine signified the blessings of the Sun God, Ra. In Persia the Eucharist was a part of the Mithraic Mysteries. In Greece the bread was sacred to Persephone and the wine to Adonis. The Rite is also referred to in an ancient fragment from India's Rig-Veda. "We have drunk soma," reads a passage, "we have become immortal; we have entered into the light; we have known the Gods."

Every age, people and religion have received this sacred ritual of the bread and wine and always it is observed as the ceremonial carrying the loftiest spiritual teachings that can be given at the time. With each succeeding age and religion, as the divine revelation is extended, the Eucharist ritual has taken on deeper meanings, reaching its highest spiritual significance when the Christ, the supreme World Teacher, celebrated the rite with His Disciples in the Upper Room on the midnight hour of Holy Thursday immediately preceding Good Friday or the Day of Passion. At that time the Christ taught His Disciples how to demonstrate the powers of the Mastership Degree.

In Pliny's celebrated *Letter to Trojan* written in 112 A.D., he states that on certain days the early Christians held two meetings, one before dawn when they sang hymns to Christ and bound themselves by a "Sacramentum" to commit no crime, and the other in the evening when the Agape or Love Feast occurred.

Wine symbolizes the cleansed and transformed desire body of the disciple. Bread represents the pure and luminous etheric body. It is through the blending of spiritual forces within these two prepared vehicles of the spirit that the powers of Mastership may be demonstrated. Each of the holy men and women who participated in the Last Supper with the Christ had so purified their desire and etheric bodies that they were able to receive and transmit the Christed powers for the healing and spiritual enlightenment of all whom it was given them to serve.

By living the pure and harmless life for a period varying in length according to previous development, the conservation of life essences in the body produces a vital force of a higher order which radiates from the body and which may be drawn upon and used at will in the service of others. This etheric emanation reached a degree of luminosity in the Disciples on the night of the Holy Supper such as they had never attained before. Each of the Disciples gave this soul emanation to the Christ at the time of the Holy Supper. Drawing this force into Himself and augmenting it with His own divine powers, the Christ appeared before them in all the glory of the body of His Transfiguration. Then it was that He poured this mighty stream of energy into the bread and the wine, magnetizing them by the magic of spiritual alchemy until they shone with the splendor of countless jewels.

In later observances of the Eucharist by the early Christians the divine powers evolved by the ceremonial magnetized the bread and wine in like manner and to such a degree that substances so sanctified were widely used for healing the sick. Rightly were they called the "medicine of immortality."

The Supper on this first Holy Thursday night was concluded with the Lord's Prayer, a mantram of tremendous power when rightly used, and with the "kiss of peace." By this token did they indicate the unity and harmony they had achieved and the common reservoir of spiritual power which they had generated for the purpose of carrying the Christ impulse out into the world for its solace and redemption. They had realized true *fellowship* which is the first requisite for effective group accomplishment. Herein is to be found the answer to the oft propounded query: Was Judas present at the Last Supper?

St. Ambrose, fourth century Bishop of Milan, writes that in the ritual practiced in the early Church the bread was broken and then placed together in the form of a human figure, thus representing the body of Christ that was broken for all the world in order that fallen humanity might be saved.

The Lesser Initiations are nine in number and correlate with nine Mysteries in the life of Christ Jesus. These are given as follows: 1. Incarnation; 2. Nativity; 3. Circumcision; 4. Transfiguration; 5. Passion; 6. Death; 7. Resurrection; 8. Glorification; 9. Ascension.

The human body is the temple of the indwelling spirit and every forward step in the expansion of consciousness produces its corresponding development in the physical body. From the standpoint of occult anatomy the consecrated bread represents the new vital force that has been created in the body through conservation and transmutation of the sacred creative life force.

The Chalice or Grail Cup represents the new etheric organ which already is beginning to form in the body of the pioneers of the New Age. This organ has its power center in the larynx which will become the instrument for speaking the divine Creative Word. This power will have been gained when the creative life force now centered at the base of the spine has been lifted to its summit in the head and the physical creative process sublimated into its spiritual counterpart.

The "flower cup," or new spiritual organ which is now being built in the throat, will form a direct connecting link between head and heart with the result that man will be able to think with his heart and love with his head. This new organ will also make it possible to recover the memory of past lives. Such recollection will then be no more difficult than it is to now recall events of past years in this life. Christ referred to this development when He said: "I will drink no more of the fruit of the vine, until that day that I drink it new in the kingdom of God."

The occult significance of the Holy Grail has been the same all through the centuries as the following quotation from Apuleius, second century Roman philosopher, well indicates. Describing this cup as symbolic of the developing etheric organ in the throat, he states that in the processional of the Mysteries: "One carried an object that rejoiced the heart, an exquisite invention bearing no resemblance to any living creature, man, bird or beast. A wonderful ineffable symbol of the Mysteries to be looked upon in profound silence. Its figure was a small urn or cup of burnished gold. The spout extended laterally, projecting like a long rivulet. Around it twined a golden serpent curling its body into folds and stretching upwards.''

The spout or stem of this cup-like organ is formed of the essence of the kundalini fire in the spine as it rises serpent-like towards the throat and head and forms into a luminous flower cup. The serpent is a universal symbol of the Arcane Wisdom. Hence the Initiate in the Egyptian Mysteries was called a Serpent. In the Christian School he is referred to as the Son of Man, and when the Mysteries it teaches shall have come to full flower we shall have entered the sign of Aquarius, or the Age of the Son of Man.

In the exalted state of consciousness into which the Disciples had been transported during the Supper ceremonial they were able to look upon nature's Cosmic Scroll and to see therein the events awaiting fulfillment in the remaining years of their earth lives. These events they were now in position to accept or reject as they would. That they chose to follow the events therein outlined, hard as it would be to endure them, is evidence of the high spiritual status they had attained since in every case that course led through diverse persecutions and often to martyrdom. But the personal self had been renounced; they now went forth as Christed souls, and so fortified, no matter what might befall the physical body, the soul marched on, sure and serene, toward certain triumph.

*The Agony Rite in the Garden*

From the Upper Room the Master went directly to Gethsemane. The agony that He there experienced marked another step on the upward way for Him, even as it does in the life of every aspirant when undergoing a like experience as he journeys on the Path that leads to illumination.

The Agony in Gethsemane may also be termed the Rite of Transmutation. After the elevation of consciousness gained in the Upper Room, and the accession of power that comes with it, the next forward step on the Path requires that this added light and strength be applied to the transmutation of evil into good and darkness into light, both in one's own life and in the world at large. In the case of Christ Jesus the agony suffered was the result of opening His pure and perfect body to the influx of the currents of evil of all kinds that swept in from the world without. These forces He received within Himself in order to work on them alchemically and then to radiate them back into the world as transmuted powers for righteousness. Such is ever the work of the redeemers of man, be they of the stature of the World Saviour or those of lesser degree who devote their lives to loving, selfless service for others.

The Master had expected His three most advanced Disciples, Peter, James and John, to assist Him in His Transmutation Rite. But as they were not sufficiently purified and selfless, they "were asleep" or inwardly unaware of the work that was being undertaken in the Garden of Sorrows.

Gethsemane was on the Mount of Olives because it was, as previously observed, the most highly charged spiritual area on all the earth. It was the point where the redemptive agony could best be endured and consummated. That the earth has special areas where the spiritual forces are most sharply focused and highly charged is in keeping with the localized centers of perception, physical and spiritual, in the body of man.

What the Christ performed in the divinely charged Garden of Gethsemane under the overshadowing wings of Angels and Archangels had a significance for all humanity. It marked a point when planetary evolution as a whole received a new, powerful impulse that was destined to carry it forward another step on its ever ascending way.

Peter came to know this Rite of Agony after his triple denial of the Lord when he returned in abject contrition to the Garden, there to face his own Gethsemane. There in its highly charged area and in communion with invisible Hosts, Peter, through repentance and purification of heart, lifted himself in consciousness to that high place where he would be further prepared and sustained for the higher Initiation that awaited him in the interval between the Resurrection and the Ascension.

To the Mount of Olives, vibrant with spiritual power, John the Beloved and Mary, the Holy Madonna, made frequent pilgrimages in later years when the Master walked no more beside them in earthly form. For here it was that the gates of Heaven opened and Angels and Archangels came to commune with men. Mystic legends of the early Church contain many references to Mary's meeting with the disciples in the Garden of Olives, such meetings always having reference to some aspect of the work of transmutation.

The olive possesses rare occult properties and is one of the most highly sensitized of all fruit trees. It will grow only in certain rightly favored areas. It is among the pioneers of the plant kingdom and all through the ages it has been associated with healing and regeneration, qualities which are inseparably connected with the process of transmutation. Hence other legends there are which state that both the cross and the crown, symbols of the attainment following the transmutation process, were made of the wood of the olive tree.

# CHAPTER XI

The four Gospels are formulas of Initiation. Matthew, Mark, and Luke begin with the Nativity, or the Holy Birth, for they are formulas of the Lesser Mysteries. The Gospel of St. John begins with the Rite of the Mystic Marriage. This Gospel is a formula of the Greater, or Christed Mysteries. St. John's Gospel is the most profound initiatory treatise ever given to man. Rudolf Steiner, the eminent occultist, states that this Gospel should not be considered merely as a textbook, valuable as it is as such, but *as a spiritual force*. Esoteric students of the western Mystery Schools are taught to meditate daily upon portions of this Gospel.

At the time of the Spring Equinox all nature lies under the spell of the mystic blending of the Water and Fire principles. The fruitage of this blending is beauty, harmony and perfection. In the spring nature manifests this beauty because the blending has been consummated under the great stellar Hierarchies. Man must also find the key in this sacred Rite to the Greater or Christed Mysteries but he must learn how to perform this Great Work himself. The Christ was referring to this Rite of the Mystic Marriage when he admonished the Master Nicodemus (who was already familiar with the work of the Lesser Mysteries) that he must be born of Water and of Fire before he could enter the Kingdom of God (the Greater or Christed Mysteries). This was also the meaning of the supreme Master's words when He said, "I am the way, the truth and the life. No man cometh unto the Father but through me." The supreme purpose of His mission to Earth was to bring the Greater Christed Mysteries to man.

Each event connected with the life of the Lord Christ as given in the Gospels represents some definite step along the Path of

Initiation. The beautiful ceremonialism of Good Friday outlines the consummation of Christed attainment. The orthodox Christian world observes this day as a time of sorrowful vigil. The mystic Christian experiences on this day a rare spiritual exhileration. He sees the Crucifixion as a means unto a greater end and the agony of the Path is lost sight of in contemplation of the supreme joy which lies just ahead. He understands that the crucifixion of the body must always precede the liberation of spirit. A Master once admonished his pupils, "It is only in moments of dire distress that thou wilt find thy weapons and also thy brothers in the Great Cause."

The musical Initiate, Richard Wagner, who understood much of Christian esotericism, has given many glimpses into the deeper meanings of this wonder day in his sublime soul drama, *Parsifal*. This transcendental work may well be considered a treatise dealing with the magic of Good Friday. Much of the beauty and mystery of this day has been woven into the Good Friday Spell music which he incorporated in the final act of his sublime music-drama, *Parsifal*.

Every aspirant who endeavors to walk the Path is a Parsifal in some stage of his development. He, too, as did Parsifal, will know the way of the cross, and if he be patient and persistent in well doing he will eventually, like Parsifal, know the supernal soul revelations which constitute the spiritual magic of Good Friday.

The scene of Parsifal's return is laid amid the beauties of nature on a bright spring morning. It is Good Friday, and a benediction of peace lies over all the landscape.

There is a strange contradiction between the ecstasy of nature in the springtime and the Lenten ceremonial observed at this season by the orthodox Church. Places of worship are swathed in somber black while penitents kneel in tears and contrition, meditating on the Passion of Christ. Nature, on the contrary, is arrayed in her most beautiful robes of the year and everywhere are heard songs of gladness and rejoicing. Parsifal describes the one as "the day of darkest agony divine"; of the other, he says, "How beauteous the morning meadows are, they speak of the infinite love of God!"

When man fell, that is, lost perfect attunement with his spiritual consciousness, he also lost equilibrium between the two poles of spirit within himself, the masculine and feminine or balance between head and heart. This want of equilibrium brought sorrow, poverty, disease and death into the world. The cross on which the Christ permitted Himself to be crucified is the great cosmic symbol of this loss of equality between the two polarities in nature, humanly represented by man and woman. The cross is found in all lands and has been used by all peoples because the whole human race suffered this loss of equilibrium in the early days of its evolutionary journey.

As Christ hung upon this cross, which, according to esoteric Christian tradition, was both literal and symbolical, an historical event and a spiritual dramatization, He opened the Way of Initiation whereby all mankind might again find completeness within; and by means of that completeness or integration, rediscover the Edenic state of abundant well-being and immortal life.

Nature already manifests the "boundless love of God" as polarity. Each year with the crossing (crucifixion) of the Sun at the Vernal Equinox from south to north, northern latitudes enter upon their resurrection season and all nature demonstrates the beauty and joy of a perfect alchemical blending of life forces. Parsifal refers to this, the great Easter Mystery, when he baptizes the repentant Kundry with the words, "Rejoice with all nature harmoniously redeemed."

Kundry represents the Divine Feminine which fell through emotional instability as typified by the horizontal bar of the cross. Later, accompanied by the triumphant Parsifal, she enters the Temple to the joyous pealing of Temple bells. Together they pass between the two upright columns which have replaced the cross and which are symbolic of Initiation through polarity. These two columns will replace the cross as universal symbols of religion in the Aquarian Age now dawning.

Parsifal tells of nature under the Good Friday Spell:

*True, I did meet some marvelous flowers*
*Which sought around my neck to twine their tendrils;*
*And yet so fresh never seemed before*

*The grasses, frondage and blossoms;*
*Nor did their fragrance seem so sweet,*
*Or speak with such appeal to me!*

"That is Good Friday's Spell, my Lord!" says Gurnemanz.

"How can that be?" asks Parsifal. "Surely instead of joy and blossoms nature should mourn and sorrow for that day of agony?"

Gurnemanz explains that the great glory of the Eastertide is due to the tears of sinners, wept in contrition and falling like holy dew upon the earth to bring it to flowery fruition. "Hence it is they flourish. All living things rejoice, they hear the Saviour's voice, and Him they cherish!"

The groves and fields, he goes on to say, cannot look to Christ upon the Cross, but they look to man redeemed. In the blossomings of flowers may be observed the counterpart in nature of the process of transmutation as it takes place in the lives of individuals.

Gurnemanz continues to expound the inner mystery of this sacred season:

*Each blade of grass, each twig and tiny blossom,*
*Knows that on this day can come no harm,*
*But that as God, with mercies manifold,*
*Remembered man, and for him died,*
*So man this day will be less bold*
*And walk with careful stride.*
*Now grateful all things animate*
*Which live a moment and go hence,*
*That all-absolved they may await*
*And greet this Day of Innocence.*

In the exquisite soul enchantment which Wagner wove into the Good Friday music he blended all the sadness and sorrow of the exoteric religionist with the ecstasy manifest throughout nature in the spring season. It is music that typifies the culmination of the great transmutative process whereby the personality (Kundry) is raised into atonement (at-one-ment) with the spirit (Parsifal). It is this alchemical blending which raises the aspirant to the Third or Master's Degree, described in the opera as the Crowning of Parsifal. The crowning is accompanied by that most ethereal of earthly music, the combined Eucharist and Grail motifs.

The descent of the Dove on Good Friday to replenish and bless the Grail and to nourish and sustain the Knights for another year has reference to exalted occurrences belonging to the Degree of Mastership as observed upon this day in inner plane Mystery Temples. According to ancient legend, it is on this holiest of days that nature puts forth her loveliest tribute of blossoms. Also, the animal kingdom responds to the accelerated life rhythms of the planet by drawing closer to one another and to man. Thus, all nature contributes to the holiness of Good Friday. The mystic knows it to be one of the supreme holy days of the year, because it is the time when Temple doors open wide to permit "the qualified and worthy" to pass through the portals of glory.

All this Wagner incorporated in his Good Friday Spell which, like the alchemy of nature herself, reveals life where there seems to be naught but death. This music, drawn from the fount of the Mysteries, shows us the human lifted to the divine, to that world beyond our world which is the sole reality. Even upon the unilluminated this "other world" casts its magic spell with indescribable loveliness.

With the crowning of Parsifal, the cycle of illumination is brought to a close. The music dies away in the haunting beauty of the Grail motif, growing ever more ethereal as Angels wing their way through translucent golden mists and are lost to human sight and hearing. Man will eventually come to understand that out of this Temple music of *Parsifal* he can build a golden bridge of sound whereby he may commune with angelic and archangelic hosts.

Richard Wagner, the musical prophet of the New Age, has in *Parsifal* brought to light an ancient Christian Mystery which both conceals and reveals much of the esoteric deep and high spiritual meanings which compose the magic of Good Friday.

# CHAPTER XII

On Good Friday the successive steps taken on the Path of Discipleship were symbolically enacted in the events that occurred on the Via Dolorosa, or the "Way of Sorrow." He that does not take his cross and follow me," said the Master, "is not worthy of me."

The Passion of our Lord on Good Friday touched the very heart of the Mysteries. The fourteen Stations of the Cross represent certain steps pertaining to spiritual development, each Station correlating with a specific center in the body. The distance each disciple traversed on this Way was, therefore, determined by his own soul status. Only the Divine Mary, John and Mary Magdalene were sufficiently advanced to make the journey to the end. This is why these three, and these only, are always pictured beside the cross that bore the crucified body of the Christ. The number three also indicates that they had each passed the Third or Mastership Degree.

In the three trials before Annas, Caiaphas and Pilate, the scourging, the crown of thorns, the three times the Christ fell under the weight of the cross and the three meetings with the holy women upon the steep ascent to Calvary, the candidate for Initiation into the Christian Mysteries discovers corresponding experiences in his own climb toward the Mount of Illumination as he takes up the cross to follow the Christ.

The various events mentioned in the Gospels, which took place during Passion Week in the lives of the men and women who composed the inner group of the Master's followers, all bear a veiled reference to some phase of their own development in connection with one or more of the three Degrees belonging to the Christian Mystery School. Each Station of the Cross thus becomes a milestone on the Christian aspirant's path as he journeys along the Via Dolorosa which becomes in truth what the California Mission Fathers called the *El Camino del Rey*, or the Highway of the King. At its terminus, the sorrows of the Way are swallowed up in the joyous ecstasy of the resurrection.

The principal obstacles on the Path are represented in the trials before Annas, or mortal mind; then in the trial before Caiaphas, or worldly ambition; and next before Pilate, or weakness and vacillation of mind when required to take a stand for truth and principle at the risk of endangering personal position or prestige in the eyes of unenlightened associates and benefactors.

The scourging represents the discomforts and sometimes pain that accompanies the birth or awakening of the successively higher centers located along the spine as the serpent fire makes its ascent from the sacrum to the centers in the cranium. The Crown of Thorns has a like significance, referring specifically to the revivification of certain areas in the head. It is because they have a similar meaning that the two incidents are usually mentioned together.

With the ascent of the spinal spirit fire to the head, the cranial nerves are progressively sensitized. These nerves surround the head like a crown, and in the Degree of Mastership they radiate a veritable halo of light.

Three times the Blessed Lord fell beneath the weight of the cross. What he so enacted physically is representative of corresponding moral failures to which frail humanity succumbs again and again as it treads the sorrowful way toward the light. As the Way-shower for all humanity, no aspect of the Path was omitted from His pattern-life. Man falls beneath the weight which the veils of matter have placed upon his spirit; also he falls because of his earth-bent desires, and yet again he falls because of the glamour to which his spiritually unillumined mind gives way. Thrice over he falls because of hindrances springing from his physical, his desire and his mental bodies.

As the Master ascended Calvary, He was confronted three times by holy women. They represent the activity of the feminine principle of love-wisdom which works for a purification of the physical and the desire bodies and a spiritualization of the mind.

After the third fall Simon the Cyrenean took the cross and carried it the remainder of the way. This act, translated into terms of spiritual achievement, indicates that his dedicatory vows of discipleship were then and there made, whereupon he took up his personal cross and followed the Christ to the place of liberation. Simon, having already passed the Rite of Purification, was ready to undertake the work leading to the Second Degree of Illumination.

According to the mystic legend, the Master was comforted by Veronica who wiped His brow with her handkerchief as He was struggling up Mount Calvary. Having done so, she discovered to her enraptured amazement that His features had impressed themselves upon her kerchief. This incident points to an experience of one of the women disciples who had succeeded in making the impress of the desire body centers upon the centers of the etheric body, thereby causing her to become clairvoyant, or to possess the ability to read the Cosmic Scrolls. This is the signature of the Second Degree.

According to the Gospels, Pilate's wife Procula, ''had a dream pertaining to this good and just man.'' This is another way of saying that she had the ability to function consciously on the inner planes when out of the body at night and that from the Akashic Record she learned the truth about the mission of the Christ as the Saviour of mankind. Her experience also bears evidence of Second Degree Attainment.

### THE STATIONS OF THE CROSS

The Stations of the Cross mark the places where the Christed Jesus halted as He carried His burden along the Via Sacra to Calvary, the Mount of Liberation. Originally these Stations numbered only seven and were known as the Seven Falls. During the Turkish occupation of the Holy Land the location of these Stations on the Sacred Way underwent some change and also much of the esoteric significance attached to them was lost.

The deeper meanings of these Stations did not originate with Christianity. They are linked to the nature of man and the processes involved in the unfoldment of his divine nature. Their meanings are, therefore, common to the Ancient as well as to the Christian Mysteries. In the Mysteries of Eleusis, for example, there was a Sacred Way which led from the city of Athens up the slopes to nearby Eleusis. These Stations, or Huts, as they were called, represented certain stages of development, and no disciple was permitted to proceed farther on that Way than his attainment warranted. Within each Hut or Chapel, the disciple received instructions that assisted him in going on to the next Station. In early Medieval times devout Christians commenced the practice of reproducing in their churches the Stations of the Cross by sculptured or painted scenes from the Passion. They would also frequently place shrines or chapels representative of the several Stations along the way leading to the church. When this was first done there was a knowledge of the mystic import of these Stations but gradually this faded, except for the very few, as materialistic thinking encroached more and more upon true esoteric understanding. Today they serve at best as little more than objects of veneration, stimulating the devout to prayer and devotion, and giving rise in many instances to nothing more than superstitious beliefs and practices.

The Stations that originally numbered seven were later doubled in number. Esoterically they represent the way of development by means of awakening the seven flower centers, in their double positive and negative aspects, that come to bloom upon or within the cross of man's body. The experiences in the life of Christ Jesus marking the fourteen Stations are as follows:

| | |
|---|---|
| I. | Christ Jesus is condemned to death. |
| II. | He carries His Cross. |
| III. | He falls the first time. |
| IV. | He meets His mother. |
| V. | Simon of Cyrene helps Him carry the Cross. |
| VI. | Veronica wipes His face. |
| VII. | He falls the second time. |
| VIII. | The daughers of Jerusalem weep for Him. |
| IX. | He falls the third time. |
| X. | Is stripped of His garments. |

XI.      Is nailed to the Cross.
XII.     Dies on the Cross.
XIII.    Is taken down from the Cross.
XIV.    Is laid in the sepulcher.

In all esoteric literature the seven centers are described as follows:

Number One is situated at the base of the spine. Here sleeps the kundalini or spinal-spirit fire. Dark red in its latency, this fire when awakened is transformed into a clear, ruby red.

Number Two is located in the solar plexus. Its color of reddish-orange is modified in the processes of transmutation by a touch of clear vernal green.

Number Three correlates with the spleen which, like a miniature sun, radiates a golden light. In early development there is a blend of green-gold light which later on becomes pure gold.

Number Four, the cardiac or heart center, emits a soft yellow radiance which in higher stages of transmutation becomes tinged with ethereal blue.

Number Five is located in the throat just over the larynx. Its color is azure blue through which, when fully expanded, gleam sparkling silver lights.

Number Six is situated near the center of the head toward the crown. When completely awakened, this emits kaleidoscopic color patterns of indescribable beauty. Its primary tones are rose, yellow, blue and purple.

Number Seven is in the topmost part of the head. When fully developed it is a crown or halo radiating an effulgent, white light.

The awakening of the two lower centers correlates with the First Degree of Purification and the spleen and heart centers with the Second Degree of Illumination. The throat center is the doorway connecting personality and spirit, and comes into its perfect flowering only when the personality has become spiritualized, or, in other words, is ready to obey the behests of Spirit in all things. The two head centers correlate with the Third Degree of Mastership.

In the esoteric understanding of the early Church the disciples who journeyed on the way to Calvary did not *meet* the Master on the way but *followed* Him. This is the true interpretation since the Christed One was the Supreme Way-shower for all mankind. The Stations mark the most important steps leading to the Christed Initiation.

### Station One—Christ Jesus Condemned to Death

In the transforming experience of Initiation man dies to the outer world and is born to the inner life of the spirit. The first station represents the supreme dedication. One is the beginning of all things. As One is the great White Flame which holds all the seven colors in latency or suspension, so also the pre-initiatory dedication becomes the seed from which spring forth in due course all the spiritual forces latent within the consciousness of the disciple.

### Station Two—Christ Jesus Carries His Cross

After the supreme dedication, the cross becomes a familiar object to the aspirant. It confronts him in all the experiences of his daily life and makes its impress upon his inner and outer life. It is at this Station that the beginning of the Way becomes so difficult that many turn back to the world and walk with the Christ no more.

As One belongs to the sphere of the infinite so Two belongs to the sphere of the finite. Two represents the descent of spirit (One) into matter. Station Two typifies the crossroads of decision, the halting place from which the disciple either turns back to the old ways or moves forward toward a more perfect alignment with spirit.

### Station Three—Christ Jesus Falls the First Time

To consider the Stations merely in relation to their historical significance as external events in the life of one unique man is to lose sight of their true significance for all mankind. Clearly, if the Christ is the Supreme Initiator, then His Way must have a significance for all. Esoterically each Fall along Via Dolorosa is symbolical of an experience in the life of the disciple, under which he may fall, or fail. It is important, therefore, to understand the nature of these tests so that they may be met with understanding.

The One added to the Two produces the Three. The early sages defined the outpourings of the Triplicity as the World of Emanation. It is through the forces of Three that Spirit descends to abid in flesh. The rhythm demonstrated through Three depends upon the harmony existing between One and Two, and therein rests the key to man's future evolution. The Third Fall relates to man's present stage of evolution in which he becomes deeply involved in the world of matter.

### Station Four—Christ Jesus Meets His Mother

Pythagoras termed Four the sacred number because it signifies the soul. Hence the inspired chant: "The Four from the One and the Seven from the Four."

The Kabbala states that the first feast is that of the Great Mother. The Mother represents the Divine Feminine, or the image-making faculty and love principle of the spirit of man. Since it is the realization of the Divine Feminine and its consequent unfoldment of spiritual powers toward which the disciple aspires he encounters the Mother, or the perfect pattern of attainment in the early stages of his quest.

### Station Five—Simon of Cyrene Helps Christ Jesus Carry His Cross

In the early stages of the initiatory processes the work of development is concerned with the masculine and feminine poles of the spirit alternately. In the *Book of Concealed Mystery* it is affirmed that the Father and the Mother contain all things and that all things contain them, also that whenever sins are multiplied in the world and the sanctuary is polluted, the male and female are separated. This preparation represents the present imperfect and unbalanced state of man's development. Consequently, the primary work of the initiatory Path is the restoration of the lost equilibrium.

Five, therefore, is the number of change or transition. It is the number of good in the making. It has been called the dual number because it represents the higher and lower natures in their struggle for supremacy. Here the Path narrows and the Cross looms large.

### Station Six—Veronica Wipes the Face of Christ Jesus

The Song of Solomon is an apostrophe to the Divine Feminine. In no other literature is the pure soul ecstasy of an Illumined One more vividly described: "My beloved is mine and I am his." Thus this inspired song describes the uniting of the masculine and feminine poles of spirit.

In the Five occurs the struggle of the human with the divine. In the Six the forces of creative construction work toward establishing a harmonious interrelationship. Six is human love dedicated to Venus. Through the suffering engendered by human love the soul is resurrected or reborn. The number Six spells preparation through purification; under its powers the illumined vision of seership is born.

### Station Seven—Christ Jesus Falls the Second Time

The ascent through Station Six comes only with purification. At Station Seven further progress depends on the strength of will and purpose.

Seven is the point of the Sabbath, or rest; not cessation of activity. It is the point at which the disciple emerges from a lesser to a higher order and from which he proceeds to spiritual victory and mastership. At this point the experiences of life are synthe-

sized and their essences transmuted into usable powers of the
soul. From this place further progress, though difficult, is continuous and uninterrupted.

*Station Eight—The Daughters of Jerusalem Weep for Christ Jesus*

It is the separation between the masculine and feminine principles that has caused all the pain, sorrow and death in the world.
This separation brought about the submergence of the feminine and
it is for this that the daughters of Jerusalem weep.

The Supreme Master and His works demonstrate the perfect
powers of the two poles in equilibrium. The Cross He bears and
the Path He follows up Calvary typify the way of restoration for all
humanity. "I am the way, the truth, and the life" is a chant of
profound mystic significance. The lament of the daughters of
Jerusalem (the awakening soul) arises from the fact that man has
not more nearly approached this Christed ideal.

Eight is the "free" or resurrection number and carries the
high powers of the golden Christ Ray. It is the highest feminine
number and holds the ideal of the feminine in exaltation (equilibrium). It represents soul powers of transcendent quality. It is the
number of intuition or the voice of the soul.

*Station Nine—Christ Jesus Falls for the Third Time*

The Third Fall is concerned with the powers of the unChristed
mind. St. Paul referred to these as the powers of darkness. Had the
feminine soul quality not been submerged by the purely mental
forces, man's unillumined mind would never have attained the
disproportionate power that it now possesses. The mind is the Path
and its Christing is the most important work of human evolution.

The number Nine represents the evolutionary ladder which
extends from man to God, hence this has been termed the number
of man and the number of Initiation, or the Christing of man.

From the sixth to the ninth hour the earth was darkened as the
Master, bound to the Cross, became the supreme Way-shower for

all mankind in demonstrating perfect spiritual equilibrium. Nine marks the beginning of this reunion of the powers, and the mind, as previously noted, is the way of attainment. "Let the Christ be formed in you," is the foremost Christian mandate.

### *Station Ten—Christ Jesus Is Stripped of His Garments*

The Tenth Station marks the beginning of the Great Renunciation, symbolized in the Master's parting with His seamless garment. This beautiful robe represents the active consciousness of Good, which is esoterically likened to the extracted essence of the good of all our earth lives, and which is visible to the interior vision as a "soul body" or "golden wedding garment," a luminous halo encircling the entire body and extending far beyond it in a radiant gleaming glory, as exemplified in the lives of many illustrious saints. This glorious soul-sheath was renounced by Christ Jesus, so that its powerful emanations might permeate the etheric envelope of the earth. Man continues to receive both physical healing and spiritual inspiration from this released power, for Christ's sacrifice was not only of the body but of the soul as well. It was an outpouring of light and love from which the earth and its humanity will benefit until the end of time.

The number Ten signifies the very substance of being. All numbers lead up to it. Numbers beyond this are merely combinations of preceding digits. Ten is formed of both the masculine (1) and feminine (0) potencies and represents man and woman working through the laws of generation. The sublime purity of soul typified in the Seamless Robe, and the renunciation in yielding it up in service to less advanced beings, are here beautifully portrayed as the high attainment of the Tenth Station.

### *Station Eleven—Christ Jesus Is Nailed to the Cross*

Station Eleven marks the full and complete renunciation of the personal life in favor of the spiritual, as the Tenth Station marks its beginning.

The esoteric philosopher, Franz Hartmann, writes: "Woman represents man's beauty and will, while the male part of humanity represents reason and strength, but neither a male nor a female being is perfect. Only that being is perfect in which the male and female elements are united."

The cross is the symbol of the prevailing disunion between the masculine and feminine principles in mankind; and the spirit of man, or the Christ within, is bound to this cross of limitation until it frees itself through Initiation whereby the perfect balance is effected.

As the cross (+) represents the lack of equilibrium between the masculine and feminine, so the number Eleven (11) represents equilibrium, the supreme goal of the human race. Therefore Eleven is called the master number. When the forces of Eleven become fully operative in man he has the power to change his environment, to create new conditions, to build a new body and a new life, all in harmony with the divine image in whose likeness he was fashioned in the beginning.

Renunciation of all belonging to the physical plane brings the divine compensation of unlimited scope and power in the higher spiritual realms. As the soul disengages itself from materiality, it achieves a corresponding freedom in its own true world.

The ancients thus defined the powers of Eleven: "In my grasp are all things held in perfect equilibrium. I bind all opposites together, each to its complement."

### Station Twelve—Christ Jesus Dies on the Cross

Through Initiation the disciple dies to the finite, the personal, the material, only to be born anew into the wonder and glory of the infinite, the impersonal and the spiritual. The mortal is exchanged for the immortal, the terrestrial for the celestial. With the words, "It is finished," the glorious Christ Spirit was freed to function in realms of immortality. Such, too, is the attainment of the disciple when reaching this place upon the Path. Death has been met and conquered. Never can that dread specter touch him again for life eternal has become his heritage.

The number Twelve may be applied to all concepts which deal with extension, expansion and elevation. It transcends the three-dimensional. The consciousness belonging to it is posited in a higher dimension.

The Tarot symbol for Twelve is the crucified man, or one who has renounced all and thereby gained all. The ultimate purpose of the human ego's pilgrimage through the earth sphere is to bring into manifestation the Christ force latent within. Number Twelve sounds the keynote of this accomplishment.

*Station Thirteen—Christ Jesus Is Taken Down from the Cross*

The Thirteenth Station is the Degree of the Great Liberation. When the sacred body was freed from the cross it was given into the arms of the Blessed Mother. In other words, through equilibrium the ego is freed from the cross of materiality and is lifted into the sublime exaltation of union with the Divine Feminine.

The Kabbala states that "when the male is joined with the female, both constitute one complete body and all the Universe is in a state of happiness, because all things receive blessings from this perfect body. And this is an Arcanum." In other words, this is the supreme evolutionary consummation of the human race.

Under the power emanation of Twelve, lessons are learned through the masculine rhythms of One and the feminine rhythms of Two. Twelve grouped around the One form a unity which vibrates to Thirteen. Herein lies the secret of peace, plenty and power for all mankind. In the formula of Thirteen is to be found the occult key to the Master's words: "Where two or three are gathered together in My name, there am I in the midst of them."

Much of the work of Christ and His Disciples is concerned with the mystic formula of Thirteen. Under its powers the New Dispensation was established. The Thirteenth Station governs the transition from a lesser to a higher state. Its forces are therefore especially operative in this day when the new Aquarian Age is coming into manifestation. As if pointing to this fact there are thirteen stars composing the celestial urn from which the constellation Aquarius, the water bearer of the skies, is pouring out the waters of life upon the earth.

### Station Fourteen—Christ Jesus Is Laid in the Sepulcher

The Christ was placed in a "new tomb" in which no man had ever lain before. The masculine principle is laid low in death, or inequality, that it may be raised together with the feminine in equality. The number Fourteen represents the combined forces of the masculine One and the feminine Four. Here Four becomes the entrance gate into realms supernal. This was the Degree Work demonstrated by the supreme Master along the Via Sacra and symbolically perpetuated in the Stations of the Cross.

The burial of Christ Jesus in the "new tomb" indicates that He who was placed in it came to experience the Mystic Death that leads to a new Initiation, or rather an Initiation of a higher Degree than any that had ever preceded it. For Christ's mission to earth was to found the new School of the Christian Mysteries. This tomb, therefore, was not a mournful sepulcher of death but a gateway to life more abundant.

The Fourteen Stations or Degrees of ever ascending and expanding consciousness, have their parallel development in the interior stars or flower centers which adorn the body of an illumined one. "After this, I looked and behold a door was opened in heaven." Such is the biblical expression for this exalted experience.

Among Christ's nearest and dearest only a few had the strength to follow Him all the way. Among those who did so, some turned back, not having the strength to make the final renunciation of losing their life in order to gain it. Others forsook the Christ at this stage because they did not have the strength of character and conviction that would enable them to remain steadfast in the face of an apparently ignominious end for their Master and the taunts and jeers of the crucifying crowd about them. The test that here confronts the candidate for the next higher step on the Path is one few are ready to pass.

In the words of the Rosicrucian mystic, Max Heindel, ''This step is for those who close their eyes to all the sights of earth, those who have ceased to care for the praise or blame of men, but who are looking to their Heavenly Father. Those who are ready and willing to uphold Truth and Truth alone. Those who see with the heart and see into the hearts of men, that they may discern therein the Christ, the Son of the Living God.''

# CHAPTER XIII

THE CROSS—A UNIVERSAL SYMBOL

"The cross is a sublime hieroglyphic possessing mysterious power and virtues." It is a "symbol of devotion and sacrifice."

Across the star-strewn face of the heavens is emblazoned this oldest of earth's symbols, the cross. It is formed by the four cardinal signs of the Zodiac: Cancer to the north and Capricorn to the south forming the vertical bar; Aries to the east and Libra to the west forming the horizontal arms.

These four signs comprise the thirty degrees of the Zodiac nearest to the two Solstices (north and south) and the two Equinoxes (east and west). Thus it is that above the busy and restless heart of this little planet there gleams the steady guiding light of the great cross of the heavens.

It is significant to note that the Aries-Libra Dispensation heralded the first coming of the Lord Christ, "the Lamb who was slain from the foundation of the world." It has been predicted by spiritual astrologers that His second coming will be in the Capricorn-Cancer Dispensation.

The earliest symbol to receive the homage and adoration of man was an upright pillar. It represents the masculine force in nature, the positive generative force. Later, the horizontal bar was attached to the perpendicular column, forming a cross. The horizontal bar signifies the passive or productive feminine force in nature and in woman. The cross which surmounts the steeples of many churches proclaims that this is a man's world and that the position of woman is secondary. The inequality between man and woman has been the cause of so much sorrow and suffering down through the ages that the cross stood as a symbol of pain and punishment for centuries prior to its association with the Christ. Before the end of the Aquarian Age the cross as a universal symbol will have been superseded by two upright columns, for the New Age is to witness the establishment of perfect equality between the masculine and feminine powers, symbolized by two upright columns side by side.

The Masonic Fraternity, the most magnificent school of symbology now existing, has accepted this equality in principle. The cross is seldom used by it, while the two upright columns is the most familiar emblem of the Lodge. Named Jachin and Boaz, they are prominent in all Degree work. If Masons accepted this ideal in practice as well as symbolically, doors of their lodge rooms would be open to women as well as to men.

## The Antiquity of the Cross

Origin of the cross appears to be coincident with the earliest history of mankind. It was an object of reverence and adoration among the most primitive peoples, and it has been a sacred motif of decoration in the finest temples and cathedrals of highly advanced nations the world over. The great pyramid of Gizeh in Egypt brings to light two kneeling figures holding between them a cross bearing an upright serpent. The serpent on a cross was a commonly used symbol throughout Egypt, the former typifying esoteric wisdom. Their traditional form of the cross was the Crux Ansata, the one with a circle above it. This they termed "the key of life," and it was entombed with priests, kings and queens.

The Tau cross was sacred with the Hebrews. Tau, the twenty-second and final letter of the Hebrew alphabet, means *eternal life*. It was their custom to stamp upon the foreheads of released prisoners the sign of the Tau as an evidence of freedom and innocence. According to early Bible history it was a Tau cross drawn in blood upon their doors that caused the Angel of Death to pass them by at the time the tenth scourge was visited upon the peoples of Egypt who held them in bondage.

The cross was also a sacred object of worship in China, India, Persia and among the Indians of both North America and South

America. The Temples of the Druids were built on the cruciform plan, as indicated by ruins still to be seen in Scotland and Ireland.

The caduceus was essentially a Greek cross. In it the horizontal bar is replaced by two wings, and two serpents are entwined about the staff. It is frequently referred to as the Staff of Mercury. In this connection it is significant that Mercury was the God of Initiation, and that in Greece Initiation doubtless reached its greatest heights of sublimity. Modern aspirants recognized in the caduceus the most complete symbol of Initiation ever conceived.

At the time of the Advent of the Christ the cross in general use had a lamb resting at its foot. This was to herald His coming, for He has ever been associated with the lamb (Aries). In the New Testament He refers to Himself as "the good shepherd," while one of His most beautiful teachings is the Parable of the Lost Sheep, also known as the Parable of the Ninety and Nine. Quite some time elapsed after the Christ departed from this earth before a human figure was placed upon the cross, which then became the crucifix so familiar to modern devotees.

The keynote of spiritual attainment is sacrifice. Primitive man ofttimes offered up his fellow man. Later, as he became more advanced, animal offerings took the place of human. The Lord Christ came to teach the nobler lesson that man should offer *himself* upon the altar of sacrifice. That loving, self-forgetting service is the shortest, safest and most joyful road to God is the mantram of a school of Christian esotericism. It was only after this concept of self-sacrifice was given to man that a human figure was placed upon the Christian cross and became a universal symbol of devotion. A human figure so placed has been a hieroglyph of Initiation from time immemorial; but it was known as such by only the few who recognized self-sacrifice as the one key to that high state of illumination. The Ancients spoke truly when they said "The mysteries of God are concealed in the cross."

As the concept of the Christos has unfolded, it differs in certain respects from that which prevailed in centuries past; and so has His image as related to the cross taken on a different form. By comparing those of the closing Piscean Age with those of the dawning Aquarian Age, we discover that each out-pictures the

Christ and the cross in terms of the dominant phase through which Christianity was and is passing. Pisces being the sign of sorrow and suffering, the bleeding agony of the crucified Christ became its symbol. It portrayed the essential character of the experiences through which humanity was passing. As Pisces placed emphasis on death, the Aquarian Age will place emphasis on life immortal. The cross which is the symbol of the incoming New Age will not bear a human figure nailed upon it; instead, it will be the resurrected Christ imposed upon the beautifully symbolic Rose Cross, emblem of New Age attainment.

Symbology has ever been the language of the wise, for symbols can both conceal and reveal important truths. And all truths have two meanings, an inner interpretation for the few and an outer for the many. St. Paul describes them as meat for strong men and milk for babes. Though couched in symbols, the deeper truths are always plainly discernible to those who are ready for them.

### The Rose Cross—The Cross of Transmutation

As previously stated, the crucifix is the Piscean cross, marking the Age as one of sorrow and suffering. The Rose Cross belongs to the coming Aquarian Age and points to the glory of conscious eternal life. The cross itself symbolizes religion while the rose connotes science; thus it heralds the glad Aquarian day when religion shall be scientific and science shall be spiritualized.

In ancient Greece the rose was dedicated to Aurora, Goddess of the Dawn, and it signified resurrection into a new consciousness of life. This flower has always typified secrecy; hence, the Latin *sub rosa* meaning *under the rose* or *confidentially*. In medieval Europe it was the custom to paint roses on the ceiling of rooms wherein certain assemblages were held; this indicated that nothing pertaining to the meetings was ever to be divulged. Then there is an ancient masonic hieroglyph showing a man standing before a closed door with a rose in his hand, and he is admonished that not until the rose is in full bloom will the door open. It is apparent that there was an intimate connection between the Rosicrucian Order and the first Order of Knights Templar.

We repeat that the caduceus is deeply symbolic of initiatory truth. Its perpendicular rod typifies to alchemists the spinal cord within the human body. Along this cord lie certain centers that in eastern Schools of Wisdom are termed lotus blossoms; in western Wisdom Schools they are known as roses blooming upon the cross of the body. The two serpents entwined about the rod of the caduceus symbolize the two nervous systems, the cerebrospinal and sympathetic. As the centers are awakened definite changes take place in these two nervous systems. Alchemists speak of the two columns of the Sun and Moon; the two elements of gold and silver; the Red and White Servitors—all of which refer to the processes of transmutation that occur as one learns to walk the path of true discipleship. The seven roses upon the cross symbolize definite spiritual attainments, such as clairvoyance, clairaudience, the gift of prophecy, ability to leave the body at will and speaking the divine word. The beautiful Rosicrucian salutation, "May the roses bloom upon your cross" is an aspirant's loving prayer that all may know the glory of this high attainment.

In Rosicrucian symbology the white cross with its seven roses is placed against a background of azure blue. The background shadows forth infinity, while the roses on the cross connote the limitless possibilities offered by the Path of the Rose Cross. The four terminals of the cross end in three loops each. Together they symbolize the twelve creative Hierarchies which surround the universe of which the planet earth is a part. The celestial Beings who comprise these Hierarchies give of themselves in loving service to aid the entire human race in its ascent toward Christood.

### The Cross of Light

"The person of Jesus having disappeared, there was seen in His place a cross of Light, over which a celestial Voice pronounced these words: "The cross of Light is called the Word, Christ, The Gate, Joy, The Bread, The Sun, The Resurrection, Jesus, The Father, The Spirit, Life, Truth, and Grace."

—Albert Pike in *Morals and Dogma.*

The highest attainment of the Rose Cross is symbolized by a pure white balanced cross with a single full-blown white rose at its center. This represents completion of the Great White Work, when both body and mind have been fully spiritualized. The single white rose represents the conscious Invisible Helper. To such an one the physical body is no longer a prison house; he is free to go and come at will on errands of love and mercy. He has learned that fire cannot burn the spirit and that water cannot drown it. He descends into the bowels of the earth and goes far into outer space, to bring aid and succor to all in need of them. The new Air Age will greatly increase the ministry of conscious Invisible Helpers. Each night before going to sleep Rosicrucian aspirants repeat the following dedicatory prayer: "Tonight while my body is peacefully resting in sleep may I be found faithfully working in the vineyard of the Christ, for as spirit I need no rest."

### The Cross Superseded

Toward the end of the Aquarian-Leo cycle the cross as a universal symbol will be superseded by two upright columns, as we have already observed. These two pillars will stand for Aquarius and Leo. The keynote of Aquarius is law; of Leo it is love. In a civilization based on these two precepts, the vision of the prophet will be a reality: "The earth shall be full of the knowledge of the Lord (spiritual law), as the waters cover the sea" (Isaiah 11:9). Between these two columns man and woman shall walk hand in hand in perfect equality and shall pass into the initiatory Temples of the New Age.

The four arms of the cross relate to the four elements: Fire, Air, Water and Earth; also, to the four fixed signs of the Zodiac; Taurus-Scorpio and Aquarius-Leo. Previous reference has been made to the work of these four Hierarchies in the closing days of this, the Piscean Age. The nations are liquidating their karmic debts under Taurus-Scorpio and are being prepared for the Aquarian Age under Aquarius-Leo. This is also true of individuals who are cleansing their karmic slates and making ready for the new Air Age

The four symbolic beasts referred to in the Bible likewise belong to the four fixed signs. These four signs work upon man's four lower principles—physical, etheric, astral and mental—by means of purification and transmutation. Taurus, symbolized by the bull and whose element is salt, works upon the physical. Scorpio, symbolized by the eagle and whose element is quicksilver, works upon the etheric. Leo, symbolized by the lion and whose element is sulpher, works upon the astral or desire principles. Aquarius, symbolized by man and whose element is azoth, works upon the mental vehicle. (Azoth is a cipher representing the quintessence of the other three elements). So, by the processes of purification and transmutation under the ministry of these Hierarchies, the spiritual essences of man's three lower principles are incorporated into the next higher, the mental. He will then live, move and have his being in a vehicle made of mind substance. The wonders of such development can be only faintly comprehended. As we reflect on the miracles already performed through the instrumentality of the human mind, even though its latent powers have scarcely been tapped, we get a vague concept of its almost infinite possibilities. For one thing, man will be able to travel in his mental body to the farthermost solar system or visit the most distant stars at the speed of merely thinking himself there.

In the opening pages of life's great textbook, the Bible, we read of Adam and Eve and of the Garden of Eden where they dwelt—but which they lost by their descent into materiality. In the closing pages of Revelation, the final Book of the Holy Bible, St. John depicts the redeemed Adam and Eve and the celestial Garden wherein they shall abide, whose gates will no longer be barred by the guardian Cherubim. Instead, they will be flung wide by the supreme Initiate of the archangelic Host, the Blessed Lord Christ.

In the Capricorn-Cancer Dispensation, Capricorn symbolizes the Christed man, the new Adam, while Cancer symbolizes the new Christed woman, the new Eve. These are the regenerated pioneers who will meet the Christ when He comes, and aid in building the new heaven and new earth, as described in the Book of Revelation.

The feminine or reproductive principle within man has been crucified. That which should be a sacrament of chastity and love has been degraded into passion and lust. Woman, the objective counterpart of this feminine principle in the outer world, has also been crucified down through the ages. With the coming of the Aquarian-Leo Dispensation she will be restored to her rightful state of equality with man. Every organ in the human body-temple possesses a masculine and feminine potency, one of which predominates. It is a fact of profound occult significance that as the body is changed to meet New Age conditions, each feminine organ will undergo a further spiritual development. The heart will become the true light of the body, so bright and lustrous that the entire form will be made luminous by its shining. Circulation of the blood will be controlled by the spirit. Man will be able to withhold the blood from any specific physical area when necessary, and to send it in increased volume to any other area where needed. The blood will not be a red liquid as at present, but will consist of a white-gold essence. The Church has many beautiful legends about saints whose blood has turned white. The sympathetic system, which is the feminine nervous system, will be changed into a second spinal cord, causing man to become androgynous (male-female) again. The creative power will be lifted to the larynx, and creation will be effected through the power of the spoken word. The Lost Word of Masonry will have been restored.

The building of this glorified human vehicle will begin in the Aquarian-Leo Age. It will receive further development in the Christ Dispensation of Capricorn-Cancer, and it will attain to its highest state during the Sagittarius-Gemini Dispensation. The Hierarchy of Sagittarius is known in esoteric parlance as the Lords of Mind, who function entirely in vehicles of pure mind substance. They radiate from themselves those germs of mind which long since became man's most priceless gift. They will continue their ministry to the human kingdom until its every member is ready to function in a body composed of subtle mind substance. As under the ministrations of Sagittarius man will eventually live and function in a body of pure mind substance, so under Gemini he will perfect the androgynous power within himself; that is, bring the masculine and feminine potencies of his body-temple into perfect equilibrium. God, the Father of this solar system, is the supreme head of the Hierarchy of Sagittarius and the highest Initiate of the Lords of Mind.

Sacrifice always brings its spiritual compensations. The greater the sacrifice the greater the reward. The Blessed Lord Christ, by reason of His crowning sacrifice for the redemption of the world, was caught up into the realm of the Sagittarius-Gemini Dispensation, as evidenced by His utterance from the cross: "My Father, how hast thou glorified me!" (a modern translation).

This is but a brief preview of the exalted attainment that awaits mankind. St. Paul doubtless caught something of the wonder of this vision when he declared in ecstasy, "Thou madest him (man) a little lower than the angels; thou crownedst him with glory and honor" (Heb. 2:7).

# CHAPTER XIV

## THE SUPREME MYSTERY: THE SACRIFICE ON GOLGOTHA

The Master was crucified between two thieves, these thieves being, in terms of initiatory experience, the desire body and the lower mind, both of which tend by their very nature to appropriate to themselves the light that belongs to the spirit.

The five sacred wounds which Christ Jesus suffered at the time of His elevation upon the cross allude to certain sheaths which encase the spirit within the prison-house of flesh and which the disciple learns how to remove as he follows the Master through the Rite of the Mystic Death into the full glory of the Resurrection Morn.

"From the sixth hour there was darkness . . . unto the ninth hour." These are the hours from twelve to three, indicating the period when the spiritual overcomes the personal and the higher nature wins its final victory over the lower. This is the sacred interval between twelve and three on Good Friday, hours to which the Church gives special emphasis in its solemn vigil on this holy day.

During these hours the light in the outer world begins to decline. Similarly in terms of inner experience this is the time when interest in external things grows less and less and that pertaining to the spirit grows more and more intense and vivid. They are three crucial hours when the transforming power that has been awakened in the fire centers of the body-temple produce "a light such as never yet lay on land or sea." In the body of the earth the corresponding three centers, which in the holy Eastertide become reservoirs of tremendous spiritual energies, are located at the poles, north and south, and at the equator.

When the Christ Spirit passed from the cross a glorious, golden light flashed throughout the desire or astral body of the earth. What then happened can perhaps best be imagined by reflecting on the effect produced on the physical plane by the release of an atomic explosive. As the latter is capable of "evaporating" steel towers and leveling whole cities in a flash, so can the energies of a vastly higher order such as those at the command of the Christ, instantly flash through the inner, psychic worlds and "evaporate" long accumulated miasmas that for ages past have been generated by an unregenerate humanity. From the moment the Christ made such a release of divine energy mankind has lived in a healthier psychic atmosphere. By a stupendous cosmic act of redemption conditions were made more favorable for man to contact his better self, to lay hold of higher values, and to save himself from the pit of self-deception and degeneration into which he had fallen.

But this redemptive act of the Christ was not limited to this one single spiritual "atomic" release. Since its first occurrence, at which time He became the Regent of the Earth, He has served humanity on a planetary scale, re-enacting annually the cosmic outbreathing of His purifying spirit as this rises yearly with all nature at the Spring Equinox or Easter and reascends to the throne of the Father at the Summer Solstice or Ascension time after having functioned in and with the earth from the fall of the year or the Autumn Equinox through the Vernal Equinox or Eastertide. Such is the redemptive rhythm of the Cosmic Christ. Such has been His work with humanity since His coming to our planet in the body of the Master Jesus; and such it will continue to be until humanity shall have arrived at a point where it will be able to carry on its own collective redemptive work without His further immediate aid. Once this truth and all it implies is realized, the lover of the Christ makes it his greatest aim to qualify himself that he may become more worthy to be a partaker in the fellowship of the suffering of the Christ, thus hastening the day when the age-long sacrifice which He is still making, that man might have life and have it more abundantly, may come to an end.

Because of this cosmic aid that the Christ has rendered humanity, the door to Initiation has been opened to whosoever will enter. Before His coming Initiation was possible to a few only and, as previously noted, under abnormal conditions such as no longer prevail. The sublime Rite on Golgotha rent the veil. A new spiritual force entered human evolution. By availing himself of this every man can achieve Initiation into the Mysteries and conscious entrance into the kingdom of the spirit.

Thus the initiatory process has been rendered universally possible through the forces released on earth by the Christ and transmitted to humanity through the planetary fire centers previously mentioned. One of the effects of this released energy is to loosen the connection between man's desire body and his vital or etheric body. When this is accomplished man need no longer take his Initiations in a disembodied trance state, but under altogether normal conditions.

Upon leaving the body of Jesus, the Christ penetrated to the heart of the Earth. This raised the planetary vibration and attuned the earth's physical sheath more closely with the World of Divine Spirit. The earth's etheric sheath has lightened and cleansed with the result that it could henceforth transmit added energies from the universal or Christed realm which Rosicrucians term the World of Life Spirit and the Theosophists call the Buddhic Plane. Similarly the desire or astral sheath of the earth was made the clearer channel for transmitting into earth life the forces of the World of Abstract Thought or the realm of spiritualized mind.

As already intimated, the crucifixion of the Christ did not end with His death on the cross of Calvary. His spirit continues to suffer on the cross of matter and will do so until the entire world and all its humanity have been redeemed. He is in very truth the World Soul crucified. And not until mankind through high and noble living shall have attained to the spiritual stature where it can bear its own cross, will the World Redeemer relinquish it. The time is yet to come when every knee shall bow before Him and every voice proclaim Him the Lord of Lords and King of Kings.

Through His sublime sacrifice on the cross for all mankind the Christ attained to an Initiation beyond that reached in the Christian Mysteries; He was elevated even unto the spiritual consciousness of God the Father. The Christ's last words on the cross referred to this exalted experience when, according to a true translation of His words, He did not sorrow over being forsaken but exalted in His elevation.

Among the powers bestowed by this Initiation is the ability to range at will among the twelve zodiacal Hierarchies. The zodiacal doorway to such celestial journeyings is Cancer and the lowest level at which that door can be entered is the plane of the World of Life Spirit which is sometimes spoken of as Christ's own home World.

It was at the foot of the cross that Mary, the mother of Jesus, passed into the Third or Master's Degree. An early Christian hymn relates the promise she made to the Master to watch with Him until the mystic sunrise of Easter Morn. This is another way of saying that during the interval between the Crucifixion and the Resurrection Mary was able, by virtue of the powers of Mastership, conferred on her, to accompany the Christ into the inner worlds where she learned firsthand about Christ's planetary mission and the manner in which it was being carried out on a cosmic scale.

### The Three-Hour Vigil

Since in the Passion of Christ is re-enacted the most important trials belonging to the Path of Initiation, the disciple who aspires to walk this Path must experience tests similar to those which beset the way of Christ on that eventful day. He will encounter the humiliations, the ridicule and the persecution, the same desertion by those close to him, as did the Christ. These disciplines come that he may gain inner strength for standing alone. They are succeeded by even greater trials, such as bearing his heavy cross up the steep slope to his personal calvary. Taken together, the trials represent definite steps along the initiatory Path, steps culminating in final liberation of the spirit from the cross of the physical body, the liberation of the spirit's activities for a three-and-a-half day period on inner planes, and finally its triumphant resurrection.

Good Friday, commemorating the events of Passion week which come to a climax in three hours of agony for the Lord

Christ, is the most momentous day of the year. Inner work then accomplished by Him was, and is, of supreme importance to all mankind. More and more its tremendous significance is being recognized, as evidenced by increased church observance of these three hours. Formerly such observances were confined largely to the Catholic Church, but now they are a regular part of the Holy Week ceremonies in many Protestant churches. Whether the deeper esoteric significance of the Three-Hour Vigil is recognized or not, it nonetheless deepens the spiritual realization of the sacrifice made by a cosmic Being on the plane of human history by relating it to specific process of spiritual unfoldment within the life of every aspirant. The three hours of agony depict three stages in progressive liberation of one's spirit from the cross of matter on which it is crucified during physical incarnation.

Thus we find that the three hours correlate to three steps in the ascent of the spinal spirit fire (kundalini life force) from the base of the spine through the three most important centers of the body. The First Hour correlates with the awakening of the fire force at the solar plexus and its ascent to the heart center; the Second Hour with the lifting of his force to the throat center; the Third Hour with its further ascent to the center at the top of the head. For man is the *way,* and the spinal cord is the *path* to the goal of perfection. All life experience is designed to carry further this process that the human body may become in very truth a temple of the living God, holy and inviolate, wherein the spirit may reign supreme. Then, luminous and serene, it will look out from this eminence upon light eternal and love immortal.

The First Hour correlates with the preparatory period of the First Degree, which has to do with the cleansing and purification of the desire nature, as we have shown, and which is therefore called the Degree of Purification. In this Degree all negative factors of the desire nature must be brought under control—the phases of self-delusion such as envy, jealousy, anger, hatred and resentment must be recognized for what they are.

The life of Christ Jesus in the New Testament pattern of Initiation, as the Tabernacle in the wilderness is the Old Testament pattern. The Tabernacle also consisted of three divisions. The first section, the outer court, contained the altar whereon bodies of slain sacrificial animals were burned. This ceremony symbolized the cleansing and purification of man's lower nature. Overcoming negative qualities increases the virtue of selflessness, and complete subjugation of self is the cornerstone of all occult work—a long and difficult process. This accounts for the lengthy probationary period exacted by Pythagoras and other wisdom teachers, for lack of discrimination is responsible for the failure of many an aspirant. Their work will never be complete until they can say with the Christ: "I speak not of myself; but the Father that dwelleth in me, He doeth the works."

During the Second Hour or Degree, as the spinal fire is lifted to the power center located in the throat the Path narrows and temptations become increasingly difficult. Tests of the First Hour are overt, undisguised, clearly defined. They may be seen easily for what they are. But the tests of the Second Hour or Degree are often subtly hidden beneath a mask of beauty, their thorns concealed by the petals of roses. In this Second Degree as presented in *Parsifal,* one of the most sublime initiatory legends of all time, the Knight Parsifal is tempted by the beauty of the flower maidens as they disport themselves in exotic gardens of unsurpassed color and fragrance. Discrimination is the aspirant's paramount lesson in the Second Hour upon the cross. He must learn, as did St. Paul, to distinguish the real from the unreal, the true from the false.

During this period the negative aspects of desire are distilled into additional soul powers and the work of the Second Degree is that of Transmutation or Illumination. In the second or inner court of the Tabernacle the fires on the altar are fed only by purest olive oil. It is also significant to note that in *Parsifal* the second act passes into the third act to the music of Transformation, and in this third act the Knight Parsifal becomes King of the Grail Temple and Teacher of its Knights.

In the Third Hour or Degree the spinal spirit fire is lifted from the throat to a point at the top of the head. This is the crowning attainment of the Great Work. Likewise, in the third or high court of the Tabernacle is placed the Holy of Holies. When the sacred illumines the aspirant's head center he is brought into that most sacred place, for he has found the key which unlocks the gates of heaven and can say with the Lord Christ, "All power is given unto me in heaven and in earth.'' His Third Hour upon the cross was climaxed by the Master with the words, ''How hast thou glorified me!''

This Third Degree correlating with the Third Hour is the Degree of Glorification or Mastership, the work of which consists in learning to focus consciousness at will upon the various inner planes, the celestial realms. Further, the aspirant must be able to maintain continuity of consciousness that never falters or fails. He passes from the waking to the sleeping state without any interval of unconsciousness; and upon returning to his body he is cognizant of his extraphysical experiences, being able to recall them as vividly as he can the events of the preceding day. This continuity of consciousness must also hold during the transition called death. Such an one is radiantly aware as he passes from one plane of expression to another. This the highest meaning of Christ's Resurrection and many advanced disciples throughout the world are now working to attain its development. It will become the common ability of all men in the New Age. With its attainment all fear and mystery connected with death will disappear and the spirit, radiant, triumphant and forever free, will joyously roll aside the stone of physical limitations and arise to greet the dawn of a new life.

### Meditation for Good Friday

When meditating upon the mystery of Good Friday and Holy Easter Sunday, let the aspirant consider them in the light of these truths. By thoughtful and reverent meditation upon the high attainment of these three hours there will accrue an increase in knowledge of inner plane work which will greatly enhance the aspirant's soul powers. Then, looking down the long vista to the coming ages, there will come in clear realization the words of St. Paul: ''Now are we the sons of God, and it doth not yet appear what we shall be.''

That the Christ might become the indwelling Planetary Spirit was the secret of the mystery of Golgotha. The Christmas events mark His divine yearly entry, and the Easter events mark its divine consummation.

# CHAPTER XV

Round about the empty sepulcher, row after row and circle after circle, were hosts of glorious Beings. They were the celestial Hierarchies that encompass this universe, beginning with Angels and Archangels and concluding with Cherubim and Seraphim, all singing triumphantly, "O death, where is thy sting? O grave, where is thy victory?"

These same heavenly Beings gathered about the manger in Bethlehem on that first Christmas night, when they sang "On earth peace, good will toward men." They were then celebrating the glad day which brought Christ Jesus to work upon Earth. Around the empty sepulcher they were celebrating an even more joyous day that brought Christ Jesus to work on and in the earth as its indwelling Planetary Spirit, for He was now able to work with both man and planet, not only from *without* but also from *within*.

There is an ancient legend stating that the cross on Golgotha was erected at Earth's exact center; also, that this spot is the burial site of Adam. It was Adam (early humanity) who brought mankind under the influence of Lucifer spirits and under bondage to death. The blessed Christ Jesus came to teach man how to overcome this Luciferic influence and so free himself from the claim of death.

At the sepulcher the vast assemblage of exalted Beings flooded earth with dazzling light. Viewing this sublime vision and walking in the light were the so-called "dead." During the interval from Good Friday afternoon, when the Lord was liberated from the cross, until He made His appearance in the outer world at dawn of Easter, He ministered to these "dead." teaching and pronouncing blessings upon them.

*For it is better, if the will of God be so, that ye suffer for well doing, than for evil doing.*

*For for this cause was the gospel preached also to them that are dead, that they might be judged according to men in the flesh, but live according to God in the spirit.* —*1 Peter 3:17; 4:6*

In his outstanding book *The Three Years,* Emil Boch writes: "Through Christ's descent into Hell, the 'beyond,' as the true source of immortality, was given back to mankind. The Descent into Hell rescued the 'beyond' for man; the Ascension rescued 'this side' for the divine."

When the ancient Mysteries flourished there were always Masters who taught their most advanced disciples about the coming of the Great One; the latter, in turn, gave these teachings to all who would listen. Conditons then were much the same as they are at the present time. Few listened and still fewer believed. Today there are comparatively few who believe in the mystic Brotherhoods and the reality of esoteric Temple instruction.

At the hour of transition the most advanced egos pass into higher spiritual realms. In the lower realms of the inner world are those who are still heavy with the dust of the earth, along with those who refuse to believe in the continuation of life after death. In esoteric parlance these spheres are termed the lower realms of the Desire World. They are the purgatory of the Catholic Church. It was in these dark realms that the Lord Christ spent the interval between the afternoon of Good Friday and Easter Dawn. There are some individuals upon earth today who bear in memory the glory of His presence and the wonder of His words. Such privileged persons devote their lives to His teachings and His mission.

Memory is a most important asset of both mind and spirit. Its cultivation and development have a foremost place in the work of true discipleship. Psychologists have divided man's mind into three areas: the conscious, the subconscious and the superconscious. Experiences of every-day life are associated with the conscious area; memory of past lives with the subconscious. Many interesting experiments are being conducted in the subconscious area to uncover memories of past incarnations. Memory of the future, which may be defined as cosmic consciousness, is correlated with the super-conscious. Rarely does anyone have any concepts of the powers available when the mind is fully awakened, or of what these powers will mean to humanity.

It has been said previously in this volume that modern disciples are learning to bridge the chasm which normally lies between waking and sleeping, life and death, present and past incarnations. One of the most effective exercises for recovering such remembrance is to faithfully and persistently review *in reverse* the events of each day before going to sleep at night. Events so viewed can then be evaluated for the purpose of strengthening what is good and eliminating whatever is of the opposite nature. By this means spiritual growth can be greatly accelerated. Also, continued practice of this nightly review will gradually improve the faculty of memory. It will be stimulated and vitalized, and becomes increasingly retentive. Little by little experiences of the inner world will become clearer, more ordered and more sequential until at length it will be possible to review events of the sleeping state as easily as those of the waking hours. As memory is enhanced and unified it will bridge one chasm after another.

*Memory working through the conscious mind is building a bridge between waking and sleeping.*

*Memory working through the subconscious is leaping the gap between past and present incarnations.*

*Memory working through the super-conscious will eventually span the chasm of forgetfulness that lies between life and death.*

The various processes for the development of memory were included in teachings given by the Christ during that wonderful interval between His Resurrection and Ascension.

From Good Friday to Easter dawn the inner-plane teachings of the Master dealt with the beginnings of the Path. Between the Resurrection and Ascension His teachings were concerned with the consummation of work upon the Path of Light, when a new and glorified race shall have passed through the sublime experiences of both the resurrection and ascension in its daily living.

When man has attained to such a level of unfoldment, transition from earth life to another world will be a glorious and conscious adventure. The ego, alive and alert, will know no fear. Instead, in a state of exaltation, it will be able to pass joyously into the next and larger life. Such an one will join the triumphant chorusing of Angels and Archangels, of Cherubim and Seraphim, in singing "O death, where is thy sting? O grave, where is thy victory?"

## Holy Saturday

The culminating event on Holy Saturday occurred at the midnight hour with the observance of the profoundly esoteric Baptismal Rite. This had to do with the Second Degree or the Rite of Illumination. Those who aspired to pass into the inner sanctuary of this Degree began a rigorous preparation under the teacher's care at the beginning of Lent and were known as "those who are being illuminated." A number of the holy men and women prominently mentioned in the Gospels passed this Degree on Saturday night and were thus enabled to greet the Sun of that momentous Easter dawn as new-born brothers of the risen Christ. These included the women to whom Christ appeared in that early dawning.

Water has a special affinity for etheric substance, hence when the etheric body of a candidate for Initiation has been sufficiently sensitized by pure and holy living, the immersion of the body in water tends to loosen the normally firm bond that holds the etheric and physical bodies together. When a separation between the two is effected, and the centers in the vital or etheric body are awakened, consciousness is opened to the inner planes and the soul encounters transcendental experiences which leave a lasting impress upon the future life. To undergo the Baptismal Rite unprepared would be to invite a condition fraught with danger since the influx of spiritual power accompanying the Baptism, while bringing illumination to the duly prepared, will carry destruction to vehicles not properly cleansed and qualified.

Certain centers in the invisible bodies of man are especially susceptible to the spiritual influence accompanying the Baptismal Rite. When the administrator of this ceremony is sufficiently advanced, he will direct his inner vision to these centers and condition the work in accordance with the aspirant's development. It was John the Baptist's possession of this ability that revealed to

him the exalted status of Jesus and caused him to feel his great
unworthiness to baptize a soul already illumined. The invocation
used by the early Christians at the Baptismal Ceremony were
words of music to the eager, expectant devotee: "Open your eyes
and ears and draw in the sweet savor of eternal life."

Although the Church has largely forgotten the inner truths
associated with the ceremonials they continue to practice, much of
their symbolism remains perfect as anyone will quickly realize
when becoming familiar with the processes involved in taking the
several Degrees pertaining to the Christian Mysteries and leading
to the Mount of Illumination. To illustrate: The Lenten Season
culminates with the Sun in Pisces when the rays of this watery sign
are poured out upon the earth. It is the final act of the zodiacal
Hierarchies immediately preceding the release of the heavenly fire
through the sign of Aries which ushers in the birth of the new
spiritual year, or the Rite of the Resurrection at Eastertide. Then it
is that an alchemical union takes place between the water of Pisces
and the fire of Aries, with the resultant increment of light and
power leading to the life more abundant. In the individual this
means the blending of the fire in the desire body, the element to
which it is primarily linked, with the water of the etheric body,
which is the element to which it belongs. In commemoration of
this alchemical act in nature at Easter time, the Church of this day
has retained a ritual observed on Holy Saturday in which a blessing
is placed upon the "new fire" as this is carried in elaborate
processional and later "united" with holy water which is then
rightly called the "Easter Water." No water can be so called
except that which blends symbolically the blessed fire with the
equally blessed water.

In the processional the "elect" who receive the blessings of
the "new fire" chant triumphantly: "Christ is our light"; to which
comes the response from the other songsters: "May His light shine
in our hearts." In the early Church the baptismal fount was
tomb-shaped, representing the death of the old and the birth of the
new when undergoing the Rite of Baptism.

So rich and so true is the symbolism which the modern
Church has preserved in many of its rituals, although but few of

those observing them realize their inner spiritual significance. Truly the light which Initiation bestows upon these Mysteries has been lost to our time, not only for the multitudes but for most of those who teach and lead as well. Long since, the priesthood ceased to be recruited from the Initiated, with the result that whereas old and true forms persist, the spirit informing then has been largely lost.

The Song of Solomon was the textbook used by aspirants on Holy Saturday, since it outlines the process of the Mystic Marriage. The Church later added the thirteenth chapter of John's Gospel to the contemplative studies on this holy day. This was used during the Footwashing Ceremonial for the newly baptized. Referring to John's Gospel, Rudolf Steiner, who approached it with the illumination possessed by the early Church, declared, as previously quoted, that it "is not a textbook but a spiritual force which is to be incorporated within the soul."

### The Empty Tomb

In the Ritual of the Empty Tomb, the Christ as the Wayshower for all mankind demonstrated to his followers the final and most difficult work to be accomplished on this physical earth. That work is the transmutation of matter into spirit. When this has been learned, man will have gained mastery over sickness, age and death. In esoteric terminology, this attainment comes with the Initiation belonging to earth, the densest of the four elements. It is the last of the four Great Initiations. When the light of this sublime illumination has been spread abroad, altars will be erected to the Christ in our physical laboratories as well as in our churches. The spirit behind and within matter will have been recognized.

With the Earth Initiation comes liberation from the wheel of birth and death. The necessity for reincarnation is over because earth's lessons have been learned. Man's spirit is henceforth free to pursue its further development on other and higher spheres, or to remain with humanity in order to help man mount the sooner to the level to which it has attained. Such are the graduates of humanity, the Masters of Wisdom and our Elder Brothers of Compassion.

Peter, too, passed through the Ritual of the Mystic Death on this Easter morning preparatory to attaining the Degree of Mastership. Together with Mary and John he came to the empty tomb and, according to the Gospel record, entered it alone, the other two remaining outside. This incident translated symbolically points to the fact that the two had previously undergone the experience of entering the "tomb" and arising triumphantly therefrom. Here they were assisting Peter to pass into the exalted glory of the consciousness which was theirs.

Through the processes of Initiation mortality puts on immortality. This is its all-inclusive end and aim. To the consciousness of the Initiate life and death are but different aspects of the spirit's progressive unfoldment. Realizing this, the burial ceremonial among the early Christians was a glorious Rite. Life was its theme. Leaves of ivy and laurel were placed in the casket and a complete text of the Gospels laid over the heart. Palms and olive branches were carried by those attending and the procession to the grave was marked, not by mourning and lamentation, but by the sound of glad hosannas. In keeping with this spirit was their garb which was not in the darkness of the grave but in the brightness of the light that greets the soul upon its birth into realms of spirit. Early Christian graves were cross-shaped in recognition of the fact that the body of mortality which is laid aside is the cross of matter from which the soul is liberated in death as it is the body from which the spirit rises free when attaining to the light of Initiation.

During the interval between the Crucifixion and the Resurrection (Friday evening until Sunday morning) the Christ Spirit was active within the earth planet, as previously described. "He descended into hell." Such is the creedal phrase for His entrance into the lower astral or desire sphere of this earth, whereunto He went to bring His gospel to discarnate souls still in the realm of darkness. Thus the Christ came to minister not only to incarnate humanity but also to its discarnate members. Moreover His mission extends to the redemption of the fallen Lucifer Spirits, whose place of activity is the Desire World, and also all the other kingdoms of life on earth who suffer evolutionary retardation because of the "fall" of man, their elder brother. This is the all-inclusive cosmic aspect of His redemptive work.

In the early morning hours of the first Easter, several women came to the empty tomb beside the Blessed Mother Mary and Mary of Magdala. These included the Virgin Mother's sister; also Mary, the mother of James and Jude, Salome and Joanna, the wife of Herod's steward, Chuza. These women were all there in preparation for entering into the Mystic Death and experiencing the illumination that follows upon passing through the Rite of the Resurrection. The two Angels that they saw guarding the open grave represent the purified desire body and the luminous etheric body of the ready candidate. That even greater attainment was awaiting these women appears from the words which the Master addressed to them when He bade them to "Go on into Galilee and I will meet you there." According to the Zohar, "The complete resurrection will begin in Galilee. The resurrection of bodies," it goes on to say, "will be as the uprising of flowers. There will be no more need of eating and drinking for we shall be nourished by the glory of the Shekinah."

The Essenes, who so reverently preserved the knowledge of the Easter Mysteries, continued throughout the years of their group activity to keep the night hours of Holy Saturday and the sunrise hours of Easter sacred with prayers and hymns of praise.

# CHAPTER XVI

## THE EASTER DAWN

The Rite of the Resurrection is the rite of the impersonal life. In the experience of the Mystic Death the disciple becomes aware of the illusions of matter and the limitations of finite life. The Resurrection consciousness brings the realization of the oneness of all life with God. The stone of separation has been rolled away. Henceforth one who has passed into this sublime experience knows that no ill can affect a part without hurting the whole, and that no good can come to the one without at the same time benefiting all.

One who comes to know the glory of the resurrection can never again wound or kill even his younger brothers of the animal kingdom for they, too, are living expressions of the same divine life that lives and moves and has its being in man. In the resurrection consciousness the passion of the unregenerate desire body is transformed into the compassion of the all-embracing spirit. The newly awakened is bathed in the golden refulgence of the Risen Christ and becomes one with Him in the realization that death has been merged into the victory of eternal life.

Meditation upon the transcendent experience of the Resurrection Rite brings a deeper understanding of and reverence for the inner significance of that salutation with which the esoteric Christians greeted one another in the early radiance of the mystic Easter dawn in the light of their own inner illumination: "The Christ is our Light."

In later years the night of Holy Saturday and the morning of Easter Day were times of Initiation for those advanced souls whose life and works are mentioned in the Gospels. And there must have been many others not so mentioned for in the words of John's Gospel, "Many other signs truly did Jesus in the presence of the disciples, which are not written in this book." Still later, St.

Gregory wrote a beautiful hymn describing the Holy Mary's dedication at the mystic sunrise, and early legends declare that it was to her that the Risen Master made His first appearance.

Mary, the Madonna, passed into the Third or Mastership Degree at the foot of the cross and Mary of Magdala entered it in the dawning of the first Easter Sunday, when she met the Master in the Garden.

In this Degree consciousness is lifted to the higher spiritual planes. This is possible only under the supervision of a teacher. Hence, before this elevation of awareness had occurred Mary did not recognize her Master in His resplendent spiritual body. Only as He helped her to gradually lift her consciousness to the levels whereon He now functioned did she know Him in all His transcendent glory. It was then that she sank to her knees in humility and addressed Him as "Rabboni," meaning *most* high Master.

### Easter Afternoon

In the Gospel of Luke is recorded the memorable walk to Emmaus. Cleophas, the father of James and Jude, together with another of the Disciples, were walking to the little suburban village near Jerusalem when the Master suddenly appeared and accompanied them into their home, where He blessed their evening meal. But it was not until He broke the bread for them that they recognized His true identity. In the ceremonial of the Last Supper they had seen Him pour His radiant life force into the bread until it became a luminous magnet of healing power. By this same sign it was that He now broke their bread, whereupon they knew that He who was among them was none other than the Risen Christ Himself. While they had not reached the development that enabled them to recognize Him on their first encounter on the road, it indicated no mean attainment to have merited coming thus intimately unto His presence and to have recognized Him at all on the level from which He now functioned. Immediately the Christed One had disappeared from their sight, they hastened to Jerusalem to proclaim the joyous news of His appearance.

*Easter Evening*

On Easter evening the disciples that had been most intimately associated with the Master met again in the Upper Room which was still vibrant with the power released there on the eve of the Holy Supper. And as they there received the two from Emmaus and listened eagerly to their joyous report, lo He Himself stood in the midst of them and said, "Peace be unto you. See my hands and my feet," said He further, "that it is I myself."

This is but a cryptic fragment of what then occurred. The Master was then imparting to His Disciples instructions pertaining to "pulling the nails" from the hands and feet at points where the etheric body is tied, as it were, to the physical body. There are also other points where the two bodies are similarly linked, but it is those in the hands and feet that are the most difficult to sever. Hence the pain, and the "Sacred Wounds," in the language of the Church. Since the work of detaching the etheric from the physical body belongs to the Third Degree of Illumination, it follows that the assembled company to which the Christ now appeared were being prepared for this Degree of the Christian Mysteries.

Thomas was not among that company. He had not yet taken the Second Degree of Clairvoyance. But on the following Octave Sunday in that same Upper Room, Thomas, the doubter, was bidden by the Christ, who again appeared, to place his hands in "the print of the nails." Doing so "he believed"; that is, he came into firsthand knowledge of truths that opened for him the door to the Initiation of the Second Degree.

*Easter Monday*

On Easter Monday the Master appeared again to His most advanced Disciples at the sea of Tiberias. In the company were Peter, James, John, Nathaniel and Phillip. Peter, around whom this incident chiefly revolves, announced his intention to go fishing. Thereupon his companions joined him, and stepping into a boat they put out to sea. During the night they caught nothing. In the morning they saw Jesus standing on the beach. Addressing them He said, "Cast your net on the right side of the boat and ye shall find." They did so and the catch was great. When Peter learned from John that it was the Lord who stood before them, he cast himself into the sea and drew the net full of fishes to the land.

This incident is recorded in the twenty-first chapter of St. John, the most esoteric of all Gospel records, written as it is by the Master's closest and most beloved Disciple. The experience here described is altogether spiritual and occurred on the inner planes. The sea symbolizes the etheric realms and the boat the soul body in which man functions in that realm. Fish is a symbol of the hidden Mysteries or esoteric truth. The number of fishes caught which is given as 153, gives the numerological value of nine, or the number of man's evolution, indicating that humanity as a whole will be caught up or saved when the Cosmic Christ will be universally acknowledged as the World Saviour.

Peter was then undergoing instruction leading to the Third or the Master's Degree. He, together with those with him, were taught by the Master how "to throw the nets on the right side of the boat," or, in other words, how to attune themselves to the positive or right-hand currents of the earth. These currents are under the control of Mercury, God of Wisdom, whereas the negative or left-hand currents come under the direction of Mars, ruler of the emotions. That man has not yet well learned how to "cast the net on the right side" is amply demonstrated by the discords and upheavels through which the world is now passing.

In order to attune life to the positive earth currents it is necessary to unite the right and the left-hand currents or the forces of head and heart, respectively. This was part of Peter's instruction as he jumped into the sea and came to Jesus. He was learning to walk the Way that He taught. Peter furthermore demonstrated his readiness for added instruction when he "went up, and drew the net to land."

We read that when the Disciples reached the shore they saw a fire on which were laid bread and fish. This is the spinal spirit fire which must be ablaze with light before the candidate can receive and assimilate the fish or esoteric truths that have to do with the great transmutation. The bread represents the powers of the pure body temple of a Christed one.

After the Master had broken the fast with His Disciples He

asked of Peter, "Lovest thou me?" "Yea, Lord," was the emphatic reply. Thrice the Lord repeated the question and thrice Peter gave like answer. To these affirmations the Christ enjoined him to feed His sheep.

In this incident is outlined the Three Degrees of the Christian Mysteries, all of which Peter had passed successfully. He had, therefore, earned the privilege or attained to the powers that enabled him to "feed the sheep," or to become a teacher of men and, in fact, the very rock of Initiation upon which the Church was founded. That the Church has lost the power it had when first established is due its having forsaken the teachings of the Mysteries. Only when these are again restored will the mystic powers wielded by the early Church be regained.

Peter "feeds the sheep" of the Church Path while John, following the Master's injunction to "tarry till I come," works continuously on the building of a spiritualized state. Initiation, centered in awakened soul power, must be the corner stone of both. Then the Christ will return to a civilization in which their forces unite to serve a glorified race wherein the Christ principle has already been made manifest, and man is prepared to pass into a higher phase of development known as the Religion of the Father.

Other disciples of Christ there were who did not attain to the sublime Degree of Mastership until the outpouring of the spirit forty days later at Pentecost. Then added numbers became clothed with the powers of the Mastership Degree which enabled them, in the words of St. Mark's Gospel, to cast out demons "in my name." And, "they shall speak with new tongues; They shall take up serpents; and if they drink any deadly thing, it shall not hurt them; they shall lay hands on the sick, and they shall recover." *Mark* 16:18, 19.

Since the first great outpouring of the pentecostal fires, humanity has drifted far into the world of materiality wherein the powers of the spirit have become less and less manifest. But from their long "burial" they are due to experience a universal resurrection in the New Day that is now dawning. Another time of "miracles" is at hand; a second Pentecost approaches. From the urn of Aquarius there is being poured out on all the earth a new fire from the heavens, which is destined to awaken humanity to new spiritual realizations and to create the conditions that will make it possible for the Christ Spirit to return to the full consciousness of men, even as manifested to those near Him in Palestine in the days of His first coming.

The Resurrection of Christ is not primarily a historical event for mere ecclesiastical commemoration. It is a recurring cosmic festival. It is an annual spiritual as well as physical upsurge of life for man's present experience and upliftment. Only as that experience is inwardly appropriated can man enter into the realization of the transcendent significance of the Holy Easter Mysteries.

# CHAPTER XVII

## The Interval between the Resurrection

### and the Ascension

One of the most important phases of Christ's mission to earth was to bring the Christian Mysteries to mankind. The early Church Fathers make many references to these secret teachings. Origen, one of the most important of these Fathers, frequently alludes to the hidden teachings as also does Tertullian, who should be familiar with these hidden truths as he was alleged to have been an Initiate of the Mithraic Mysteries before contacting Christianity.

When Christ said to a number of chosen ones, "Follow thou me," He was formulating the first Path of Discipleship leading to the Christian Mysteries. The modern aspirant, as he notes the magnificent churches of the present day, with all their comfort, ease and luxury, dedicated to the memory of the various Disciples, is prone to forget the life which these men and women lived when they walked the earth. They were driven from place to place amid the direct persecutions, living in cellars and caves and not daring to show their faces in any public place. No visitor to Rome can ever forget the catacombs, dark, somber subterraneous passages running for miles underground, where hundreds of the early Christians lived for many years. The only apparent recompense for their years of sacrifice and fortitude was the wild beasts in the arena or martyrdom upon the cross of their own Golgotha. Yet, despite all this, these brave men and women possessed an inner courage and ever deepening joy of soul such as few persons have ever known. They had found that great "peace which passeth understanding." They had learned to say with St. Paul, "none of these things move me," for they had accomplished one of the most difficult attainments upon the Path of Discipleship: they had found the kingdom of heaven within themselves.

During Passion Week, the interval between Palm Sunday and Easter Day which is termed Holy Week, the Christ gave to His Disciples many keys relating to the work of discipleship in the *outer* physical realm. In the week between Easter and the following or octave Sunday of Easter, which is termed Easter Week, He gave to His Disciples many keys relative to discipleship as manifested in the *inner* or spiritual realms.

It was in the mystic sunrise of that memorable Easter dawn that the followers of the Lord Christ first beheld the effulgent glory of the Master's Sun-body. The three most advanced Disciples were permitted to behold this body of light on the Mount of Transfiguration, but this high privilege came only to the majority of His Disciples in the Resurrection Rite of Easter morn.

During the three years of Christ's ministry upon Earth, He appeared in the physical body of the Master Jesus. This human instrument, for this earth plane, faded into a pale shadow beside the luminous radiance of Christ's Sun-body, which was His natural vehicle upon the spiritual Sun and also in the Capricornian realm, which is the home of the Archangels.

It was during that wonder time of the spirit which marked the interval between the Resurrection and the Ascension that the Disciples saw the Christ daily in this glorious body which St. John described as whiter than snow and brighter than the Sun. The events which occurred during this transcendent period of forty days, as has been previously noted, took place largely upon the spiritual plane and it was only the disciples who were able to function consciously in the higher realms who could take part in them. These sublime events which are described in the last chapters of St. John's Gospel were a part of the preparation by which the disciples were conditioned for that highest of all spiritual occurrences in human life, which is biblically described as the Feast of Pentecost.

It was in the early Easter dawn when the Christ appeared in the glory of His archangelic body that He tested the powers of extended vision and clairvoyance possessed by Mary Magdalene, one of the highest of His women disciples. Later that same morning, the Scriptures tell us, "to other of the holy women He appeared in another manner" (St. Mark 16:12). Man possesses a number of bodies, of finer or more tenuous substance than the physical. The desire or astral body is composed of the substance of the astral world; the mental body of the substance of the mental world; the spiritual body of the spirit substance of those realms. The Master Initiate can easily attract to Himself the atoms belonging to these planes, clothing Himself in a body of that particular substance. He can also as easily dissolve this body when it is no longer needed and return the atoms to the universal substance from which they came, which explains the mystery of the empty tomb that has been so long a matter of such disputation among the churches. Anyone who has passed the high stage of illumination, known as the Earth Initiation, has obtained complete control over every atom and can disassociate and disintegrate these atoms at will, which the Christ did before the Resurrection, as He no longer needed a physical body when His mission on earth was terminated.

The Master appeared to these women robed in His etheric body as their vision was not as high as that of Mary Magdalene. On the way to Emmaus, the Scriptures report that for a time ''their eyes were holden,'' so they could not recognize Him. Later, it states, ''their eyes were released,'' so they could recognize Him. These statements refer to the development of clairvoyance. The power of clairvoyance and the ability to leave the body at will as a conscious Invisible Helper are two of the most familiar phases of Christian discipleship and many references to these two steps are to be found throughout the Books of the New Testament.

On Easter evening, in the event previously described, when the Master appeared to the Disciples in the Upper Room with doors locked and barred, He was teaching them that physical matter can never be a barrier to the body of spirit. This is a truth to which many students of psychic phenomena can attest.

The next day by the sea of Galilee, the Christ was teaching His advanced disciples how to develop and use certain spiritual currents within themselves. The proper development and use of these currents will always protect the disciple from psychic onslaughts, from sinister influences of earthbound discarnates, and from the terrors of obsession. No disciple should attempt to work in the psychic realms unless he has learned how to protect himself with the shield and armour of the pure white Light.

*But when the morning was now come, Jesus stood on
the shore: but his disciples knew not that it was Jesus.*

*Then Jesus saith unto them, Children, have ye any
meat? They answered him, No.*

*And he said unto them, Cast the net on the right side
of the ship, and ye shall find. They cast therefore, and
now they were not able to draw it for the multitude of
fishes.*

*Therefore that disciple whom Jesus loved saith unto
Peter, It is the Lord. Now when Simon Peter heard that
it was the Lord, he girt his fisher's coat unto him, (for
he was naked,) and did cast himself into the sea.*

*And the other disciples came in a little ship (for they
were not far from land, but as it were two hundred
cubits), dragging the net with fishes.*

*As soon then as they were come to land, they saw a
fire of coals there, and fish laid thereon, and bread.*

*Jesus saith unto them, Bring of the fish which ye have
now caught.*

*Simon Peter went up, and drew the net to land full of
great fishes, an hundred and fifty and three: and for all
there were so many, yet was not the net broken.*

*Jesus saith unto them, Come and dine. And none of
the disciples durst ask him, Who art thou? knowing that
it was the Lord.*

*—John 21:4-12*

Herein, as previously stated, is contained one of the deepest
occult teachings given by the Christ during His entire ministry. It
is a continuation of the deeply esoteric work previously noted as
occurring on Easter Monday. Its action did not take place upon the
physical plane but was an inner world experience which the Disciples underwent in their spiritual bodies. Fish, being a dweller of
the deep, has been a universal religious symbol of the deepest
esoteric knowledge. This symbol was used extensively by the early
Christians during the period of their intense persecution. These
were not men who caught and sold fish as a means of livelihood
but Disciples trained under the guidance of St. John the Baptist to

receive the teachings of deeper esotericism as taught by the Master. A key to this fact is given in the mention made of the honeycomb. If this were a natural physical occurrence, certainly not a very appetizing meal could be served with a mixture of fish and honey. The latter has been used from time immemorial in initiatory ceremonialism. In the ancient Mysteries when the aspirant successfully passed certain steps he was joyfully received and welcomed by his fellow Initiates and together they partook of the ambrosial drink of thanksgiving which was composed largely of honey and certain herbs. Thus these most advanced Disciples of the Master through the symbolic use of fish and honey were being introduced into the deepest esoteric truths of the earliest Christian Mysteries.

In the interval between the Resurrection and the Ascension the Disciples received recompense for their long years of sacrifice and self-effacement. The wondrous glories of these holy days filled with divine revelation the hours of intimate and tender communion with their Risen Lord. Only those who were sufficiently advanced to function consciously on the inner planes could experience the glory of the interval between the Resurrection and the Ascension. For this interval truly lay between heaven and earth. These holy days could never be described in mere words. St. John refers to them in the final words of his Gospel: ''And there are also many other things which Jesus did the which, if they were written every one, I suppose that even the world itself could not contain the books that should be written.''

# CHAPTER XVIII

## THE ASCENSION

These blessed days were climaxed with the Ascension. Always the Master emphasized to the Disciples the wonder of that time when they should develop all the Christed powers within themselves, which He termed being invested with powers from on high. On that great day of Pentecost they would step forth inspired and illumined ones, messengers and teachers of the perfect Christ Way.

In the Rite of Ascension, Christ gathered His most advanced Disciples about Him and as He blessed them they saw Him rise like a golden cloud, ascending ever higher and higher into the spiritual realms, so far that at last even their extended vision could no longer follow Him, as hosts of Angels chanted joyously, "As ye have seen Him rise, so shall He come again."

During the forty-day interval between the Resurrection and the Ascension, not only the Disciples knew a richly, spiritually rewarding experience, the Lord Christ Himself was also a channel for an ever renewing inflow and outflow of increasing spiritual power. It has been stated many times throughout the New Age Bible Interpretation that every important event in the life of Christ represents an important initiatory step in man's spiritual development. These events also represent progressive Initiations in the life of the Master.

In the Ascension He passes into the highest spiritual realms of the earthly sphere, which is described biblically as the throne of the Father. Here He becomes a channel for the downpouring forces of the twelve celestial Hierarchies including the Seraphim, Cherubim and the Lords of Flame. At the Ascension, or the Summer Solstice, every atom of the earth is flooded with the glory-light of this divine spiritual power. At the Winter Solstice the heart of the earth is made luminous with Christ light. At the Summer Solstice every atom of the entire planet is suffused with this same Christ light. However, its emanations are so high that the vast majority of humanity has little or no realization of them. The Christmas Season receives a universal commemoration, but the Feast of the Summer Solstice passes almost unnoticed. While this is true on the physical plane, it is very different in the spiritual world. There the festivities are enhanced by Angels and Archangels. The beauty, splendor and spiritual power which permeate both heaven and earth in this high season can never be adequately described by the human tongue any more than it can be seen by human vision. The exalted glory of the Feast of the Ascension belongs to an advanced state of being which aspiring and developing humanity will someday attain in the course of its progressive ascent toward Illumination.

There is a legend which relates that a short time after the Ascension, the Christ, in the heavenly realm, was surrounded by a number of the Old Testament prophets. As they were leaning over the rim of the world watching His Disciples on earth busily engaged in teaching and healing the multitudes of people who followed them, one of the prophets said to the Christ: "It is a pity that you left the world so soon when there remained so much for you to do." The Christ replied: "But I have not left the earth. So long as there are Disciples who perform My deeds and who speak My words, I am still among them."

Is this not the most arresting and challenging test for the disciple of all ages and all time? To know a dedication and a consecration so complete that the feet shall walk only in His ways, the hands shall minister only for Him and the lips shall speak only of Him, *This is the meaning of true discipleship.* One who qualifies in this test will be found worthy to participate in the same glorious interval of communion with the Lord Christ that the first Disciples knew in the interval between the Resurrection and the Ascension.

# PART III

# The Path of Holiness
# or
# The Way to Christ

## A Study of the Path through the

## Twelve Zodiacal Gates

*I am the way, the truth, and the life.   —John* 14:6

*Enter ye in at the strait gate: for wide is the gate, and broad is the way, that leadeth to destruction, and many there be which go in thereat:*
*Because strait is the gate, and narrow is the way, which leadeth unto life, and few there be that find it.*
*—Matthew* 7:13, 14

*And an highway shall be there, and a way, and it shall be called The way of holiness; the unclean shall not pass over it; but it shall be for those: the wayfaring men, though fools, shall not err therein.*
*—Isaiah* 35:8

*There is a path which no fowl knoweth, and which*
*the vulture's eye hath not seen:*
*The lion's whelps have not trodden it, nor the fierce*
*lion passed by it.*                    *—Job* 28:7,8


*Thine eyes shall see thy teachers:*
*And thine ears shall hear a word behind thee, saying,*
*This is the way, walk ye in it, and when ye turn to the*
*right hand, and when ye turn to the left.*
                                        *—Isaiah* 30:20,21


*But he knoweth the way that I take: when he hath*
*tried me, I shall come forth as gold.*
                                        *—Job* 23:10


*This is the only (Way) my son,—the Path (that leads)*
*to Truth, (the Path) on which our forebears, too, did set*
*their feet, and, setting them did find the Good.*
*Solemn and smooth this Path, yet difficult to tread for*
*soul while still in body.*
*For first it hath to fight against itself, and make a*
*great dissension, and manage that the victory should*
*rest with the part (of its own self).*
*For that there is a contest of the one against the*
*two—the former trying to flee, the latter dragging*
*down.*
*And there's great strife and battle (dire) of these with*
*one another,—the one desiring to escape, the others*
*striving to detain.*
*The one longs to be freed; the others love their*
*slavery.*
*Thou must, (my) son, first leave behind thy body,*
*before the end (of it is reached), and come out victor in*
*the life of conflict, and thus as victor wend thy way*
*towards home.*
                                *—Thrice Greatest Hermes*

*Sacrifice, study, gift, asceticism, truth, forgiveness, mercy and contentment constitute the eight different paths of righteousness. The first four of these may be practiced from motives of pride, but the last four can exist only in those that are truly great.*

*—The Mahabharata*

# CHAPTER XIX

*Spiritual Meditation for Libra*

Every nation has celebrated New Year in relation to the Sun's passage at a certain point on the ecliptic. There are four such points, called by astronomers Solstices and Equinoxes. Some observe New Year at the Vernal Equinox; others at the Autumnal Equinox; still others at the Summer or the Winter Solstice.

Ancient Hebrews developed two calendars, the one secular and the other sacred. New Year of the older secular calendar began with the month of Tishri near the Autumn Equinox. The sacred New Year—which they seem to have adopted from the Babylonians but which was sanctioned by Moses (Exod. 13:4)—fell near the Vernal Equinox. Their Feast of the Passover was celebrated as one observance of that season. Hebrew feasts were all determined by the relative positions of the Sun and the Moon, and the New Moon was counted as the first day of each month.

While this arrangement emphasized the Jehovistic lunar influence, it was designed by Initiates who understood the correlation between spiritual and material forces. The civil New Year and the Day of Atonement or Judgment were celebrated in the season of the Autumn Equinox, and are so still observed. They were attuned to forces flowing through the universe with particular intensity at that time, and impinging upon earth in a special way. The constellation in which the Sun crosses the celestial equator at autumn is Libra, sign of the Scales in astrological symbolism and associated with ideals of justice and equilibrium.

Since Christ's coming spiritual emphasis has been upon the Sun, the solar calendar and the Vernal Equinox, but this has not changed the truths known to ancient Initiates. For neophytes on the Path of Holiness leading to Initiation in Christ, there is still the *soul's New Year* celebrated in autumn, at the time of the Sun's crossing the celestial equator in the sign (not the constellation) Libra—for reasons which will appear in the following pages.

According to Christian astrological legend, which naturally seeks to correlate astronomical phenomena with biblical teachings, Virgo and Scorpio were united as one constellation before the Fall; after the Fall they separated and Libra was inserted between them. The astronomical pattern for this legend is still discernible in the sky. The constellation Virgo is one of the most extensive in the heavens, reaching in its natural state from about twenty-four degrees of the *sign* Virgo, throughout the *sign* Libra, and to five degrees of the *sign* Scorpio, as these are measured at the present time when the Vernal Equinox is in about ten degrees of Pisces.

Students will observe that we make a distinction between the *constellation* and the *sign*. *Constellations* are the stars visible to the eye. *Signs* are arbitrary mathematical divisions of space measured off from the Vernal Equinox along the ecliptic in thirty degree segments, the first of which is called Aries; the second, Taurus; the third, Gemini; and so on around the Zodiac. At one time these mathematical divisions of space along the ecliptic, the Sun's path, coincided with the natural Zodiac as it appears in the sky. The Greeks, in common with the rest of the ancient world, first used the natural Zodiac but later shifted to the equalized mathematical divisions for reasons of astronomical convenience. It is said that Hipparchus led this change, but archeologists have shown that the Babylonians were already using twelve divisions of the Zodiac before Hipparchus' day; and it is self-evident that the Babylonians had also calculated the rate of precession of the Equinoxes prior to Hipparchus. So far as European civilization is concerned, however, the modern system of equal signs supplanted the more ancient unequal divisions of the natural Zodiac in the time of Hipparchus (second century B.C.), and the former has been used in western astrology ever since.

To the Greek mind Virgo was Astrea, the Virgin of the Skies. She held in her hand the Scales of Judgment (Libra) which extended into that area of the heavens we now call Scorpio. Another system names Libra the "Claw of the Scorpion" for the same reason.

Thus Libra stands as a milepost at the place of the soul's decision, pointing on the one hand to the path of purity, chastity and the Immaculate Conception as symbolized in Virgo; on the other to the "fall" into generation as symbolized by Scorpio, the eighth house sign which decrees that all human forms conceived by the present mode of generation must die.

To this parting of the ways every neophyte must come, as to a testing ground, before he is deemed worthy to receive the light his soul craves. Egyptians represented this state of consciousness in the figure of a blindfolded man walking toward a precipice where a huge crocodile awaited him. No other symbol could more truly depict the present condition of humanity. Blinded by his five senses, man rushes heedlessly toward the brink of destruction where the yawning maws of materialism (the crocodile) are ready to devour him.

Personification of justice (Libra) is conventionally pictured as blindfolded because the action of justice is impersonal. Swayed neither by preference nor prejudice, it looks down upon emotional predilection and mental bias alike, seeing with clear inner vision the results of past causation in succeeding cycles of rebirth. When spiritual sight becomes a faculty common to the race, justice will cease to be represented with bandaged eyes. Rather, with open eyes it will fearlessly and compassionately gaze upon man and his world.

In other constellations of the Zodiac we find the Fall symbolized. Esoteric Christianity recognizes that it was also a cosmic phenomenon of this physical globe itself in its relation to both the universe and to the humanity dwelling upon earth. Since every man is a cosmos in miniature, he also bodies forth the story of the planetary Fall. When he enters upon the Path of Initiation—known in the Bible as the "way of holiness"—he starts from the cosmic Fall to find his way back to the Edenic state.

Holy legends record that before the war in heaven and the fall of Lucifer and his Angels, the Sun was directly over earth's equator and the Moon remained at full. There were no changes of seasons; day and night were of equal length. This was the Golden Age.

Coincident with the fall of Lucifer, a cosmic event, the axis of the earth shifted to its present position. It is now inclined twenty-three and one-half degrees from the celestial equator. This change in position introduced the changing seasons. The nature of the Fall also led to a gradual descent from the ethereal state in which Edenic man lived to the dense material conditions we have today. As man is redeemed through regeneration, the earth will slowly right itself and become more and more etherealized.

So our globe stands between the urge of Virgo and its ruler (Mercury) on the one hand, and Scorpio and its ruler (Mars) on the other. That the ultimate conquest will be by Mercury over Mars (mind over matter) is indicated by the fact that in its evolution the earth has already passed through what occultists call the "Mars half" of the Earth Period and has entered upon the "Mercury half." Paralleling the evolution of the planet is the progress of the kingdoms in nature evolving thereon, a development climaxed in the life of humanity, the life wave astrologically correlated with the constellation Pisces.

### The Path of Holiness through Libra

The twelve zodiacal constellations are definitely more than a collection of stars adorning the heavens. Each constellation is the home of great spiritual Intelligences possessing wisdom and power beyond all human comprehension. Every year, when the archangelic Lord Christ makes His journey to earth while the solar orb completes its circuit of the Zodiac (as seen by earth dwellers), these mighty Hierarchies unite their spiritual forces with that of the Christ for sustaining and nourishing every living thing upon the globe.

When the Sun enters Libra at the time of the Autumn Equinox, the Sublime Christ touches the outer surface of the earth. Then it is that a cosmic quickening occurs. Little by little during November and December, the Christ Ray penetrates the planet's various inner layers until it reaches the very heart of the sphere at Christmastime. To higher vision, the Christ Ray is golden like the spiritual Sun whence it emanates. It truly constitutes the Path of Holiness for any disciple who has sincerely and earnestly dedicated himself to the Quest at the period of the Autumn Equinox. At some future Winter Solstice he will greet the Divine Light *newborn* in the heart of earth. This is the time for dedication to the Christ Path.

Before he can achieve this goal, an aspirant must learn the cosmic lesson of Libra:

> *Then shalt thou understand righteousness, and judgment, and equity, yea, every good path.''*
>
> *Proverbs* 2:9

Knowing the real from the unreal, the true from the false, is also the biblical keynote of Libra.

The principal work given to a disciple on his dedication to the Path is establishing contact with the living god within himself. In this work the Hierarchy of Libra, Lords of Personality, are divinely qualified to assist. The testings of a disciple at this point are for the purpose of developing his powers of *discrimination*, a most important asset to one on the Path of Discipleship.

### Biblical Parable for Libra
The Builders upon Rock and Sand

> *Therefore, whosoever heareth these sayings of mine, and doeth them, I will liken him unto a wise man, which built his house upon a rock.*
>
> *And the rain descended and the floods came, and the winds blew, and beat upon that house; and it fell not: for it was founded upon a rock.*
>
> *And every one that heareth these sayings of mine, and doeth them not, shall be likened unto a fooiish man, which built his house upon the sand:*
>
> *And the rain descended, and the floods came, and the winds blew, and beat upon that house; and it fell: and great was the fall of it.*

*And it came to pass, when Jesus had ended these
sayings, the people were astonished at his doctrine:*
*For he taught them as one having authority, and not
as the scribes.*

*Matthew* 7:24-29.

Libra is the sign which marks the crossroads where one is
called upon to make a decision. Here an aspirant stands before two
paths, the positive and the negative. Also, it is the season of the
year when earth is balanced between light and darkness, between
summer and winter.

In the life of the Supreme Lord the event which correlates
with Libra was His temptation, when He had to choose between a
promise of everything the world has to offer and the glories of
heaven. "He was in all points tempted . . . yet remained without
sin," so He became the Way-shower for all mankind. To follow in
His steps and overcome every worldly allurement is to become a
New Adam, a pioneer of the New Race and the New Age. Hence,
in esoteric astrology Libra is termed the sign of the New Adam.

The parable of the two builders correlates with Libra. The
foolish builder is one who erects his house on sand only to have it
destroyed by wind and wave. Being a person who has not yet
contacted the divinity within himself, he is prey to every negative
current of thought that comes his way. He is centered in material
law, ascending and descending according to the eventualities in his
purely objective life. The wise builder is one who establishes his
house on rock so it withstands whatever storms may assail it. This
man has found the Christ within himself and is, therefore, immune
to outer conditions. He knows he is stronger than anything that can
happen to him. Despite the raging of wind and tide, he declares in
triumph, "Be still, and know that I am God." Truly his house is
built upon a firm foundation and shall stand forever.

Under Libra there is a shuttling forth and back of the contrasting forces of its two ruling planets: Saturn, the law of materiality,
and Venus, the law of love. Here it is that each individual stands
at the place of decision and chooses whereon he will build,
whether on sand or rock according to his folly or his wisdom.

# CHAPTER XX

*Spiritual Meditation for Scorpio*

Since the beginning of the Earth Period the creative Hierarchy of Scorpio has given to mankind patterns of cosmic thought forms. By these patterns man has learned to build his characteristic embodiments. Hence, members of the Scorpio Hierarchy are termed Lords of Form. Dr. Rudolf Steiner states that man's brain-mind is but a cup for dipping into these thought archetypes. In the early days of human evolution students of Temple Mysteries were able to contact the celestial Hierarchies directly, and to observe the tremendous service they were rendering to the human race. For this reason the message of the stars was included among Temple studies, and no candidate was permitted to receive this instruction without long and arduous preparation.

*Transmutation* is the dominant keyword of Scorpio. During the period between the Autumn Equinox and the Winter Solstice, when the golden Christ force is penetrating ever more deeply into this sphere, The Archangel Michael, second only in glory and power to the Christ Himself, is engaged in cleansing and transmuting an accumulation of man's evil desires which hangs like a dark miasmic cloud above the earth. Together, they purify and transmute man's negative thought forms which permeate the planet's mental atmosphere. Due to the work they perform, purer thought and desire substance is available for man's use in building stronger mental and astral bodies. These, in turn, impinge upon and strengthen his etheric and physical vehicles.

Scorpio is the mystery sign of the Zodiac. It has two symbols: a scorpion, which carries the sting of death in its tail, and an eagle, which can fly closer to the Sun than any other bird. These symbols portray two widely divergent aspects of this sign. Under the scorpion influence man can descend to the depths of degradation; under the eagle influence his lower nature is transmuted so he can soar to great spiritual heights.

Another phase of the Scorpio paradox are the water and fire influences exerted through this sign of opposing elements, for Scorpio, a watery sign, is governed by the fiery planet Mars. This is a further indication of the mystic properties of Scorpio and of the part it plays in the regeneration that must precede illumination. The latter can be accomplished only after the fire and water principles have been brought into harmonious union.

Such a union was demonstrated when the fiery Ray of the archangelic Christ took possession of the body of the Master Jesus. As a member of the human race, the latter came under the Hierarchy of Pisces so was attuned to the water principle. What was thereafter accomplished by the composite Being known as Christ Jesus was the supreme demonstration of an ideal state that all humanity will realize to some degree when it has learned to blend the principles of fire and water. Christ taught this truth to Nicodemus when He said: "Except a man be born of water and spirit he cannot enter the kingdom of God"—spirit being the fire principle.

External conditions can never be mastered until discordant or opposing forces within oneself have been brought into harmony. Once this has been accomplished, the largely concealed mystery of Scorpio will stand revealed. Generation will have been transmuted into regeneration, so there can be no repetition of tragedies like those of Cain and Abel, of Solomon and Hiram Abiff. Factors which divided these opposing streams of humanity will have yielded to the principle which units all in harmony. In many myths and legends, both religious and profane, this precept is variously presented. But only through a study of the spiritual science of the stars can its full significance be grasped with definiteness and clarity.

Ancient Egyptians who were well versed in the deeper mysteries of star lore, gave out teachings on polarity in pictures so

those who could not apprehend them in terms of science could lay
hold of them intuitively through appropriate symbols. Their glyph
for Scorpio was a skeleton within an open grave spanned by a
rainbow. In a horoscope Scorpio governs the eighth house, the
house of death. But the house of death is also the house of
regeneration. In it are found both the scorpion and the eagle.
Imperfect and impure forms are subject to death. This is benefi-
ciently true because not everything pertaining to this plane is
worthy of immortality. Only the *essence* of mortal experience,
gathered and incorporated into man's higher nature—assimilated,
that is, into his soul—becomes immortal. It is through Scorpio's
power to effect regeneration that an incarnated spirit is able to
utilize physical forms and the death incident thereto as stepping-
stones to a higher life and rebirth into vehicles possessing elements
of immortality.

Returning to the skeleton as symbolic of Scorpio's powers,
we find it also represents the workings of karmic law. In this
aspect it is shown with a scythe for mowing down humanity; in
other words, for removing forms that are transient by nature. But it
also reveals that while life has been identified with these forms, it
is not dependent upon them for existence. Amidst the forms being
mowed down arise new hands and feet and arms, indicating the
supremacy of spirit over matter and pointing to the cyclic law of
rebirth. The rainbow which spans the grave is a symbol of immortality. Therein is given yet another signature of the regenerative
aspect of Scorpio: the promise of a time when sorrow, pain and
death shall be no more.

### The Path of Holiness Through Scorpio

A disciple treading the Path of Holiness as he follows the
golden Christ Ray to the heart of earth uses the Scorpio period as a
time of transmutation. He endeavors to sublimate evil into good,
darkness into light, negatives into positives, in every phase of his
daily living. He dedicates himself to the task of transmuting the
base metal of his lower nature into the pure gold of spirit. The
laboratory wherein he performs this great work is the spinal cord,

sometimes termed the Path of Discipleship. When its purifying fire is awakened, it is first active at the base of the spine. As the spirit fire ascends it unites with a corresponding spiritual fire from above, the two gradually increasing in volume and strength until the disciple's entire body is filled with light. He thus attains to an illumination that is visible to those possessing inner vision. It is then, for the first time, that his lower nature is literally consumed by celestial fire and he himself becomes a torch by which he finds his way to the heart of earth where abides the Christ splendor. The more sincere his dedication, the farther along the Path he will be with every return of the season, until at last he will be declared worthy to partake of the Feast of Light consummated on Holy Night.

Biblically as well as astrologically, Scorpio is said to have two keynotes illustrating what has been written concerning this sign: for the neophyte, "Blessed are the pure in heart: for they shall see God"; and for the illumined, "I will utter things which have been kept secret from the foundation of the world."

## Biblical Parable For Scorpio
### The Barren Fig Tree

*And he left them, and went out of the city into Bethany and he lodged there.*

*Now in the morning as he returned into the city, he hungered,*

*And when he saw a fig tree in the way, he came to it, and found nothing thereon, but leaves only, and said unto it, Let no fruit grow on thee henceforward for ever. And presently the fig tree withered way.*

*And when the disciples saw it, they marvelled, saying, How soon is the fig tree withered away!*

*And Jesus said unto them, Verily I say unto you, If ye have faith, and doubt not, ye shall not only do this which is done to the fig tree, but also if ye shall say unto this mountain, Be thou removed, and be thou cast into the sea; it shall be done.*

*Matthew 21:17-21*

Scorpio is a sign of tremendous power. Its forces run the gamut from the lowest phases of degeneration to the highest phases of regeneration. It possesses unsuspected depths and unsurpassed heights. When one learns to place himself in perfect attunement with the powers of Scorpio, he becomes a miracle worker on both the physical and spiritual planes. The parable correlated with this sign is one of the most controversial of the entire Bible. There are profound esoteric truths concealed therein.

In spiritual symbology the fig tree represents generation. The Christ, Lord of Life and Love, would never curse any living thing causing it to wither and die, for His word and His touch could give only life. The parable contains not a curse but a statement of an eternal verity. The law of generation is impermanent. It was not in the original plan so its misuse has resulted in war, disease, old age and death. By it Adam and Eve lost the Garden of Eden. The Book of Revelation tells of a hundred and forty-four thousand who bear the mark of the Christ upon their foreheads and are permitted to enter the portals of the Temple. They are the pioneers who have transmuted generation into regeneration.

Generation as practiced today is a transitory phase of the present evolutionary cycle. In the dawning New Age, pioneers will discard the unreal for the real, the transitory for the permanent. Lust will be superseded by love and immortality will take the place of mortality. In the words of St. Paul, man will find within himself the Christ who is the "hope of glory." This was the meaning of the words of our Blessed Lord when He said to the fig tree: "Let not fruit grow on thee henceforward," and presently the fig withered away.

In the sign Scorpio we get a kaleidoscopic view of mankind's evolutionary status. Sublimation of generation into regeneration is symbolized, not by the scorpion crawling upon the ground and with the sting of death in its tail, but by the eagle soaring straight into the heart of the Sun.

# CHAPTER XXI

## SAGITTARIUS

### Spiritual Meditation For Sagittarius

Sagittarius, like Scorpio, is dual in nature. Its pictorial symbol is a centaur, half horse and half man. The former symbolizes man's lower nature; the latter, his higher. Immortal spirit is forever aspiring toward the heights despite appearances to the contrary. From the time humanity elected to follow the way of materiality (Scorpio) instead of the way of spirit (Virgo), Sagittarius has been the sign of promise, of hope, of aspiration.

Basil Valentine, an early Rosicrucian Initiate, illustrated the story of Initiation by a series of pictures. In them Sagittarius is portrayed by a number of ever-burning lamps, a glyph that calls upon humanity to rise above materiality and achieve union with Divinity that it may partake of true spiritual ecstasy.

It is interesting to note that when the spinal spirit fire rises upward from the level of generation toward the plane of regeneration, the point where it leaves the former is the sagittal plexus located at the base of the spine and ruled by Sagittarius.

This sign is governed by Jupiter, planet of benevolence and expansion. It points the way to the birth of the Cosmic Christ that occurs annually on Holy Night, when the Sun leaves Sagittarius to enter the first decanate of Capricorn.

The pictorial symbol for Sagittarius shows the human half of the centaur aiming an arrow at the stars. This pictograph found modification in a representation of Cupid, god of love, originally shown with his arrow aimed toward the pineal gland instead of toward the heart. Later, as man gradually lost consciousness of his higher spiritual objective, and the affections were centered in the personal rather than in principle, Cupid's dart was redirected to the heart instead of to the spiritual center located in the head.

Sagittarius correlates to the Hebrew Vau, meaning *Sun* or *eye*. This letter stands for whiteness and brilliance, the spiritual light of Genesis and Revelation. It is the light that shineth in the darkness but the darkness comprehendeth it not. The Tarot symbol for Vau is a man standing between two women. One of them is crowned with the gold of spirit; the other with a vine, symbol of the false spirit. Fruit of the vine stimulates man's body to a point of ecstasy, but his urge for such an experience is his personality's mistaken response to the call of his ego. Thomas DeQuincy made this clear in his *Confessions of an Opium Eater*. Detachment of the mind from personality and linking it with spirituality is the prompting of Sagittarius; and this is the purpose and end of the Great Work. Modern Masonry has adopted this symbol to depict the same idea.

Thus it may be seen that the message of the stars reveals the path of evolution for all humanity. For the half-asleep masses the Path winds round and round the mountain of attainment; but for awakened souls there is a short, narrow and direct ascent to the summit.

Sagittarius rules man's higher mind, the mind capable of abstract reasoning. Its biblical keynote is found in Paul's admonition: "Let this mind be in you, which is also in Christ Jesus."

In Greek mythology the virgin Ariadne led Theseus out of the labyrinth by means of a thread. Both the virgin and her thread have been lost to modern man, but the higher intuition of Sagittarius serves in their stead—for spiritual intuition (the thread) is, in fact, the essence of reason. When, having made the circuit of the Zodiac, a liberated spirit returns to its starting point, it will find the Virgin of the Skies awaiting it as Ariadne awaited Theseus in the ancient myth.

## *The Path of Holiness Through Sagittarius*

The golden Christ force penetrates still more deeply into the earth as the Sun passes through Sagittarius, and the inner realms become intensely luminous with its glory light. From outer space this planet would appear like molten gold. All the light and color of Christmas observances are but a dim reflection of its light and color at this time. If a disciple on the Path of Holiness has learned to work well with the forces of transmutation under the influence of Scorpio, he will now find himself drawn into that great and glorious radiance.

Each event of the sacred Christmas celebrations symbolizes the development of a specific spiritual power within the disciple himself. As he awakens these powers he will experience an increasing measure of at-one-ment with the cosmic activities of the winter solstitial period.

We have already said that Sagittarius has been symbolized by a series of lighted lamps. If the disciple be faithful and persistent in his efforts, during this holy season each year he will become aware that there is increased power and luminosity of the seven lights (centers) within his own body-temple. When these centers have attained their full climactic glory, the disciple will be found worthy to follow the Path of Holiness to the very heart of earth, and there stand in the presence of the Light of the World. He will then receive Christ's blessing and hear Him intone the mantram that has been used in every Temple of Initiation, ancient or modern: "Well done, thou good and faithful servant . . . enter thou into the joy of thy Lord."

### Biblical Parable for Sagittarius
#### The Great Supper

*Then said he unto him, A certain man made a great supper, and bade many:*

*And sent his servant at supper time to say to them that were bidden, Come; for all things are now ready.*

*And they all with one consent began to make excuse. The first said unto him, I have bought a piece of ground, and I must needs go and see it: I pray thee have me excused.*

*And another said, I have bought five yoke of oxen,*

*and I go to prove them: I pray thee have me excused.*

*And another said, I have married a wife, therefore I can not come.*

*So that servant came, and shewed his lord these things. Then the master of the house being angry said to his servant, go quickly into the streets and lanes of the city, and bring in hither the poor, and the maimed, and the halt, and the blind.*

*And the servant said, Lord, it is done as thou hast commanded, and yet there is room.*

*And the lord said unto the servant, go out into the highways and hedges, and compel them to come in, that my house be filled.*

*For I say unto you, That none of those men which were bidden shall taste of my supper.*

—Luke 14:16-24.

Sagittarius is the sign of high idealism, of inspiration and aspiration; also of priests and poets, prophets and seers. Under its influence an illumined and awakened mind strives to soar amid the stars. It is also the sign of preparation for the holy Christ Feast just ahead. Hence, the correlating parable is that of The Great Supper (Luke 14:16-24). This feast symbolizes the opportunities for a spiritual life that are so bountifully spread before us. Guests who are bidden to partake typify average humanity—those for whom the Christ made His supreme sacrifice, and for whom He opened the way of illumination by His invitation: "Come; for all things are now ready."

The keynote of this parable is not discovered by an aspirant until he learns to live an impersonal life. In this connection the words of the Lord Christ are simple and direct: "If anyone comes to me without hating his father and mother, and wife and children and brothers and sisters, and his very life too, he cannot be a disciple of mine" (Goodspeed Translation). By "hate" is meant *undue attachment*. Christ thus declares that excessive attachment in all relationships must be renounced before at-one-ment with the Most High is possible. While a true disciple may be *in* the world, he must not be *of* it.

Every negative or destructive emotion has to be overcome by its opposite. Hate ceases not by hate, but by love. Love is the one true solvent. Good will is a paramount reconciler. Not until we have made complete renunciation of our baser selves have we become worthy to hear our Lord say "Come; for all things are now ready." Then we are privileged to sit beside Him and partake of the Great Supper; in other words, partake of celestial joys.

No one can fully share this holy repast until he has effected a union between the feminine and masculine principles within himself; that is, until he has established a balance between the powers of head and heart. From this mystic union are born four children—two sons, Fire and Air, and two daughters, Water and Earth. These four represent the transmuted essence of an aspirant's personal life after the energies of head and heart have been lifted up and united with the radiance of spirit. This is the Great White Work of the alchemist; the White Stone of Revelation; the White Rose of the Rosicrucians. The Sagittarian month, November 23rd to December 22nd, is the time to make preparation for participating in the Great Supper, when the most sacred significance of the Christmastide will be revealed.

# CHAPTER XXII

## *Spiritual Meditation for Capricorn*

The physical body of the earth reaches its highest vibration when the Sun enters Capricorn. The pictorial symbol for this sign is a goat; and a goat was the sacrificial animal during the Age of Aries when the Winter Solstice was in the constellation Capricorn. These ancient sacrifices have been sublimated into their spiritual equivalents; but their esoteric meaning—the meaning known to candidates for Initiations—has always been the same. Even to the Ancients a goat symbolized wisdom because of general recognition that attainment on the Path can come only through sacrifice.

In early Israelite ceremonials two goats were sacrificed for the sins of the people. One was slain before the altar while the other was laden with their sins and sent into the desert after priestly imprecations had been placed upon it. The goat that was slain represented the straight and narrow Path of Initiation taken by the few, whereas the other had reference to man's slow progress by means of the unaided evolutionary impulse. The Rite of the Two Goats also points to a truth underlying vicarious atonement as it was enacted at a later date by Christ Jesus when He took upon Himself the sins of humanity. These had become too heavy for the race to bear alone so could not be liquidated without divine assistance.

St. Germain represented Capricorn by a picture showing a brilliant borealis on either side of an inky background, above which shone a lone star.

In his beautiful love song, Solomon compares the teeth of his beloved to a flock of goats; also to a cluster of camphire beside the

164

vineyards of Engedi—a name meaning *goats' fountain* which, in turn, refers to the waters of everlasting life. This gives a deeper meaning to many biblical references to the waters of life. David thirsted for the waters of Bethlehem. The Israelites left for a time their own natural waters for strange, cold waters. Christ told the woman at the well of Samaria that if she would drink of the waters He had to give her, she would never thirst again. All of these references correlate with the spiritual symbolism of Capricorn.

Mystically speaking, there are two "gates" through which egos pass in and out of physical embodiment. Cosmically, these are the gates of Cancer and Capricorn. Egos take upon themselves garments of flesh through the powers of Cancer and the Moon; for Cancer is the sign of the cosmic Madonna and the Moon is its ruler. Through the powers of the opposite sign of the Zodiac, Capricorn which is ruled by Saturn the Reaper, dissolution of the ego's mortal body comes about, thus liberating it that it may return to higher planes. The stream of souls descending and ascending through these two celestial gates is the cosmic reality of what Jacob saw in his vision. The biblical story states that Jacob saw Angels ascending and descending the ladder; but biblical writers used the term *angel* in the same sense as it is now generally used to indicate many classes of non-material beings including discarnate egos.

Each constellation has its shadow side which belongs, not to the stars but to the earth whereon the shadow falls. The spiritually unawakened Capricornian manifests a strong desire for the acquisiton of personal power. Those in this sign often seek power for its own sake, whether that power be material or spiritual. Capricornians are therefore inclined to be ambitious, yet not so much for things in themselves as for the power inherent in their possession.

The biblical keynotes of Capricorn are "Blessed are the poor in spirit: for theirs is the kingdom of heaven" and "Blessed are the meek, for they shall inherit the earth."

Capricorn has been described as extending over three distinct stages of human evolution, namely, those of slave, slave driver and master.

### Path of Holiness through Capricorn

As previously stated, the golden Christ force touches the periphery of earth at the Autumn Equinox, passes through the desire realm during November (Scorpio), the etheric realm during December (Sagittarius), then becomes centered in the heart of earth at the hour of the Winter Solstice (Capricorn). This final penetration of the Christ force to the very core of earth marks the Holy Night of the year, when a deep calm and stillness pervades the whole world. Then follows a mighty surge of all the life forces of the planet. It is this new infusion of life into nature that has been so beautifully described in various Holy Night legends, wherein it is said that even members of the plant and animal kingdoms make humble obeisance at the mystic midnight hour.

When this mighty Christ force enters the earth, an impulse is released that quickens the life and spiritualizes the conditions of the entire planetary sphere. As this healing and redemptive work continues from year to year, the earth is being transformed from a discordant state into one of universal harmony. Hatred, enmity and conflict will eventually cease. Then that glorious ideal pictured by Isaiah so long ago will become a reality: "Man shall turn his sabres into plow shares and his swords into pruning hooks, and there shall be war no more, and peace shall cover the earth as waters cover the sea."

### The Biblical Parable for Capricorn
#### The Sower

*And he spake many things unto them in parables, saying, Behold, a sower went forth to sow.*

*And when he sowed, some seeds fell by the wayside, and the fowls came and devoured them up:*

*Some fell upon stony places, where they had not much earth: and forthwith they sprung up, because they had no deepness of earth:*

*And when the sun was up, they were scorched; and because they had no root, they withered away.*

*And some fell among thorns; and the thorns sprung
up, and choked them;*

*But others fell into good ground, and brought forth
fruit, some an hundredfold, some sixtyfold, some thirtyfold.*

*Who hath ears to hear, let him hear.*
                                                    —*Matthew* 13:3-9

The Bible is one of the greatest mystery books of all time.
Few there are who realize its infinite depths. Christ said, "Seeing,
they may see and not perceive; and hearing, they may hear, and
not understand." (Mark 4:12).

In very ancient symbology the word *ship* referred to the soul
while the word *sea* had reference to psychic currents. It is said that
Christ Jesus sat in a boat teaching people on the shore. This meant
that He was teaching those on both the inner and the outer planes,
for His mission was to instruct the discarnate as well as the
incarnate.

When Christ finished giving the parable on the sower, He
said, "He that hath ears to hear, let him hear." The sower is the
teacher; the seeds are the truths he disseminates. Students and
disciples receive according to their ability to understand and make
use of the teachings. The Lord also said that some received
thirtyfold; in other words, they could accept only a literal interpretation. Others received sixtyfold; these are the ones who grasp
deeper meanings. To understand the Bible as the supreme textbook
of life must be one of the first attainments of a true Christian
disciple.

Then He added further, there were others who received an
hundredfold; these are Initiates who lay hold of truths in their
fullness. They are the good ground into which the seeds falls,
springs up, and bears fruit. Some seed, however, falls by the
roadside and is devoured by birds; that is to say, it is taken by
those who are emotionally insecure so can give it no spiritual
anchorage.

Every disciple is admonished to learn how to contact his own
inner being and, through prayer and meditation, awaken and in-

crease its powers. A wise aspirant makes this center the focal point from which to work for attracting the good, the true and the beautiful. Care must be taken, however, that it never becomes circumscribed by narrowness of thought or bigotry of interpretation. One who has not cultivated persistence and perseverence along with constancy to his innermost center will be apt to meet with disappointment and disillusionment. Immature enthusiasm tends to turn into bitter repulsion. When this happens, a neophyte not only forsakes the things of spirit, but he places stumbling blocks in the way of others. Then the biblical warning in Luke 9:12 is verified: "No man, having put his hand to the plow, and looking back, is fit for the kingdom of God."

According to the parable, other seed falls among rocks and dies for lack of moisture. This is a symbol of the purely mental type of person, one whose heart is not yet awakened. The mentality alone can never solve the problems of life or teach others how it can be done, for it can be accomplished only through the love of a spiritualized heart.

Some of the seed falls among thorns and the thorns spring up and choke it. Thorns stand for base desires. Since the days of ancient Atlantis the human mind has been more closely linked to the desire nature than to spirit, the latter being the divine plan. Hence, to a great extent, humanity has been motivated by desire rather than by reason. This self-centered motivation has resulted in the present chaotic condition of the world. Races, nations and individuals are now so torn with strife and confusion that mankind approaches a state of general panic and despair.

One of the chief purposes of repeated earth lives is for man to free his mentality from the toils of his desire nature that it may become an instrument of spirit. He must return again and again until he has learned his lesson. Persons whose lives are motivated by reason rather than desire are exceptional, and an individual who is guided by a spiritually illuminated intellect is extremely rare. Still some seed did fall on good ground and bore fruit an hundredfold. This refers to the few who have balanced heart and mind, the superior state that is the Christ ideal for all humanity. When an aspirant learns to bring these two powers into balance he is worthy to receive and disseminate the mysteries of the kingdom of God.

# CHAPTER XXIII

## AQUARIUS

*Spiritual Meditation for Aquarius*

The pictorial symbol for Aquarius is the Water Bearer, a man pouring from an urn the waters of life, shed upon earth for its refreshment and renewal.

Aquarius rules the dawning New Age. Already the Sun by precession has touched the aura of its electrifying influence, with the result that human life in its every aspect is experiencing a tremendous acceleration. Through its planetary ruler, Uranus, Aquarius governs the finer forces in nature. Hence, under its inspiration the material world has been transformed by tapping sources of light and power such as are found in electricity and the now unlocked atom. Correspondingly, processes that quicken and awaken man's latent powers of mind and soul are being activated as the teachings of Initiation are being restored to him.

The Water Bearer is an androgyne figure, one in whom the masculine and feminine principles are equally blended. The physiological result of this state of equilibrium is a perfectly balanced relationship between the sympathetic and the cerebrospinal nervous systems. In initiatory terminology this development is spoken of as the Mystic Marriage. One biblical version of the process involved is the miracle at Cana, when the Christ turned water into wine. A symbolic conception of this phase of Initiation is given by St. Germain. It portrays a stormy sea, above which shines eight brilliant stars. A nude female figure stands with one foot on land and one on the sea. In her hands she holds two cups; from one flows kindness and from the other charity, qualities that promote friendliness and brotherhood. Over her head is an eight-pointed star, its center forming a pyramid; one part of it is white and the other black, thereby symbolizing the two aspects of occult law. Near the woman is a plant with three full-blown blossoms, and above it hovers a butterfly with out-spread wings. The entire symbol points to the richer life and extended powers Aquarius will bestow upon humanity. It is under this sign that man moves toward the state of being superman, and through its power the human kingdom will give birth to a fifth kingdom, the kingdom of souls.

The tarot symbol is similar in some respects to that of St. Germain. It represents the kneeling figure of a woman bearing an urn in each hand. From one liquid is being poured into the sea; from the other, upon the land. Just behind her appears that glorious realm described by St. John as the new heaven and the new earth. Above her head is the glowing light of an eight-pointed star. Beneath the figure are inscribed the words: "He who would enter here must die to his lower self." Then it goes on to state that by contemplation (a deeper degree of meditation) the eyes of the soul will be turned from the outer realm of appearances to the inner realm of reality. The occult interpretation of the liquid being poured upon the earth and the sea is the downpouring of the Christ ether—for the Christ is drawing ever closer to earth, and the spiritual ethers are becoming more dense, more potent in their effect. Their downpouring is making it easier for man to awaken within himself his own Chirsted powers that he may use them for helping others; also to hasten the Lord's return.

St. Paul was referring to the natural working of spiritual law when he said that there is milk for babes but meat for strong men. Every great world religion has two phases of teaching: profound esoteric truths given only to the few who are ready to receive them, and a simplified version of these truths for the masses. As the Vernal Equinox shifts backward through each zodiacal sign, the religion given to the people in general is in harmony with the current sign. The deeper esoteric truths come under the opposite sign, that of the Autumnal Equinox. For example, the Aquarian religion for the masses will be centered in the Fatherhood of God and the Brotherhood of Man. The esoteric teachings reserved for the few will be centered in the opposite sign, Leo, whose keynote is described biblically in the words of St. Paul: "Love is the fulfilling of the law."

Under Leo the illumined or sacred heart will become the light center of the body, and the power of love will be the principal motivating factor in life. *Sharing* rather than greed will be the chief aim of the business world, so cooperation will take the place of present-day competition. Tolerance will supersede bigotry and rehabilitation will take the place of capital punishment. Each individual will place his neighbor's good beside his own, and the supreme ideal of life will be to serve one another with love. The biblical keynote for this new Aquarian civilization can be found in the words of Christ Himself: "Ye are my friends."

Aquarius is the eleventh house, sign of friendship, fellowship and brotherhood. The incoming Aquarian Age will shift the emphasis of spiritual development from the individual to the group. This is already noticeable in the increasing attention given by educational institutions to the training of students for social service. In occult schools a similar trend is evident. The familiar statement of the Christ, "where two or three are gathered together in my name, there am I in the midst of them," acquires a deeper meaning in the light of Aquarian unfoldment.

Aquarius has two rulers, Saturn and Uranus. The former governs what is old and belongs to the past. Uranus governs all that is new and belongs to the future. The ancients depicted Aquarius as a tree of life with two branches, one branch terminating in a figure indicative of old age and representing the product of Saturn; the other branch terminating in the figure of a beautiful youth bearing in his hands the Holy Grail, symbolic of attainment under the transforming influence of Uranus.

At the present stage of evolution all humanity, individually and collectively, is in a period of transition, moving gradually from an old established order into a newly emerging civilization. The old is crumbling; the new is in process of formation. Consequently, nothing is settled or stable. Everything is in a state of flux. The turmoil and conflict now engulfing the world stems from the disturbing and dislocating conditions attendant upon passage from one order into another. It is the function of Saturn, the ruler of the material side of Aquarius, to confine, to limit and to provide fixed and dependable forms through which the life forces of the individual and of society can be effectively channeled on the material plane. This is its constructive contribution to life as expressed on this plane of existence. However, since evolving life is constantly expanding its powers, the forms which Saturn provides must be replaced periodically by others of greater elasticity and wider dimensions, so along with Saturn in Aquarius is Uranus, whose task it is to dismember inadequate and crystalized forms that others may take their place. Uranus destroys only what has become a hindrance to evolving and progressive life; hence, it is called *the transformer*. It is also termed the Christ planet, for its influence is that of the Voice in Revelation, associated with the redemptive Christ impulse which declares, "Behold, I make all things new."

On all sides are to be noted evidences of the incoming Aquarian age. In daring underwater adventures, in those high in mid-air and in preparation for space travel are revealed the Uranian impulses that are beginning to permeate the entire sphere. Children today speak as casually about making trips to the Moon, to Venus or to Mercury as they did some years ago about going to cities or towns in their own native state. As preparation for the exploration of other planets require long and arduous planning plus severe discipline, so also are similar preparations necessary for the New Age disciple. As material scientists seek to explore outer realms of other planets which correspond to the physical body of earth, so New Age disciples are being prepared to enter the more refined spiritual bodies of both the earth and other planets.

The forces of the two higher ethers are becoming increasingly potent in their effect upon mankind. The Life Ether aids in the development of extra-sensory perception, while the Reflecting Ether awakens a disciple's latent forces in preparation for Initiation. The time is not far distant when the word *Initiation* will be a familiar one, and the work of Initiation will be restored to its rightful place as the supreme attainment of a spiritual life. An evidence of this trend may be noted in the fact that in a number of orthodox church bodies groups have been formed for the study and development of the latent spiritual faculties in man that have hitherto been regarded as belonging exclusively to the realm of metaphysics, and, therefore, quite apart from the sphere of religion as currently understood.

### The Path of Holiness through Aquarius

The constellation Aquarius is the home of the angelic Hierarchy. The Angels, when working on earth, use the etheric realms of the planet as their vantage ground. The bodies of the Angels are fashioned of etheric substance so are visible to those only who have developed etheric vision. Many children have such extended sight and thus have first-hand knowledge of angelic Beings. They are also familiar with nature spirits which, like the Angels, function in etheric bodies.

Angels are expert in working with etheric substance. Many and varied are the beautiful flower patterns they fashion in the blue and gold of the higher ethers; and nature spirits transmit these to earth as blossoms to adorn the flower kingdom throughout the world.

When the Sun is transiting Aquarius the Lord Christ, in His annual passage through the earth, centers His activities in the etheric realms. He pours His love and blessings upon both Angels and the disembodied souls of earth's humanity who are living and serving in these realms. They are also the heavenly homeland of children—those egos who pass from earth in infancy—where they are taught and companioned by Angels.

In the etheric realms are to be found initiatory Temples that formerly existed on this planet but were lost to it when dense materiality descended thereon. Frequent references have been made to the Christian Temple located in the ethers just above Jerusalem. Angels are closely associated with Temples of Initiation. They are free to enter such sanctuaries at will, and are happy to serve in these holy places.

It is said a Guardian Angel hovers above the chair of each Knight who sits at the Round Table in King Arthur's Temple. Profound spiritual truths are concealed in Grail legends, for the work of Grail Temples is part of the Christian Mystery Temple work. The deeper meaning of these legends is veiled by poets and artists, who relate them to the manners and customs of the period in which they first appear. Grail legends center around the Holy Cup. The deepest mysteries of esoteric Christianity center in the Grail. The most profound teachings of the Christ were given at the Last Supper, when mysteries connected with the Sacred Rite of Holy Communion were revealed to His Disciples.

As was noted in the Path of Holiness through Capricorn, a disciple is taught to become an Invisible Helper who ministers to those living in the physical world. As the Path of Holiness passes into Aquarius. the work of the disciple is enlarged. Here he learns to minister under the guidance of Angels and to work with Beings who inhabit the etheric or heavenly realms.

A qualified disciple who has learned to follow the Christ upon the Path of Holiness through Aquarius is able at this stage of his unfoldment to enter *consciously* into the etheric realms. There he is permitted to observe the varied and beautiful ministries performed by Angels for the benefit of humanity and all forms of life on the earthly planet. Many of nature's inner secrets are revealed to him through the activities of the nature spirits. Thus, the disciple finds himself in an enchanted world, that tenuous world wherein fairy lore has its origin—for the realm of the higher ethers in a veritable fairyland. It is upon the activities of this sphere that many an illumined seer or mystic has woven his most beautiful fantasies concealing spiritual truths. A delightful example of these is Maeterlinck's *Blue Bird*.

During the month that the Sun transits Aquarius the higher ethers become more golden and luminous as the Christ force is being lifted toward the surface of earth in preparation for His triumphant Easter liberation.

### Biblical Parable for Aquarius
The Good Samaritan—Luke 10:25-37

Aquarius, being the sign of fellowship, brotherhood and cooperation, correlates to the biblical parable of the good Samaritan. There was a man who, for purposes of trade, was going from his home in Jerusalem to Jericho. Upon his camel he loaded many precious jewels and much gold. On the road he was waylaid by robbers and all of his goods, including his camel, was taken from him. After he was severely beaten he was left by the roadside to die. As he lay there pleading for help a priest came along, but passed by on the other side of the road. Next came a Levite who, though seeing the man, also went his way unheeding the cries for help. Later came a Samaritan. Now in the days of Christ Samaritans were considered utterly unworthy; they were looked upon as rank materialists who did not believe in God. Children were not permitted to play with the offspring of Samaritans or to attend the same schools. The situation was much the same as the race problem today.

But this Samaritan stopped, cleansed the man's wounds with wine and healing oil, and bound them up. Then he placed the injured one on his own beast while he himself walked beside the animal, leading it to the village. There he went to an inn-keeper and left with him two coins, saying, "Take care of him; and whatsoever thou spendest more, when I come again, I will repay thee." Christ concluded His parable by asking, "Which now of these three, thinkest thou, was neighbor unto him that fell among the thieves?" "He that shewed mercy on him," was the answer. Whereupon the Lord commanded, "Go, and do thou likewise."

Perhaps nowhere in literature is there a more beautiful interpretation of friendship than the one given in the *Parable of the Good Samaritan*. Emerson wrote that if one would have friends he must be one. The true evaluation of wealth is not based on things, but on friendship. The richest man is the one who has the greatest number of loyal and devoted friends. At the end of an earthly pilgrimage the rarest and most precious soul assets will be those centered in friendship.

# CHAPTER XXIV

*Spiritual Meditation for Pisces*

To repeat, the Egyptians, with their amazing wisdom relative to stellar science, conceived a series of pictures depicting symbolically the way of the Solar Chirst through the twelve signs of the Zodiac.

There are two important significators of Pisces in the Tarot symbolism. One represents an unawakened individual typified by the Hanged Man with one foot upon the opposite knee, thus forming a cross. The other is an illumined soul pictured by two lovers standing hand-in-hand and encircled by a wreath of green signifying immortality. The wreath points to the resurrection of the planetary Christ at the time of the Vernal Equinox.

St. Germain likened the influence of the sign to a bright comet that mysteriously flashes across the sky and gives momentary illumination to the earth as it floats above a sea of inky darkness, beneath which are two hands clasped together.

The astrological symbol for Pisces consists of two fish joined together but headed in opposite directions. A single fish has been widely used to symbolize an Initiate because it lives in the mysterious deeps. In the story of Jonah and the whale, Jonah remained for three days in the body of the creature—an allegory of Initiation. The story is a veiled description of induction into the Lesser Mysteries as they were observed in pre-Christian Temples. This same pattern is repeated in the life of Christ, Who spent three days in the inner realms of earth during the interval between His Crucifixion and Resurrection. It will also be remembered that the sign for fish was used as a password among early Christians and was variously used by them as a mystic symbol.

Pisces has two rulers, Jupiter and Neptune. Jupiter is the

planet of law and order. Under its influence the Piscean Age has witnessed the development of the esoteric Church, two prominent features of which are water (Pisces) and bread (Virgo). Christ Jesus rent the veil before the Temple of Initiation on the threshold of the Piscean Age, opening the door to "whosoever will" to enter. Those responding to this call come under the influence of Neptune, the spiritual ruler of Pisces. Under Neptune they learn to walk the Path that leads to liberation—the type of liberty belonging to the sons of God, of which Paul spoke.

In relation to man's development, the work of the Piscean Age has been directed toward purification of his desire nature. Thus, we find the battle for emotional and soul control to be the outstanding ordeal of medieval saints and of characters appearing in legends of the Holy Grail. The highest aim of Piscean work has been transmutation of base emotions into soul-power through devotion, as depicted in the ecstatic visions of cloistered religious devotees.

Pisces is the last of the twelve zodiacal signs, and it holds the final summation of karmic experience belonging to a completed life cycle. For this reason it has been termed the sign of tears and sorrow. Venus, the planet of personal love, is exalted in Pisces. When their personal love is selfish and possessive, a Garden of Gethsemane is all too familiar to natives of this sign. The biblical keynote for this aspect of Pisces is "Not my will, but thine, be done." It is only by complete self-surrender and renunciation that the gates of the Garden of Sorrow will be permanently closed.

The two linked fish representing Pisces bear a profound esoteric meaning. In their highest significance they indicate a state of perfect equilibrium. In the two columns of the physical body-temple (the two nervous systems) the force of right and left interact in harmony, establishing equilibrium between head and heart. Through the cerebro-spinal nervous system spirit contacts the objective world while through the sympathetic nervous system it contacts the subjective world. When interaction between the inner and the outer is perfectly balanced the ego is equally at home in either realm.

Only two signs have Jupiter and Neptune for their ruling planets: Cancer and Pisces. Jupiter governs the forces of soul;

Neptune, the powers of spirit. The zodiacal pilgrimage under
Pisces will unite the divine essence of soul with the powers of
spirit. This supreme ideal was given to humanity by the Hierarchy
of Cancer, and its attainment will be consummated under the
guidance of Pisces. Perfected humanity will make its abode in the
constellation Pisces, fittingly described by that figure of a man and
a maid standing hand-in-hand within a wreath of evergreen. Such
perfected ones have won immortal life and eternal youth. The
biblical keynote of Pisces, first sounded forth by the Piscean
Hierarchy in the great creative fiat "God created man, in the
likeness of God made he him," will then sound triumphantly
throughout the earth.

An ancient astrological dictum declares that the Piscean
stands so near the mount of purity and godhood on one hand and
the chaotic pit of self-destruction on the other that both Angels and
demons stand by to speed him on whichever way he chooses to go.
The hieroglyph accompanying this description is one of a beautiful
woman. A genii kneels at her feet offering her the riches of earth
while an Angel hovers overhead offering her celestial treasures—
thus vividly depicting the dual nature of Pisces. Natives of this
sign may soar to the heights of inspiration, and many of the
world's most gifted souls have come under it; but it often happens
that their gifts are wasted through their indulgences in unbridled
Piscean emotions.

Pisces is the twelfth house sign. One born under this config-
uration is completing a series of earth lives and is, therefore, busy
clearing karmic debts engendered in the past. The Piscean's life is
usually rich in varied experiences and laden with heavy responsibilities. Venus, exalted herein, proclaims that the sorrows of
Pisces usually originate in too tenacious personal attachments.
Regenerated Pisces means death to the personal self and life to the
immortal soul. The mystic death in this sign occurs under the
forces of Neptune, planet of Initiation, Those who pass through
this experience become New Age pioneers.

### The Path of Holiness through Pisces

As the Sun is transiting Pisces during the month of March, the golden Christ Force re-ascends from earth's center and rises to the surface of the planet in anticipation of the Easter resurrection. Being the sign of sorrow and renunciation, Pisces also typifies the crucifixion. As the Cosmic Christ experiences the sorrow of renunciation and crucifixion upon entering the earth at the time of the Autumnal Equinox, so the spirit of earth experiences a certain void when the Christ Spirit withdraws from the planetary body at the time of the Spring Equinox.

As the Christ Force rises and permeates the desire envelope of earth, temptations become more subtle and testings more severe. The admonition given by the Master to disciples of all Ages is: "If any man will come after me, let him deny himself, and take his cross and follow me." It is at this point that a disciple must learn to follow Him upon the straight and narrow way leading to Golgotha. Max Heindel likened this path to a church steeple which becomes narrower and more steep until there would be nothing for one to cling to but its surmounting cross, a very apt analogy. And so it is that above most churches arises a vivid symbol of the Path of Discipleship. Truths leading to this Path are now lost to the Church. These must be regained before it can once more exercise the powers and influence it had during the early centuries of its existence.

The cross of renunciation must be accepted by every true disciple who endeavors to walk the Path of Holiness. His soul body can never be built until he acquires mastery over himself, and is willing to forego the so-called pleasures of the sense world. The soul-powers attained by each self-conquest enable an illumined one to exchange the cross for a crown.

As already stated, the constellation of Pisces will be the home of the human race when all its units are perfected. Those who learn to tread the Path of Holiness and follow the Christ to that ultimate high goal will have finished their earthly cycles of incarnation. Their karmic debts will have been paid and all their earthly bonds severed. Such are known as Compassionate Ones, the Elder Brothers who no longer have need for earth's lessons. They are free to pass into a glorious existence within the constellation Pisces. However, these great ones may return at will, and in obedience to the spiritual precept that he who loves most serves best. Often they give up the privileges and opportunities of that plane for the purpose of serving less advanced members of the human race. Humility, obedience and service are the keynotes of their lives.

Such renunciation is illustrated in the life of Mary of Bethlehem who, having learned all of earth's lessons and been caught up to reign with the Angels, returned to this planet to teach humanity one of heaven's supreme mysteries, that of the Immaculate Conception. Knowing she would be misunderstood, ridiculed, persecuted, she yet persisted that she might give to mankind an ideal which, even two thousand years later, is barely comprehended by the few and is entirely unknown to the masses. Working under the law of service, she descended into mortality, saying, "Let it be according to thy word." Such a high state of spiritual attainment, builded upon sacrifice, humility of spirit, and perfect at-one-ment with the law of obedience, awaits perfected man.

The aspirant who reflects seriously on the meditation for the twelve signs will do well to correlate the Piscean meditation with the experiences of the Immortal Twelve during the season immediately preceding Christ's annual "crucifixion." Then, as its pain and sorrow are swallowed up in the golden glory of Easter morn, the disciple who succeeds in overcoming his personal self and who walks the Path of Holiness through Pisces to its very end will find that he has exchanged his cross for the golden glory of a "wedding garment" in which to function, free and triumphant, with the Risen Christ.

### Biblical Teaching for Pisces
#### Renunciation

Lent, the season when an aspirant undertakes restrictive disciplines in the interest of his higher life, comes under the sign Pisces. The supreme attainment to which man may aspire comes only through a series of progressive renunciations. At the stage of discipleship much in the nature of foregoing is required, as indicated by the Christ when He said: "He that loveth father and mother more than me is not worthy of me: and he that loveth son or daughter more than me is not worthy of me. And he that taketh not up his cross, and followeth after me, is not worthy of me.''

Ties based solely upon bonds of blood can never result in spiritual brotherhood such as Christ came to establish. Remember His asking: "Who is my mother? and who are my brethren?'' and replying to His own query: "For whosoever shall do the will of my Father which is in heaven, the same is my brother, and sister, and mother.''

Thus we are called upon to surrender the lesser to the greater, to expand the relationships of kin until they include all mankind. This can be accomplished only as the separative, self-centered personality is brought under the control of spirit—which realizes essential unity with every spirit because it is indissolubly related through the Fatherhood of God.

Humility is the true signature of illumination. The wiser a person is, the more simple and unassuming he is. The more he learns, the less he knows he knows. A true astronomer stands in awe before the vast reaches of the starry skies, knowing there are infinite worlds far beyond his vision. A true esotericist bows in lowly submission before an infinitude of wisdom that exceeds his comprehension; he feels like a child playing in the sand upon the shore of an illimitable and mysterious sea.

A most illustrious example of humility is to be found in Peter, the Piscean among the twelve Disciples. Peter considered it the greatest honor to follow the Christ and serve His cause. When Peter's time came to follow Him in the crucifixion, he declared his utter unworthiness to be placed upon the cross head upward, as was the Christ; so he asked that he be crucified head downward— and this from a man whose spiritual emanations are said to have been so powerful that when his shadow fell upon the sick they were instantly healed!

Pisces is a water sign, and water is correlated to man's emotional nature. When one has gained complete control over his emotions, he will have obtained control over the element of water. This is the lesson Christ was teaching Peter when He bade him walk upon the water. At that time, however, Peter had not yet mastered his emotions. If the Christ had not saved him, he would have sunk beneath the waves. Later, when he had become ruler over his passions, without fear Peter walked upon the water to meet the Christ—an accomplishment known in esotericism as *Initiation by Water*. After this experience Peter knew the most transcendent bliss of his life.

It was the practice of Pythagoras to take his most advanced students to the banks of a lake and there, by their combined and concentrated power, ruffle the surface of the lake and then make it so calm that the water reflected the beauties of the over-arching sky. His instruction to those with him was to still their minds so not the slightest thought caused a ripple in it. When this is accomplished by an aspirant, the full glory of his true self is revealed.

# CHAPTER XXV

*Spiritual Meditation for Aries*

Since it is the first point of the Zodiac, Aries is the place of new beginnings. In the annual cycles of the Sun's passages through the twelve signs, it heralds the commencement of the spiritual year. It has been so regarded even in nations beginning their civil year at other points of the zodiacal circle. Moses appointed the month of Abib (March-April) as the beginning of the year (Ex. 13:4) for it is the month of sprouting grain and young corn. Also, a command was given to Moses that the slaying of the paschal lamb was to occur when the New Moon was in Aries. At the time of the original Passover the Sun was near the star El Natik, meaning *pierced, wounded* or *slain*. The Full Moon was then near the star Al Sheraton, which also means *bruised* or *wounded*. As the Passover foreshadowed the Curcifixion of Christ Jesus, so the heavens proclaim the coming of great events in human destiny.

Keywords for Aries are *purity* and *sacrifice,* and the symbol of Aries is a lamb or ram. Since it was in the Dispensation of Aries that the Lord Christ came to earth, He is known as the Good Shepherd. A familiar picturization shows Him bearing a lamb in His arms.

During the early years of the Christian Dispensation, as has been said, the most used symbol was not the crucified Christ but the cross with a lamb resting at its base. It was not until about the fourth century of our era that the lamb was replaced by a human figure nailed to the cross.

There are two Tarot cards which have been ascribed to Aries; one is the Fool and the other is the High Priest. The former depicts a young lad with a knapsack over his shoulder and an open rose in his hand. He is going forth, fearless and venturesome, to meet the challenge of life. He is called a Fool because he has not yet entered upon the Quest, and no one really understands life until he enters upon the Path of Holiness. The other card shows a High Priest seated upon a throne, a halo of golden light about his head. With him are two most sacred relics, the holy Cup and the sacred Spear. In his right hand he holds the Cup filled with human passions; over it he has placed his left hand, indicating that he has achieved mastery over the elements of his lower nature. This figure accurately depicts the highest expression of Aries, self-control. The words of wise King Solomon carry the biblical key-note of this attainment: "He that is slow to anger is better than he that is mighty; and he that ruleth his spirit than he that taketh a city." On a higher level the following from Revelation applies: "Behold, I make all things new."

Upon the truth concealed in the symbology of these two Tarot cards Richard Wagner, the musical Initiate, founded his magnificent soul-drama of *Parsifal*. Parsifal, "the pure Fool," enters by chance, as it were, the grounds of the Grail castle. Unintentionally, he slays a swan floating upon the waters of the healing lake. Through his sorrow and contrition for this misdeed his soul awakens and he enters upon the Quest. Now he must go out into the world to be tempted in order to prove his strength, his courage and his perseverance. Wagner stated that the theme of *Parsifal* was to be found in the line "Strong is the power of desire, but stronger yet is the soul-power gained through resistance." At length Parsifal returns to become the High Priest of Mt. Salvat or King of the Grail Knights. Donning the white robe of mastership and carrying the sacred Spear, he enters the Grail Temple to heal the wounded Amfortas. Having accomplished this, he becomes the teacher of the Grail Knights and the trusted guardian of the holy Cup.

What is it that brings about this transition from Fool to High Priest? What is it that changes mortal man into one who manifests his godhood? It is the awakening of the great I AM principle within himself. It is the resurrection of his own Christ Spirit. This is the theme of that ancient Temple chant which sounds forth the highest concept of the resurrection:

*Before all worlds, I was!*
*Throughout all worlds, I AM!*
*When all worlds are but a memory, I shall be!*

At the time of the Passover, when the Sun ascends from the southern hemisphere to the northern, the Christ force passes from the physical to the spiritual realms of earth. The body of earth is like the body of man; it is interpenetrated by more highly attenuated vehicles which extend far into space beyond the planet's physical body.

To repeat, during the six months of the year that the Sun is passing through the six signs below the equator, and for the next six months as it passes through the six signs above the equator, the Christ force permeates earth's higher spiritual realms. These realms are the home of the so-called dead, a region where they pursue for a time their normal activities in an environment of enchanting beauty and radiance. It is here that Angels and Archangels carry on their various ministries for the planet and its progeny.

When the Sun enters Aries it ushers in the glorious resurrection, beginning the transmutation season of the year. Then the white waters of Pisces merge with the red fires of Aries, a blending which manifests in spring's floodtide of blossom and song. It is also the transmutation season for man, the most propitious time for him to roll away the stone of his old life and come forth in the full power of a "resurrected" consciousness. Just as nature exchanges the gloom of winter's sleep for the resplendence of spring, and the Christ transcends the agony of Golgotha by the exaltation of Resurrection morn, so the disciple who has faithfully and persistently followed the Christ up the steep and narrow way has his own resurrection in newly awakened Christ powers within himself.

This is the time when a marvelous transformation can occur within his own body-temple. A new force emanates from the white liquid of his nerves and unites with a new essence in the red currents of his blood, a merging that produces the golden light which infuses and surrounds the body of an Illumined One. St. John was referring to such a transformation when he wrote that we shall someday "walk in the light as He is in the light." Red and white are the colors of Aries, and they are also the colors of transmutation in both nature and man.

## The Path of Holiness through Aries

As the disciple travels the Path of Holiness leading into the higher spiritual realm, the experiences he encounters become more wonderful and transforming. At this level of existence there is no veil separating the living from the "dead," no barrier to communication with celestial Beings. Here one can observe the wondrous workings of nature spirits and see how their activities underlie what material scientists refer to as the "laws of nature." And here on Easter morning, amid the triumphant hosannas of Angels and Archangels, the Christ, following His release from annual incarnation in the earth, appears in radiant glory. In the Temple of the Christian Mysteries the glorious Easter processional is fashioned around His luminous presence, not as a mere spectacle but so the power and majesty of His blessing may be bestowed on all who have been found worthy to be numbered among His sanctified comapny.

The mystic Christian does not commemorate Easter solely as an historical event that occurred on Golgotha, for he knows that Christ's sacrifice is of annual occurrence; that each year He is entombed within the earth, from which He arises every Easter to ascend into the heavens for restoration of His powers before He returns to this physical sphere at the time of the Autumn Equinox.

It was when His Crucifixion occurred on Golgotha that the Christ left the body of Jesus, in which He had functioned for a three-year ministry among men, and transferred His Spirit into the planetary body itself to henceforth be its Regent. There is a profound significance in the words He spoke to His Disciples after the Resurrection: "All power is given unto me in heaven and in earth."

When the human race succumbed to the seduction of Lucifer spirits the atomic rhythm of man's physical body was changed so the spinal spirit fire was attuned to the Luciferic forces and received the impress of these fiery Beings. It is the mission of the Christ to counteract this condition by substituting His rhythm and impress for that of the Lucifers—for the Christ also, as an Archangel, is a Fire Being. When this has been accomplished, the atomic vibration of man's body will make it immune to disease and death. Individuals of the New Age bear within themselves the glorious image of the Christ.

The Hierarchy of Aries contains an archetypal pattern of man as he was created "in the image and likeness of God." This pattern will be increasingly manifested in the New Age. As before mentioned, the six constellations above the equator hold the cosmic patterns of that which is to manifest on earth; the six constellations below the equator contain these patterns in miniature, so to speak, and the Hierarchies of these southern constellations work with mankind to bring these patterns to fulfillment here on earth. For example, the Hierarchy of Aries holds this perfect pattern of the new Christed man. Libra, the sign opposite Aries and the home of the Lords of Individuality, steps down this cosmic pattern of Aries and is aiding man in bringing about its manifestation.

Such is the knowledge which has motivated the great teachers of the world to help mankind bring the divine pattern into manifestation on this plane. The work is arduous. But down through the ages those brave souls who have been strong enough to follow the Path of Holiness into spiritual realms have returned aflame with what they beheld of "a new heaven and a new earth" inhabited by a Christed humanity. They know, as the Christ knew, that "the Word was God" indeed.

### Biblical Parable for Aries
The Rich Young Ruler

*And, behold, one came and said unto him, Good Master, what good thing shall I do, that I may have eternal life?*

*And he said unto him, Why callest thou me good? There is none good but one, that is, God: but if thou wilt enter into life, keep the commandments.*

*He saith unto him, Which? Jesus said, Thou shalt do no murder, Thou shalt not commit adultery, Thou shalt not steal, Thou shalt not bear false witness.*

*Honor thy father and thy mother: and, Thou shalt love thy neighbor as thyself.*

*The young man said unto him, All these things have I kept from my youth up: what lack I yet?*

*Jesus said unto him, If thou wilt be perfect, go and sell that thou hast, and give to the poor, and thou shalt have treasure in heaven: and come and follow me.*

*But when the young man heard that saying, he went away sorrowful: for he had great possessions.*

*Then said Jesus unto his disciples, Verily I say unto you, that a rich man shall hardly enter into the kingdom of heaven.*

*And again I say unto you, It is easier for a camel to go through the eye of a needle, than for a rich man to enter into the kingdom of God.*

*When his disciples heard it, they were exceedingly amazed, saying, Who then can be saved?*

*But Jesus beheld them, and said unto them, With men this is impossible but with God all things are possible.*

*Then answered Peter and said unto him, Behold, we have forsaken all, and followed thee; what shall we have therefore?*

*And Jesus said unto them, Verily I say unto you, that ye which have followed me, in the regeneration when the Son of man shall sit in the throne of his glory, ye also shall sit upon twelve thrones, judging the twelve tribes of Israel.*

*And every one that hath forsaken houses or brethren, or sisters, or father, or mother, or wife, or children, or lands, for my name's sake shall receive an hundredfold, and shall inherit everlasting life.*

*But many that are first shall be last; and the last shall be first.*

*—Matthew 19.16-30*


The parable of the rich young ruler imparts a teaching appropriate to the meditation for Aries.

The foregoing biblical parable is one of the Master's most misunderstood and misinterpreted teachings. It is not the *use* but the *abuse* of wealth which engenders evil and wrong-doing. The One who is the Teacher of us all stated further: "For unto whomsoever much is given, of him shall be much required." The possessor of vast wealth has a great responsibility. To hoard wealth, to squander it in idle or foolish pleasures, or to spend it for the gratification of personal vanity, engenders a heavy karmic debt which must be liquidated sometime, somewhere, through sorrow and pain.

Children who are to be the inheritors of a great fortune should be trained very carefully in regard to its *true* value and purpose; when such training is neglected, parents suffer because their offsprings often have no proper understanding of any responsibility toward others.

As a man comes into a clear realization regarding his responsibility relative to wealth, he thinks of himself as a steward in God's vast storehouse of abundance. He understands that he is but a channel for an inflow and outflow of supply wherewith to bless and uplift those whom he contacts. Such dedication makes an individual an anointed one. Being dedicated to the All Good he attracts *only* the All Good, and his life becomes an inspiration and an example to be emulated.

It is difficult for the average person to disassociate *things* from the spirit lying within and behind things. Ralph Waldo Emerson, the American sage, wrote: "Things are in the saddle and ride mankind." This is indeed applicable to our modern world. The real purpose and goal of human life, however, is for man to so sublimate his thoughts and emotions relative to material possessions that he can identify himself with the spirit that lies above and beyond their physical properties. This spirit is the God power, the All Good; and union with it attracts whatever is high and noble, beautiful and true. This was the ideal the Master projected to the young disciple when He said, "Sell all that thou hast . . . and come, follow me." The clarion call of Aries is not to the personal self but to the I AM to come forth and assert its divinity by establishing dominion over all things.

# CHAPTER XXVI

TAURUS

*Spiritual Meditation for Taurus*

As the Sun passes from Aries into Taurus a sensitive person is conscious of a change in earth's psychic atmosphere from the highly charged masculine radiations of Aries to the gentle, caressing mood of the Venus-governed sign of Taurus. The Moon, also feminine in nature, is exalted in the sign, which further emphasizes the tender, loving quality of a developed Taurean. It is, therefore, in accord with cosmic influences that Mother's Day is observed on the second Sunday in May when feminine attributes of the heavens are in the ascendancy.

The Ancients depicted Taurus as a high priestess seated on a throne, a halo about her head and an open book resting upon her knees. A veil covers her face, symbolizing concealment of the Mysteries from the unawakened multitude. The divine feminine holds holy secrets of life which are never revealed until a seeker approaches with clean hands and a pure heart. The veil of the priestess can never be lifted so long as man wars with his fellow man and continues to kill for meat, for sport, for vanity, or to practice such cruelties as are perpetrated by vivisectionists. All life is sacred and must be held so before man is worthy to remove the veil of Isis and enter into life's deeper mysteries.

Taureans are naturally attracted to activities wherein Venusian qualities find expression; and since Taurus is an earth sign, its expression tends towards the practical arts. The healing profession is favorably influenced by Taurus, with emphasis on keeping the physical body in perfect condition for its indwelling spirit.

The keynote of Taurus is "I possess." The keynote of Venus,

190

ruler of Taurus, is "I love." In an undeveloped Taurean this inclines to a possessive love that circumscribes the freedom of its object, with the result of bringing disappointment, discord and sorrow into their relationship. Heavy karmic debts are incurred in this manner.

Under the Hierarchy of Taurus humanity is reaping a weighty toll from past causation. Under its opposite sign, Scorpio, the debt is now being liquidated on a planetary scale through war, social upheavals and terrestrial disasters.

Transmuting forces prevalent in nature are active under Taurus for transforming the life of a disciple. Every biblical character illustrates the characteristics of a zodiacal sign. A personality typifying Taurean characteristics was Mary Magdalene. Mary, the sister of Lazarus, typifies Cancer while the Blessed Virgin Mary comes under the sign Virgo, the Virgin. Thus, the three Marys most closely associated with the life and ministry of Christ Jesus correspond to the three outstanding feminine signs of the Zodiac. Mary Magdalene, alluring and seductive, was centered in the desire currents of earth; yet when the Christ touched her life, the red flame of passion was transformed into the white fire of the soul. It was this transformation that won for her the privilege of being first of all His followers to see the Risen Lord, and of being bidden by Him to go tell the others the most transcendent message of all time: "There is no death!"

### The Path of Holiness through Taurus

As the Sun passes through Taurus during the month of May, the Christ force ascends higher and higher into earth's spiritual aura. The disciple who is walking the Path of Holiness follows in the wake of the ascending Christ Light and enters a sphere where he finds himself inwardly harmonized and strengthened by the creative power of music. Celestial Beings who inhabit this realm speak a musical language. Their every motion emanates music. They mold and fashion all manner of forms through the medium of musical tones. In this realm all growing things are nurtured by the power of music, while the various flower colors are produced by variations in tone. Music is assuredly the supreme creative power of this lofty realm.

The constellation of Tuarus is the home of cosmic patterns for all that exists on earth. These patterns are shadowed forth by its opposite sign, Scorpio, home of the Lords of Form. This Hierarchy teaches form building throughout the physical plane; and from the constellation Taurus sounds forth the mystery tone God used in creation, that creative Word by which ''all things were made by him; and without him was not anything made that was made.'' This is the biblical keynote of Taurus.

The Lords of Taurus hold the cosmic pattern of a most wonderful organ destined to become a part of the future human body. This new organ, resembling a golden rose, will be located in the throat, and will be the center through which the creative word will be projected by New Age man. By its power generation will become regeneration, and man will be able to mold substance into whatever he desires. In the realm where Taurean powers are most active an illumined one can behold a vision of this perfection and meditate upon it. He perceives the glorious development awaiting him in the future and realizes literally the meaning of the psalmist's words: ''Thou hast made him a little lower than the angels, and hast crowned him with glory and honour.'' (Ps. 8:5).

### Biblical Parable for Taurus
*The Talents—Matthew 25:14-30*

Taurus is essentially the Hierarchy of karma. It is under this sign, assisted by its polar opposite, Scorpio, that in the last days of this Age both individuals and nations are clearing their karmic sheets in preparation for the incoming New Day. War has been fittingly termed an operation for spiritual cataract. While war is a terrible scourge, it is also an inexorable cleanser; and so these days are filled with wars and rumors of war.

The parable of the talents is a teaching on reincarnation and karma. A great nobleman went into a far country to claim his kingdom. Before leaving he called his servants to him and gave to each of them a specific number of talents in trust. After a long absence he returned and called for an accounting by the servants. The first showed his talents which had been doubled. "Well done, thou good and faithful servant," commended his master. The second presented his talents with a like increase, so he too received the blessing of the master. The third servant, who had received only one talent and had buried it, returned it to his master, saying, "I was afraid, and went and hid thy talent in the earth: lo, there thou hast that is thine." Whereupon his master replied, "Thou wicked and slothful servant . . . cast ye the unprofitable servant into outer darkness." This followed the Master's cryptic statement: "Unto every one that hath shall be given . . . but from him that hath not shall be taken even that which he hath."

This parable deals with the cycle of recurring earth lives. The purpose of each terrestrial pilgrimage is that man may gain additional soul-power, soul-life, soul-light.

Each talent that he brings with him from previous incarnations must be increased else his sojourn is futile. The first servant, who was given ten talents, represents an old soul who, through many incarnations, has garnered a rich harvest of soulpowers. In each new life he is learning additional lessons, largely by means of meditation, contemplation, and advanced work on both inner and outer planes. The second servant, who receives five talents, represents a younger soul in God's evolutionary school. He is learning his lessons chiefly through activity on the physical plane. His life centers principally in his five physical senses. (It is to be noted that *five* is the number of activity while the significance of *ten* is the union of 1 (masculine) and 0 (feminine) working harmoniously together. This second servant typifies the evolutionary status of the great mass of humanity.

The third servant, who through fear buried his one talent in the ground, is representative of those who are wholly unawakened spiritually so are centered in the interests of the mortal self. The casting of such a person into outer darkness is not a curse but the working of divine law, for only through much sorrow and travail does man awaken his higher nature. As Mabel Collins expresses this in her *Light on the Path:* "Before the feet can stand in the presence of the Master, they must be washed in the blood of the heart."

# CHAPTER XXVII

GEMINI

*Spiritual Meditation for Gemini*

Gemini is the sign of the Twins. On the material plane this signifies duality; on the spiritual plane, polarity. The Ancients assigned to Gemini two brilliant stars, Castor and Pollux. They taught that Mercury, ruler of Gemini, bestowed immortality upon these two stars on alternate days, thus subtly suggesting the dual nature of the sign. Under the influence of Gemini man is easily swayed one way and another: from the material to the spiritual, from the personal to the imperaonsl.

Gemini's keynote is *versatility*. Its natives are characterized by ability to do many things well. The awakened Gemini often engages in writing and speaking on spiritual subjects and sometimes becomes a spiritual healer.

Gemini is a mental sign, and mind can lead either in the direction of darkness or of light. St. Paul well understood this when he made the focal point of all his teachings the ideal that "Christ be formed in you." Until the mind is Christed, it is fraught with great dangers. To again quote St. Paul: "The carnal mind is enmity against God."

The ancient hieroglyph for Gemini was the figure of a high priest seated upon a throne. Two sphinxes, one white and one black, were kneeling at his feet—another symbol portraying the duality of the sign of the Twins.

In accordance with the nature of Gemini, those predominently under its influence often face the need for choosing one of two things or courses; hence, it is essential for them to cultivate their powers of discrimination—powers emphasized in Virgo, also ruled by Mercury, as especially important. They must cultivate stability and fixity of purpose because they are so easily influenced. The Gemini native needs much time for concentration and meditation upon the affirmation "Be still, and know that I am God."

Mercury's angelic ambassador to earth is Raphael, the guardian and director of all healing movements in the world. Raphael also presides over the higher Temple teachings, the foremost being the healing power of the mind. This principle has found wide acceptance and practice in these modern times.

A beautiful legend states that at the end of each day the Angel Sandalphon gathers up all the prayers for help and healing that have gone forth from the earth and places them before God's throne where, in tender benediction, they are transformed into a glorious array of fragrant flowers This legend was given a lovely expression by Longfellow in the following lines:

*And he gathers the prayers as he stands,*
*And they change into flowers in his hands,*
*Into garlands of purple and red;*
*And beneath the great arch of the portal,*
*Through the streets of the City Immortal,*
*Is wafted the fragrance they shed.*

The same thought applies to Raphael, the Angel of Healing who, because of his closeness to our race, has been called "the friend of man."

Raphael, the ambassador from Mercury, typifies in his own being the Lords of Mercury who are now playing an increasingly active part in humanity's initiatory work. He presides over the Mysteries, the initiatory work of the human race for the remainder of the Earth Period. Messengers from Mercury serve all those who are aspiring to Initiation and, according to Max Heindel, they will be giving man more and more help as time goes on. Many sensitive persons are becoming aware of their presence, for the Mercurians belong to our own life wave that originally had its home in the Sun. They are, however, far in advance of early humanity and Raphael is their prototype before the throne of God.

### The Path of Holiness Through Gemini

When the Sun ascends toward its northernmost point in the sky in June it transits the sign Gemini, the constellation that sets a dual impress upon the human body-temple. It governs the dualities of the body: lungs, shoulders, arms and hands in particular. It also holds the cosmic pattern of the perfected androgyne in whom the masculine and feminine potencies are in equilibrium. Such is the attainment of Initiates of the Greater Christ Mysteries. This attainment brings immunity from disease and old age. And since consciousness remains unbroken whether such be in or out of the flesh, death as we know it is never experienced by them because their consciousness is centered in immortality without interruption.

The archangelic life wave has reached the status where it functions in perfectly polarized bodies. This is not true of the less evolved angelic and human kingdoms. It is, therefore, possible for members of these kingdoms to descend from their high estate into lower forms of expression. The fall of Angels is recorded biblically in the account of the war in heaven, when Lucifer and his followers were expelled therefrom; and the Fall of man occurred, according to the Genesis account, when Adam and Eve (infant humanity) lost the Garden of Eden. Redemption from these falls required a higher power than was available to either of these life waves. It had to come from the archangelic level. And so it did. The Lord Christ, the most highly evolved of the Archangels, became the teacher and redeemer of both the fallen Angels and humanity. This is one of the most profound truths associated with the mystery of the Christos.

The pattern of the perfect androgyne was projected by the Hierarchy of Gemini into its opposite sign, Sagittarius. The Hierarchy of Sagittarius (Lords of Mind) gives this enlightened teaching to earth's most advanced pioneers. After the coming of the Christ, further development of the human mind passed from the guidance of Scorpio to that of Sagittarius. Considering the wonders of the mind, its creative powers and its ability to encircle the globe in an instant of time and to contemplate the vastness of cosmic space—even though at present only a fraction of it is active—we get a faint glimpse of the transcendent glory of the Sagittarian Hierarchy whose lowest vehicle, corresponding to man's physical body, is composed of mental substance. It also indicates the sublime powers awaiting man when he attains like development.

For an awakened soul, the supreme purpose of cultivating the mind is that it shall become Christed. As yet this is the attainment of but few only. The majority are steeped in the materialism of the concrete mind, which is focused mainly on worldly pursuit and interests of the separative self. So long as such concerns claim man's attention, there will be a lack of spiritual perception and scant realization of the realities pertaining to the inner world and universal mind. Nor will there be any continuity of consciousness and but little if any, intimation of the experiences encountered in the spiritual world during intervals between earthly lives. The result of consciousness so veiled from spiritual realities is the materialism that conditions the world today. This, however, is but a temporary phase of mankind's evolution. As added light falls on the path of those who strive for holiness, realization of spiritual realities that lie back of all physical and temporal manifestation will become clearer and stronger. The insistent impulse of such aspirants to make themselves worthy to walk in the Way of Holiness will bring more and more light.

While the Sun is transiting the sign Gemini the Christ Light suffuses a wider auric sphere of this earth, which enables Initiates on the Path of Holiness to come into the presence of mighty Beings known as Seraphim, whose grandeur and power surpass all description. Under their sublime ministry teachings are given concerning the mysteries of polarity, wherein it is learned that the harmonious interaction of the masculine and feminine forces—the positive and negative elements in nature—constitute the motive power in everything from atom to planet. Medieval alchemists referred to this perfect union, this polarity, as the blending of fire and water. It is vividly symbolized in Jachin and Boaz, the two columns of every Masonic Temple, and it is the theme of the glorious initiatory Song of Solomon. It is of polarity that Solomon sings in the words "My beloved is mine, and I am his: he feedeth among the lilies."

As an illuminated one follows the Path of Holiness which leads to this exalted spiritual sphere, he is permitted to study the marvels of the androgynous body, the form the human body will take in a future stage of development. As already stated, this glorious cosmic pattern is held above earth by the Hierarchy of Gemini, the Seraphim. Their forces will be brought down to man by the Hierarchy of Sagittarius when humanity is ready to receive them. As man learns of the marvels of this cosmic pattern and the wonders of the Sagittarian body built entirely of mental substance, he begins to comprehend something of the exalted destiny awaiting him. With profound reverence and deep humility, he intones within himself the biblical keynote of Gemini: "Be still, and know that I Am God."

### Biblical Parable for Gemini
The Rich Man and Lazarus

It has been said that Gemini, the Twins, is the sign of opposites: positive and negative, high and low, black and white. Under this Hierarchy mankind comes to know the path of light and the path of shadow, even as did Lazarus and the rich man in the biblical parable.

The rich man possessed vast worldly goods while Lazarus was a beggar living in penury. These two symbolize the contrasting states of wealth and poverty, the "haves and the have-nots"—a cleavage that has been the cause of countless wars down through history. The rich man of the parable was robed in fine linen and royal purple. Every day he made merry with feasting and entertainment while Lazarus, in his dire need, came each day to beg crumbs from the other's table.

Similar conditions exist in the world today. Such inequities cannot always be, for we live in a world governed by moral law. The balancing of accounts, however, requires more time than the brief segment of a single earthly incarnation. This fact is brought out in the parable, which reveals the operation of spiritual law in both the inner and outer worlds.

Lazarus and the rich man died. The former was caught up into heaven whereas the latter found himself in purgatory, there to suffer for his idle, useless, misspent years. Such retributive justice is not retaliatory in nature. Man reaps as he sows. Though Lazarus had lived in poverty, the seeds he sowed bore a rich harvest in comparison to those of the man who failed to rightly use his possessions or to take advantage of an opportunity for rendering service to one less fortunate than himself. The operation of law is purely corrective. By reaping the harvest of his own sowing man acquires understanding and compassion, and comes to realize his unity with all mankind.

The parable also teaches that the nature of man's experiences after death is determined by his life on earth. When the rich man, suffering from thirst, saw the felicity of Lazarus' state in the bosom of Father Abraham, he pleaded with Abraham to let Lazarus bring him a drink of water to assuage his terrible longing. To this plea Abraham replied, ''Between us and you there is a great gulf fixed.'' This barrier is one of vibration. If a person in purgatory could lift his consciousness to the heaven realm he would no longer be confined to the lower level of the astral plane.

The parable brings out still another truth. The gamut of human experience is made up mostly of the emotions of joy and sorrow. Fiona McLeod, an exquisite English writer, states that while there are no tears in Paradise, there is in a certain garden a great gray pool—a pool whose waters are constantly replenished by tears of sorrow, pain and remorse shed on earth. If one will but kneel and bathe his eyes in these waters he will be healed. Thereafter his songs will be the sweetest to be heard in Paradise.

When rightly accepted, sorrow builds a shining rung upon the ladder of attainment. It deepens compassion, broadens sympathy, increases humility and beauty in one's character, all of which are the soul signatures of him who is upon the truth Path of Discipleship.

# CHAPTER XXVIII

*Spiritual Meditation for Cancer*

Cancer is a most deeply mystical sign, the principal feminine sign. The Moon, ruler of Cancer, is the exaltation place of both Jupiter and Neptune, and its physical keynote is *fecundity*. In the cosmic waters of Cancer are the germs that ensoul every earthly form belonging to the several kingdoms of nature. Also, Cancer governs home and family, and its qualities tend to develop attributes of character that enable parents to preside lovingly and harmoniously over their household.

The mysticism of Cancer stems in part from Jupiter, planet of expansive sympathies and generosity, but still more from Neptune, the higher octave of Mercury and the planet of divinity. The Summer Solstice occurs when the Sun enters this sign, at which time the brilliant blue-white fixed star Sirius pours out its spiritual influence upon earth in greatest measure. As the cosmic mother sign, Cancer is the portal whereby human egos come to rebirth.

By means of the Jupiterian influence, creative arts are especially inspired at this season, while Neptune makes this period one of the most propitious for enlightened souls to pass through the gates of light into the inner world and there experience immortal life. One of the three principles of man's triune being is governed by the Moon, Jupiter or Neptune. In their correlations the Moon relates to his physical body, Jupiter to his soul, Neptune to his spirit.

Humanity in general responds to Jehovah through the influence of the physical Sun; Initiates of the Lesser Mysteries respond through the influence of the spiritual Sun, the body of the cosmic Christ; Initiates of the Greater Mysteries respond through the influence of Vulcan, which corresponds to the solar body of the

Father. Astronomers have not yet discovered the planet Vulcan. It will, however, become known to the world as the result of scientific observations when enough individuals have become sufficiently sensitive to receive its vibrations. This was the condition under which the planets Uranus, Neptune and Pluto commenced to register in the higher vehicles of man.

The Ancients represented Cancer by the figure of a woman with the Moon under her feet and a crown of twelve stars on her head. This symbol was also used by St. John in Revelation to represent the triumphant restoration of the fallen feminine, the Eve of Genesis, to its original divine estate. This exalted feminine figure is symbolic of that great Initiate of the Cancer Hierarchy known as the Cherubim. One of the highest Initiates of this Hierarchy is the Cosmic Mother of the universe to which this earth planet belongs.

The Moon as ruler of Cancer means generation; Neptune exalted in Cancer means regeneration. The transmuting of generation into regeneration is the new birth—that new birth about which Christ spoke to Nicodemus when he came to the Master "by night." The biblical keynote of Cancer is found in those words of Christ: "Except a man be born again, he cannot see the kingdom of God . . . Except a man be born of water [Moon in Cancer] and of Spirit [Jupiter in Cancer], he cannot enter the kingdom of God [Neptune in Cancer]." This is one of the most explicit teachings on Initiation given by Christ during His three years' ministry. All men know the natural birth under the Moon in Cancer; but few there are who learn to walk the "strait and narrow way" of renunciation of the flesh and dedication to the spirit implicit in the exaltation of Jupiter and Neptune in Cancer. Yet this is the true and only key to that elevation of consciousness whereby man is lifted from the natural or "water" birth into the divine at-one-ment of the "fire" birth in spirit.

## *The Path of Holiness Through Cancer*

The Sun in its annual transit through Cancer reaches the highest point of its northern ascension at the time of the Summer

Solstice. Its physical radiation then attains to maximum in the northern hemisphere, so the days are longest and the nights shortest. It is the high noon of the year, and its keynote is *light*.

Cancer is the foremost feminine sign of the heavens. In harmony with this fact, the sign contains a small cluster of stars arranged so as to resemble a manger. From the heart of Cancer well up the waters of eternal life, in which are germinated seed-forms that animate all the kingdoms of earth. The Summer Solstice occurs when the Sun enters Cancer (June 21st) and is also attuned to the principle of fecundity. It is in obedience to this active principle in nature that seeds burst forth into a cycle of manifestation. Light, freedom, joyousness are dominant qualities of the midsummer season. Accordingly many people, particularly in Europe, observe this time of year with music, dancing and exuberant festivities.

The Hierarchy of Cancer is known biblically as the Cherubim. It is the ministry of this Hierarchy to guard sacred places. They hover above the Holy of Holies. Through initiatory processes an aspirant is taught to build this Holy of Holies within himself. The pot of golden manna within the Ark of the Covenant is a symbol of man's own individual Grail Cup and his own sacred life force. Humanity lost the Garden of Eden through misuse of this life force, since which the Cherubim have guarded the gates of Eden lest unregenerate humanity should find its way back prematurely. The Blessed Virgin Mary and the Disciples are alleged to have communed with the Cherubim after Pentecost, meaning that they had learned these sacred truths from this divine Hierarchy.

As the Sun reaches its highest ascension the Christ Spirit ascends to the very throne of the Father. His activity is then focused at the very highest level of earth's planetary aura, where he brings added illumination and renewed blessings to the celestial Beings who inhabit this realm; also to souls who, in their spiritual progression between physical embodiments, have risen to this high plane. In harmony with this, it is also at the summer season that an illumined one who is following the Christ on the Path of Holiness rises in consciousness to this realm to commune with its celestial denizens and learn further about the nature forces. Here it is perceived how the elementals of water and fire, the undines and salamanders respectively, work in spring and summer with growing plants; and how the elementals of air and earth, the sylphs and gnomes, work in autumn and winter with disintegrating and dying plant life. On this exalted plane one who pursues the Path of Holiness stands before the actual mystery of life itself. Only the pure in heart attain to this plane. Those whose hands are stained with blood can never lift the veil of this holy place. He who seeks to discover the secret of life will never find it until his hands and heart are chaste and clean. Only to such will come the realization of the oneness of all life.

These are truths that belong particularly to the Hierarchy of Cancer, and they are not possible of direct transmission to the earthly plane. Therefore they are passed by the Cherubim to the Hierarchy of Capricorn, the sign opposite Cancer and home of the Archangels who, being of a lower hierarchical rank than the Cherubim and thus closer in consciousness to humanity, disseminate them to those of earth who are ready and willing to receive them. Hence, it was at a time when the forces of Capricorn permeated the earth that there descended into embodiment the Master Jesus, of the seed of David, who became the bearer of the Christ.

### The Biblical Parable for Cancer
#### The Prodigal Son—Luke 15:11-32

According to esoteric astrology, every incarnating soul passes through the gates of Cancer. In the waters of Cancer are formed the life germs ensouling each unit of the mineral, plant, animal and human kingdoms. This life impulse progressively raised the mineral into the plant, the plant into the animal, the animal into the human, and the human into the angelic, for all evolution is under the guidance of the Hierarchy.

The parable of the prodigal son is correlated with Cancer. It is a story of evolution. This parable is a story of evolution. This parable introduces two brothers, an elder who never leaves his father's house and a younger who goes into a far country. To the former the father says, "All that I have is thine." This brother typifies man's higher nature which is ever in attunement with all that is good, noble, beautiful, pure and true. The other brother left his father's house and wasted his substance in riotous living, eventually descending to sharing husks with the swine he tended. This one typifies man's lower nature which succumbs to sensual temptations and worldly glamor.

Because of its universal application, this parable will be found in some form in every spiritual teaching given to the world. It was an important teaching of the Mysteries of ancient Egypt. A slightly different version appears in the symbolism of Blue Lodge Masonry. As therein presented, the candidate—poor, naked and blind from having wasted his substance unworthily—lifts his eyes once more toward the Father's house and begins the journey toward the light in the east. There sits the worshipful Master who, when the candidate has proven himself worthy, will give him instructions for also attaining to mastership.

Humanity at large is enacting the role of the prodigal son. For all too long mankind has turned from the true light and, in its absorption with material pursuits, literally lived on the husks of existence. This has given rise to the fear, chaos, uncertainty, conflicts and social upheavals that fill the earth today. And they will increase until humanity begins to retrace its steps toward the light that shines in the east.

When the prodigal son returned the father met him "a great way off." Said the son, "I have sinned . . . and am no more worthy to be called thy son: make me as one of thy hired servants." But the father welcomed him with loving embrace, placed about him the best robe, and put upon his finger a golden ring.

The most comforting assurance there is for man in the midst of world chaos is the realization that he can never really separate himself from his Father's loving care and protection. "The hound of heaven" pursues him ever. In the words of the Psalmist: "If I ascend up to heaven, thou art there: if I make my bed in hell, behold, thou art there" (Ps. 139-8). No person can become so hardened in crime or so debased but what he can be assured of the Father's loving welcome when he lifts his eyes and begins to journey toward the east. The returned prodigal will have placed upon him the robe of a new life and will be given the golden ring of love and protection.

The nearness of the Father is beautifully expressed by Elizabeth Barrett Browning:

*And I smiled to think God's greatness flowed*
        *around our incompleteness, —*
*Round our restlessness, His rest.*

The two natures of the prodigal son are well defined by Emerson: "It is only the finite which has wrought and suffered; the Infinite lies stretched in smiling repose." And St. Paul illustrated the path leading from unreality in the statement: "Things which are seen are temporal; but the things which are not seen are eternal."

# CHAPTER XXIX

## LEO

### Spiritual Meditation for Leo

An ancient sage declared that as above, so below, and as below, so above. All true Mystery Temples on the physical plane are constructed in harmony with the zodiacal pattern in the heavens. In that circle of twelve constellations Cancer and Leo form a two-columned entrance into that cosmic Temple. By correspondence, symbolical columns have been placed at the entrace of all Mystery Temples; between them every candidate must pass on his way to illumination. These two pillars have borne many names down through the ages, and their significance has been emphasized in the mystery literature of all nations. They are referred to as representing the elements of fire and water; as indicating the two precious metals, gold and silver; and again, as symbolical of the two planetary bodies, the Sun and the Moon. Cancer has been called the mother and Leo the father of souls.

Between these columns New Age man and woman must pass, hand-in-hand, in complete equality, to receive the glorious heritage which that Age will bestow upon its pioneers. The Masonic Craft has yet to learn that its deepest secrets will never be understood until the Divine Feminine has been restored to its original estate of equality with the opposite masculine polarity.

The Ancients depicted the sign Leo as a high priest seated in a chariot and driving two sphinxes, one white and the other black. A similar symbol relates to Gemini; but in this instance the two sphinxes kneel before the high priest, meaning that it is for him to choose whether he will follow the path of light or the path of darkness. In Leo the decision has been made. Both his lower and higher natures have been brought under control.

The keywords of Leo are *authority, rulership* and *triumph.* One of the symbols of Leo is a sword, sign of conquest and victory. That the sword also represents the creative power within an individual is indicated in several biblical stories. In Genesis, for instance, there is the account of the expulsion of Adam and Eve from the Garden of Eden because they had eaten of the forbidden fruit of the Tree of Knowledge of good and evil. In consequence of their sin, Cherubim stand guard before the gate brandishing a flaming sword lest man, through access to the Tree of Life, should acquire the secret of the etheric body and learn thereby to immortalize his imperfect physical form.

These same celestial Beings were represented as standing before Solomon's Temple, but a full blown flower had replaced the sword. Here, in exquisite symbology, is depicted the attainment of a high Initiate, whose body is described mystically as a flower garden. In this garden the two principal flower-centers are the heart, the day star of the body, and the pituitary gland, the highest of the two spiritual head centers. It is through these flower centers, when they are awakened, that the powerful fire forces of Leo play upon the whole body.

In the life of the Christ, His Triumphal Entry correlates to the regal radiations of Leo. The Christ Spirit was at that time magnetically charged with the effulgent glory of the Father, which had been bestowed upon Him as the Sun was transiting the kingly sign of the heavens. This instinctively called forth from the populace the hosannas that accompanied His entry.

That triumphant scene was the beginning of culminating events in Christ's earthly ministry, to be followed by His assumption of the regency of this planet for the redemption of the world. It also typified the festival processional of a successful candidate entering an initiatory Temple of Light. It was then that he heard the angelic chant from heaven: "Blessed is he that cometh in the name of the Lord (law)"—that is, he that walketh in spiritual light and love.

Material science recognizes the Sun in its physical aspect only. Esoteric science recognizes two additional solar spheres or interpenetrating spiritual bodies. The first of these is the vehicle of the Solar Logos whom we know as the Cosmic Christ; the other, of still higher vibratory frequency, is the celestial body of the Father of our solar system.

Ordinary humanity responds chiefly to the influence of the physical Sun, the emanations of which correlate to Jehovah and the race religions fostered under His influence. It was during the Jehovistic regime that the Lesser Mysteries were inaugurated by the Lords of Mercury. With the coming of the Christ a new era was instituted, under which man was to look no longer to the law outside himself but to the law within as the chief purpose of life is for man to awaken his latent divinity, the Christ within. Under the influence of Mercury the early Mysteries were inaugurated. The Christ came bringing the four Greater Mysteries, an outline of which is given in the four Gospels of the New Testament. Neptune, the planet of divinity and Initiation, gives humanity the necessary aid for apprehending these Greater Mysteries, which hold the loftiest truths it can grasp at this time. Later will come the religion of the Father. When pioneers have qualified for the higher illumination inherent in that religion, the spiritual planet Vulcan will emerge within man's ken—a fact dependent upon the law that in the sequence of time outer events follow their occurrence on inner planes. This will mean the revealing of glory and power far beyond the present capacity of the human mind to comprehend or of human speech to describe.

### The Path of Holiness Through Leo

It has been said that as the Sun transits the sign Cancer and Leo during July and August the Christ ascends to the throne of the Father where He bathes in the Father's transcendent glory. It is here that He renews and revitalizes Himself, attracting higher and more spiritual forces for continuing his earthly ministry when He returns to the realm of humanity at the Autumn Equinox. During His sojourn in the high heavens the earth planet, clairvoyantly observed, appears luminous with His radiations; and the observer comes into a profound realization of the meaning of His statement that "All power is given unto me in heaven and in earth."

When the Sun is thus transiting Cancer and Leo, an illumined one who treads the Path of Holiness ascends to the highest spiritual realms of this planet and enters into a deeper consciousness of transcendent power. He begins to understand that love in its highest aspect is not passion or a sentiment, but a phase of divinity itself. It was with such power of love that Peter was imbued. He himself referred to this power of love when he said to the lame man beside the gate of the Temple Beautiful: Silver and gold have I none, but such as I have give I thee . . . arise up and walk.'' Again, it was this same power which so animated Paul that, despite all persecutions and imprisonment, he was able to utter those sublime words: ''Though I speak with the tongues of men and angels, and have not love (charity), I am become as sounding brass, or a tinkling cymbal.''

When an aspirant reaches this degree of spiritual attainment the Christ is all in all to him. To serve as He served, and to love as He loved, becomes his highest aspiration. The biblical keynote of Leo is sounded in the words ''Love is the fulfilling of the law.'' Such an one is permitted to view in the Akashic Record the sacred and illuminated heart, and to learn of the profound mysteries connected therewith. He begins to understand the intimate connection between the Hierarchy of the Lord Christ and the center of light in the human body called the heart. One of the foremost akashic pictures he studies represents the Christ standing before a door upon which he knocks. In His hand He bears a light and He is saying, ''Behold, I stand at the door and knock: if any man will hear my voice, and open, I will come in unto him.''

This passage immediately calls to mind Holman Hunt's realistic portrayal of it. His canvas has immortalized the soul-searching aspect of our Redeemer. One may reasonably conclude that the creation of this masterpiece was inspired by the higher presentation which the artist beheld, either consciously or superconsciously. Disciples working on inner planes often stand before this picture and meditate upon its profound meaning, for the door before which the Christ stands represents the heart of man.

In the approaching Aquarian Age, as the love influence of Leo penetrates the earth more deeply, more and more seekers will become conscious of the Christ's nearness and will hear His pleading words as they echo down through the corridors of time: "Behold, I stand at the door, and knock: if any man will hear my voice, and open, I will come in unto him."

### Biblical Parable for Leo
#### The King's Marriage Feast for His Son

The constellation of Leo belongs to the Fire Triplicity. *Light, love, authority* and *rulership* are among its keywords. The heart rules the human body-temple and is the center of love. With its increasing spiritualization, the heart of a disciple grows more luminous until finally he walks in the light as Christ is in the light. By virtue of its radiance, it commands attention and wins allegiance. The Hierarchy of Leo is implanting this ideal in the innermost self of mankind as it focuses its power of love and light upon the earth.

The parable correlating with Leo is that called the king's marriage feast for his son. There was a certain king who prepared a great feast in honor of his son, and he sent his servants out to invite all who would come to attend this feast. But everyone they approached "made light of it, and went their ways." The king then sent his servants into the highways and byways, telling them to bring in the lame, the halt and the blind to attend the feast. When they were assembled he observed that one man wore no wedding garment. The king demanded, "Friend, how comest thou in hither not having a wedding garment?" The man was speechless. Then the king ordered his servants to cast the offender into outer darkness, saying, "Many are called, but few are chosen."

The wedding feast is, of course, Initiation. There is no season of the year when the portals of the Temple swing wider or the light is more insistently bright than during the time that the forces of Leo are focused upon the earth. The lion, symbol of Leo, represents the cosmic fire within man. When the fire is lifted to the heart, that organ becomes the divine regenerative center of the body-temple. This is the highest meaning of the lion standing with an uplifted paw, which symbolizes the highest aspect of Initiation.

In the magnificent ceremony of the Masonic Lodge, it was the lion with an uplifted paw that raised the masonic hero, Hiram Abiff, from the darkness of death into the glory of immortal life.

Initiation as it existed before the coming of Christ was a very different process from what it is today. Ancient Initiation was termed the Path of Illuminated Mysteries, and it consisted of a magnificent ceremonial depicting important events in the life of great world teachers, from birth to their resurrection. With Christ's coming Initiation underwent a marked change, and is now termed the Path of the Solar Mysteries. Christian Initiation still depicts important events in the life of the Lord—birth, baptism, transfiguration, resurrection and ascension. Now these must become workable, vital experiences within the consciousness and the body of a disciple. Thus we see how much more difficult is Initiation under Christ than was pre-Christian Initiation. Therefore St. Paul, one of the leading exponents of the Christian Mysteries, gave what amounts to a mantram to his disciples—one applicable to those of modern times—when he said, ''The Christ be formed in you.'' All of the various schools of metaphysics, New Thought, Christian Science, and so forth, which teach the manifestation of the Christ within are preparatory steps leading toward the supreme attainment of man's life: Initiation into the Mysteries brought to earth by the Christ.

Another pronounced difference between pre-Christian Mysteries and those taught by the Christ is that in ancient times every city had its own initiatory Temple wherein the Mysteries were observed. During the Golden Age of Greece no man was permitted to hold a state position unless he was an Initiate of the Mysteries. These earthly Temples have all been closed and the true Mystery Temples are located in the etheric realm. Therefore an aspirant must build his own ''wedding garment'' before he can enter for he can never gain entrance therein in the physical body.

The ethers are divided into four gradations of density. As previously observed, so long as man is of the earth, earthy, and lives to eat, drink and be merry, his etheric body is composed chiefly of the two lower ethers. When he begins to forego the ways of flesh and to aspire toward the things of spirit he draws to himself more of the two higher ethers.

In this modern day the high and sacred meaning of Initiation has been lost to the great majority. Consequently there is little or no recognition of the deep spiritual significance attached to the initiatory feasts and rites observed in the Ancient Mystery Temples. These were not ceremonials open to any and all as some may unthinkingly assume. They were accessible only to those duly qualified to participate. This is the truth elucidated in the parable of the king's supper. Only those could enter who were arrayed in the "Golden Wedding Garment." This garment of the soul cannot be bestowed upon one by another. It must be self-woven. It comes into being through "living the life," through sublimating the lower desires into powers of the spirit and in rendering loving, self-forgetting service to one's fellow man and every lesser living creature. This is the truth emphasized in esoteric Christianity. Whereas orthodoxy places virtually the whole of the burden of man's salvation on the Christ, esoteric Christianity places it where it rightly belongs, on man himself.

While the Hierarchy of Leo is pouring its forces upon the earth, it is most fitting that an aspirant dedicate himself anew to walk the Path wherein he fashions the shining garment that will open to him these streamers of light and radiations of love. When this garment is ready he will be found worthy to attend the mystic marriage feast and be counted among the sons of the King. This feast is always blessed by the presence of the Christ. When one is permitted to attend he will stand in His presence, seeing Him face to face and knowing Him as He is.

# CHAPTER XXX

*Spiritual Meditation for Virgo*

The Immaculate Mother of all world religions is depicted in the skies by the constellation Virgo. This Eternal Feminine is Isis of Egypt, Ishtar of Babylon, Minerva of Greece, Maya of India and Mary of Bethlehem. The feminine leader of the Virgo Hierarchy is the Cosmic Mother of the planet. For man she is the embodiment of the exaltation of the divine feminine principle. The supreme feminine Masters who have come to earth as the Madonnas of the great world religions are brought to this exalted Being for instruction in the mystery of the Immaculate Conception.

The pictorial representation of Virgo is a maiden bearing in one hand a sheaf of wheat and holding in the other a glorious jewel, the beautiful blue-white star Spica, a star of the first magnitude. This star's spiritual radiations were recognized by many of the ancients. They built Temples dedicated to its heavenly light where they could receive its special benediction. When Spica is again contacted, this time by a more sensitive and spiritualized race, man will truly come under the deeper significance of its Immaculate Conception. As the Cosmic Mother, it is Virgo's office to guide humanity into ways of purity, and to quicken man's higher vehicles by means of etheric currents higher in potency than any yet generated in his body.

Spica means *a sheaf of wheat,* and so we find that both wheat and stars are emblems associated with Virgo and with the various Madonnas. These are not merely ornamental symbols but true insignia of powers possessed by those who have attained the

213

spiritual status where the masculine and feminine creative potencies are united.

Bethlehem means *the house of bread*. One of the most beautiful stories relating to the mystic marriage is the biblical account of
Ruth and Boaz. Ruth went to Bethlehem to glean wheat (the bread
of life), and brought her offering to Boaz, placing it at his feet. It
was by means of her gift that she was found worthy to receive
instruction from Boaz, her spiritual teacher; and later, under his
guidance, to take the exalted rite of the Mystic Marriage.

It is stated in esoteric lore that wheat was a gift to earth from
Venus. It is a plant capable of reproducing itself without polleniza-
tion since it contains within itself the dual creative powers—a
properly like unto that of the Lord Christ who contains within
Himself androgenous power. In this connection it is interesting to
note that wheat and Christianity are closely connected, for where
wheat will not grow Christianity will not flourish.

According to a beautiful Grecian legend, the gods and god-
desses abandoned humanity one by one after its descent into
materiality, until only Astrea, goddess of justice, was left. Conditions finally became such that she, too, had to leave for a time and
was taken up into the heavens where she was changed into the
constellation Virgo. From there, however, she has continued to
guide and bless the world and mankind.

Virgo is the sixth sign, the numerical significance of *six* being
entrance into a new life through service. Truly it has been said that
"Secret Wisdom is hid in number. Number veileth the power of
the Elohim." And Virgo is a mental sign. It is ruled by Mercury,
planet of reason, which finds its place of exaltation in this sign.
This gives the mental alertness that in its lower expression inclines
toward criticism, but in its higher aspect becomes constructively
analytical.

The first step in conservation of the life force is through
self-control. The second step is transmutation. Conservation is
accomplished by the masculine will power principle; transmutation
is achieved through the elevation of the feminine love principle.
This work is delineated in the ancient symbol of a maiden (Virgo)
closing the mouth of a lion (Leo).

An illumined native of Virgo responds to the exaltation of Mercury in this sign, which changes knowledge into wisdom, for wisdom is soul knowledge. Virgo embodies the feminine principle, always associated with sacrifice. It voluntarily subjects itself, as the negative pole of divine energy, to a lower vibratory rate in order that the masculine principle, the positive pole, may obtain a form through which to manifest. It is this feminine principle that is sacrificed for the sake of the world, as in the divine descent of the Lord Christ that earth and its people might regain the lost light and attain to life more abundant.

Virgo is the sign of purity and service. Its purity includes that of food to nourish the body and of that to embellish life. "He that humbleth himself shall be exalted." The biblical keynote of Virgo: "He that is greatest among you let him be the servant of all." Service, symbolized by the golden grain of wheat, fills the spiritual storehouse of a Virgo native, where thieves cannot break through and steal.

Virgo is also the sign of healing, a power that comes with pure and spiritual living. It is the sign of Mother Earth (Virgo is an earth sign) who protects and nourishes her children as did Diana of the Greeks. All baby animals live for the first few months under the benefic influence of the mother aspect of Virgo. In Christianity, however, Virgo is above all else the sign of the Immaculate Conception.

## The Path of Holiness Through Virgo

While the Sun is in Leo the Christ Spirit is refreshed and renewed by the glories of the Father's kingdom. As the Lord Christ's highest attribute is sacrificial in nature, when the Sun passes into Virgo, sign of service, a cosmic urge moves Him to leave the realm of the Father and descend again to Earth, which he contacts as the Sun passes into Libra.

The *Path of Holiness,* following the Christ Ray, also leaves the spiritual region of Earth while the Sun passes through Virgo. Love being the keynote of Leo and service through purity that of

Virgo, one who walks that part of the Path which traverses the higher vibratory planes of this sphere must have evolved purity as a power within himself. The quality of such power is not generally recognized, yet the Christ declared that only the pure in heart shall see God. In this connection the lines of Tennyson in *Sir Galahad* are descriptive.

> *My strength is as the strength of ten,*
> *Because my heart is pure.*

This is the attribute that rendered Parsifal immune to the attack upon him by the evil Klingsor. The spear of hate the black knight hurled at Parsifal was deflected from its course. In that same moment, and by virtue of this power, Parsifal made the sign of the cross and brought complete collapse to Klingsor's castle of evil.

While Virgo holds the secret of the Immaculate Conception, it is through its opposite sign, Pisces, that this gift was brought to earth and demonstrated by the supreme feminine Master, Mary of Bethlehem. It was under the Hierarchy of Sagittarius (Archangels) that Mary herself was immaculately conceived; and it was under the spiritual guardianship of the Hierarchy of Virgo that she was born into the physical world.

A candidate who is worthy to touch the supernal realm of Virgo finds himself before the mystery of the Immaculate Conception and learns that this divine gift was not bestowed upon one individual only, but that Mary and Jesus were type patterns which humanity as a whole is destined to emulate. In this celestial abode those who are spiritually enlightened hear Angels chanting of the day when, in a new heaven and a new earth, the Immaculate Conception will be the heritage of the entire race.

As previously stated, the Hierarchy of Taurus holds the cosmic pattern of form; the Hierarchy of Cancer, that of life; the Hierarchy of Virgo, the power by which life ensouls form. These three constellations, the Feminine Triangle of the heavens, minister to all kingdoms of life on earth.

It should be noted that one who follows the *Path of Holiness* through the six zodiacal signs above the equator has reached that high place of illumination where he is found worthy to stand before the sublime mysteries of the four Greater Initiations. The disciple who treads this Path as it is outlined in the six signs below the equator is being prepared to receive the work of the nine Lesser Mysteries.

*Biblical Parable for Virgo*
The Wise and Foolish Virgins—Matthew 25:1-13

There were ten virgins who carried their lamps as they went forth to meet the bridegroom; but when he tarried, they fell asleep. Then, at the hour of midnight, came the cry, "Behold, the bridegroom cometh." The virgins awakened and five of the ten discovered there was no oil in their lamps, so they sought to borrow some from their sisters. But the wise virgins said, "Not so; lest there be not enough for us and you: but go ye rather to them that sell, and buy for yourselves." While the foolish virgins went to purchase oil the bridegroom came, and the five wise virgins "went in with him into the marriage; and the door was shut." When the foolish virgins came and asked for admittance, the bridegroom replied, "Verily I say unto you, I know you not."

The foolish virgins are those who squander their sacred life force (oil) in worldly and sensual pleasures, and so have no light within themselves to greet the Bridegroom when He comes; in other words, they have not made themselves worthy of the Christ life within.

Many of the most profound keys to biblical interpretation are hidden in the sacred meaning of numbers. *Ten* is the number of man and woman working together as they travel the Path of Discipleship. *Five* is the number of the five physical senses, and also the number of the activity by means of which inner lamps are kept alight. An ancient utterance, that long antedates biblical literature, is the admonition: "Learn to count aright that thou mayest have oil for thy lamp." So long as man is subject to the lure of the five physical senses he can never discover the true purpose and meaning of life. When he has overcome that lure he becomes the five-pointed star and understands the real import of the Master's words: "I am the light of the world."

The oil forfeited by the five foolish virgins was the divine creative essence within themselves. When that force passes up the spinal cord, the true path of discipleship, and reaches the head, it illumines two spiritual organs located therein, the pineal body and the pituitary gland, and they shine with rare radiance. This accomplished, the disciple then bears within himself his own lighted lamp and is ever ready to welcome the Bridegroom. He who is illumined by this light never fails to attract the attention of a teacher. As the saying is "When the student is ready the master appears."

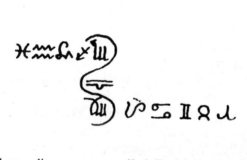

The above diagram was called Ezekiel's Wheel by the ancients. It represents the karmic wheel of human evolution. In the vast incarnation cycles every ego stands many times and in many places to be weighed and proven in the scales of Libra, whether he will choose the high way of spirit as represented by Virgo, or the low way of the senses as typified by Scorpio.

The evolutionary processes are slow. The way by which a human soul becomes a Christed one is long and arduous. Only through choice may that way be shortened. Wrote the poet:

> *To every man there openeth*
> *A Way, and Ways, and a Way,*
> *And the High Soul climbs the High Way,*
> *And the Low Soul gropes the Low,*

*And in between, on the misty flats,*
*The rest drift to and fro.*
*But to every man there openeth*
*A High way and a Low,*
*And every man decideth*
*The Way his soul shall go.*
                    —*The Ways* by John Oxenham

*He became mortal that we might become immortal*—St. Cyprian

# PART IV

# Further Elucidation of
# The Mystery of the Christos

## CHRIST IN THE OLD TESTAMENT

## CHAPTER XXXI

### TESTIMONY OF THE EARLY CHURCH FATHERS

Christ, Lord of the Sun and Regent of Earth, belongs not to time, but to eternity. He Himself declared, ''I and my Father are one,'' and ''Before Abraham was, I Am.''

Athanasius, an early Church Father, stated expressly that Christ is both Maker and Lord of the Sun. ''Our Lord the Sun'' is an expression that was used in Church prayers up to the fifth or sixth century A.D., and it was embodied in the Liturgy until altered to read ''Our Lord the God.''

Genesis relates in algebraic brevity the story of creation. St. John, the most profound interpreter of the Christ in His cosmic aspect, declares that this divine Being was present at the beginning of creation, and that everything came into existence through His creative activity. This subject is greatly elaborated by Lactantius, a fourth century commentator. As he was not a theologian but a rhetorician, he was never given a place among Church leaders—a fact which makes his comments more significant in some respects.

To quote him:

> Since God had perfect providence in counsel and perfect wisdom in action before He began upon this work of the world that good might rise out of Him like a stream, and flow in a long course, He produced a Spirit like unto Himself which was endued with the Power of God, His Father. God, therefore, when He began to frame the world appointed this His first and highest Son over the whole work, and at the same time appointed Him both as an adviser and creator in devising, arranging and completing all things since He is perfect in providence and reason and power. God therefore, the contriver and appointer of all things before He began upon this beautiful fabric of the world, begat an holy and incorruptible Spirit, whom He called His Son.

In his *Epitome of the Institutions,* Lactantius develops this same theme still further. He writes:

> God in the beginning, before He created the world, begat Himself from the fountain of His own eternity, and from His own divine and everlasting spirit a Son who was incorruptible, faithful, corresponding to the power and majesty of His Father. This is the Power, the Reason, the Word and the Wisdom of God . . . taken into a partnership of supreme power . . . for all things were made by Him and without Him nothing.

The following extract from a letter issued by the Council of Antioch gives the belief of the early Church, probably current from the time of the Apostles: "We acknowledge that the only begotten Son is the invisible God, begotten before all creation, the Wisdom and Word and Power of God, who was before the worlds . . . as we know Him in the Old and New Testaments. But if anyone should contend that we make two Gods if we preach the Son of God to be God, we consider such an one to depart from the ecclesiastical canon . . . We believe that He always was with the

Father, and fulfilled His Father's will in the creation of the universe. Then the Council quotes John 1:3 and Colossians 1:16 to show that the world was created by Christ as "really existing, acting, being at once the Word of God by whom the Father made all things . . . Nor was the Son a spectator only, or merely present, but actually efficient for the creation of the universe. It was He who, fulfilling His Father's counsel, appeared to the Patriarchs . . ."

Barnabas, a leading disciple of St. Paul, states in his apocryphal Epistle that "the Lord endured to suffer for our sins, though He is the Lord of the world to whom God said before the constitution of the world . . . let us make man after our own likeness and similitude; and let him have dominion over the beasts of the earth, and over the fowls of the air, and the fish of the sea. And when the Lord saw the man which he had formed, that behold he was very good, he said, Increase and multiply and replenish the earth. And thus he spoke to his son."

The early Fathers, some of whom received their teaching direct from the original Twelve, avowed the necessity for this resplendent Sun Being taking upon Himself human guise in order that man might make direct contact with Him. Referring to the Sun Spirit, Irenaeus, a celebrated Father of the Greek Church of the second century, says that "he might have come to us in his own incorruptible glory, but we could not have borne the greatness of his glory." Also Origen, another Greek Father (185-253 A.D.), wrote: "Who (the Word) being in the beginning with God, became flesh that he might be comprehended by those who were not able to look at him, in that he was the Word, and was with God and was God." And Origen adds further: "Coming down once to that which was not able to look at the dazzling brightness of his divinity, he became in manner flesh."

To again quote Lactantius: "Scriptures teach that the Son of God is the Word or Reason of God," and adds as substantiation: "If anyone wonders that God should be begotten of God by putting forth of the voice and breath, he will cease to wonder if he knows the sacred sayings of the prophets."

Tertullian, a celebrated ecclesiastical writer and another

Father of the Latin Church (150-250 A.D.), explains: "God could not have entered into conversation with man unless he had assumed human feelings and affections, by which he could temper the greatness of his majesty, which would have been intolerable to human weakness . . . but necessary for man."

St. Clement of Rome, who lived in the first century A.D. and is said to have been the third Bishop of Rome after St. Paul, affirms of the Chirst: "Who being the brightness of His majesty is so much higher than the angels, as he hath by inheritance obtained a more excellent name."

The Lord Christ is the most advanced of the Archangels, who are one stage higher in evolution than the Angels. In the apocryphal Book of Hermes (2nd century A.D.) appears the statement: "The Son of God is more ancient than any created thing, so that he was present in counsel with his Father at the creation." God the Father is the highest Initiate of the Hierarchy of Sagittarius, the Lords of Mind. The Lord Christ is the highest Initiate of the Hierarchy of Capricorn, home of the Archangels.

This great Being was with the Father in the days of creation; and it was in the Second Creative Day, the Sun Period, that He dedicated Himself to serve as Regent of earth and Saviour of mankind. Thus it may be seen how these two glorious Beings worked harmoniously in the creation of this planet and all that exists therein. The original twelve Disciples, together with their disciples as referred to by the Church Fathers of the first three centuries, were Initiates able to study the Akashic Records (the Memory of Nature) wherein these truths were indelibly inscribed.

Hence, St. Paul refers to Christ in Colossians 1:15 as "the firstborn (first begotten) of every creature." We gather from this that Paul was saying Christ Himself was not created, but that He existed before creation; in other words, that He was self-existent with the Father. Justin Martyr, a first century Greek Father, expressly names the Christ as the "first begotten of God, and before all created things." Origen makes a similar statement, indicating that the doctrine regarding the cosmic nature of the Christ was a general teaching among founders of the early Church. Says Origen, placing these words in the mouth of God: "I have begotten thee before every reasonable creature''; and adds: ''Christ was the image of the invisible God begotten before every creature, and is incapable of death.''

The Christ theme, like a beautiful symphony, sounds throughout the Old Testament and is echoed in writings of the first Christian votaries. According to both Tertullian and Irenaeus, it was Christ who spoke with Adam in the Garden of Eden. Irenaeus also declares it was the Christ who counseled Noah in reference to the destruction by flood.

# CHAPTER XXXII

## ABRAHAM AND MOSES CONTACT THE COMING ONE

Egos that come to earth as great spiritual messengers, often called sons of destiny, are given special care and protection from inner realms—although their lives are usually filled with sorrow and travail, for it is pain that sensitizes and refines the nature of man. Such are often conscious of the angelic ministry, as exemplified in the lives of Abraham and Moses, both of whom were chosen and prepared for becoming leaders of the Fifth Root Race.

Justin Martyr and Clement of Alexandria—the latter a second century Father of the primitive Church, and most noted as the founder of the Alexandrian school of theology—held that it was Christ who appeared to Abraham and said, "I am the Almighty God; walk before me, and be thou perfect" (Gen. 17:1). These same Fathers, together with Tertullian and Origen, assert that it was also Christ who appeared to Abraham on the "plain of Mamre." There He is called Lord and Judge of all the earth. Cyprian, a third century ecclesiastic and martyr of the African Church, considered that Christ was the Angel who called to Abraham when he was about to sacrifice Isaac.

It was after Abraham's intimate contact with the spirit of the Cosmic Christ that he developed extended vision, expansion of consciousness, and an ever-deepening spiritual awareness. His development led to the birth of Isaac as foretold by angelic visitors—the name Isaac meaning *all abiding spiritual joy* which, once acquired, is dimmed by no vicissitudes of the mundane world. It is what the psalmist had in mind when he sang: "Though I walk through the valley of the shadow of death, I will fear no evil: for thou art with me."

Again, Cyprian attributes to Christ the guidance given the people of Israel during their wandering in the wilderness, as recorded in Exodus 13:21 and 14:9. "And the Lord went before them by day in a pillar of a cloud, to lead them the way; and by night in a pillar of fire, to give them light" . . . "And the angel of God, which went before the camp of Israel, removed and went behind them; and the pillar of the cloud went from before their face, and stood behind them." He also conceived Christ to be the Angel promised in Exodus 23: "Behold, I send an Angel before thee, to keep thee in the way (v.20) . . . obey his voice (v.22) . . . for my name is in him" (v.21).

Every disciple being prepared for service in the Christ Dispensation meets upon the Path, in some form or other, the paramount test—such as Abraham's being called upon to sacrifice his beloved son Isaac. At this point the disciple must be able to say with the Christ: "Not my will, but thine, be done." It was the Comforter, the Lord Christ Himself, who attended upon Abraham during this supreme trial, a fact recorded by both Origen and Cyprian, a contemporary of Origen. The sacrifice was not really required of Abraham, but only his willingness to renounce *all* for his Lord. This is beautifully demonstrated in the biblical sequel telling how a ram was substituted for Isaac, the ram being a symbol of the coming Arian Dispensation when the Lord Christ would descend and, in human embodiment, make the supreme sacrifice. In this test Abraham had proved his worthiness, and also his ability to study profound truths directly from the Akashic Records.

*Polarity* is the fundamental teaching underlying esoteric Christianity. The High Priest Melchizedek gave it to Abraham in the ritual of the Holy Supper to prepare him for his mission as pioneer leader of the incoming Fifth Root Race. The same teaching was the final pronouncement of Christ's ministry on earth, given to His Disciples at the Last Supper on Holy Thursday preceding His sacrifice on Golgotha. This ritual is now largely regarded as mere ceremonial. Few persons have any concept of the power that can be communicated to its recipients when this divine ordinance is worthily and understandingly observed.

The hidden power of the fruit of the vine was realized by the early Fathers, as the following passage from Justin Martyr indicates: "The words *blood of the grape* are used purposely to express, that Christ has blood, not from the seed of man, but from the power of God. For in the same manner that man does not produce the blood of the vine, but God; so also this passage foretold, that the blood of Christ was not to be of human origin, but from the power of God: and this prophecy shows, that Christ is not a man, begotten of men according to the common law of men." Eusebius, a fourth century ecclesiastical historian, writes of the same text: ". . . men are redeemed by the blood of the grape, which has God dwelling in it, and is spiritual."

Such statements make plain that the "blood of the grape" has a deep significance. It refers to the purification and transmutation of the blood of man. Christ told His Disciples: "I am the vine, ye are the branches." A consecrated aspirant places himself into closer and more perfect attunement with Christ by means of the bread and wine, and is thereby able to develop and manifest greater Christed powers within himself.

Both Justin Martyr and Clement of Alexandria claim that it was the Christ who appeared to Jacob in the dream where he beheld a ladder reaching from earth to heaven, with Angels of God ascending and descending upon it. Above it stood the Lord, who said, "I am the Lord God of Abraham thy father, and the God of Isaac" (Gen. 28:13). Cyprian, quoting from Genesis 35:1, writes: ". . . believing as all the Fathers did that the God there spoken of who appeared to Jacob when he fled from Esau was Christ."

As mentioned in the third volume of *New Age Bible Interpretation,* illumined Masters down through the ages have understood and have taught their disciples that the work of Mystery Schools and the various forms of their Initiation were but preparatory steps for the coming of the Supreme World Teacher, the Lord Christ. This statement holds true regarding seer-teachers of the Old Testament Dispensation. They were preparing themselves and their followers to later serve the Christ. In his dreams Jacob was being taught to read in the Memory of Nature. There he saw the involutionary-evolutionary ladder which extends from heaven to earth and from earth to heaven, with multitudes of spirits descending into incarnation and reascending into heaven after earth's lessons have been learned.

The Path of Discipleship has been similar in all ages. Aspirants must meet the same tests and make the same over-comings. Only particulars change in the course of succeeding epochs. This initiatory Path is outlined with exceptional fidelity in the life of Jacob.

It is recorded in Genesis (32:24) that when Jacob was left alone "there wrestled a man with him until the breaking of day." At the conclusion of this incident it was made clear that the One who prevailed over Jacob was invested with super-human authority, for He gave Jacob the new name of Israel: "for as a prince hast thou power with God and with men." The experience here related is a most meaningful one. That the Lord Christ was herein the Teacher and Guardian of Jacob is noted by Justin Martyr, Clement of Alexandria and Irenaeus.

Jacob's experience of wrestling all night with the Angel and refusing to let it go until he received a blessing is a familiar one upon the Path of Discipleship. Spiritual powers latent within each aspirant thereby become sufficiently dynamic for him to manifest them within his life. St. Paul's admonition to his disciples was, "Let the Christ be formed in you." This must be accomplished by a candidate before he becomes a pioneer of the Christ Dispensation. Through it the life of Jacob was completely transformed. He parted from Esau (the lower nature) for all time; and in conformity with his inner change he was no longer called Jacob, but Israel (those who see God). Jacob was now an heroic conqueror and a dedicated server. He was qualified to become a worker in the vineyard of the Lord Christ, who declared: "Whosoever of you will be the chieftest, shall be the servant of all" (Mark 10:44).

Referring again to the verse in Genesis (32:24) which says that "Jacob was left alone, and there wrestled a man with him," Origen writes: "Who else could it be that is called at once man and God, who wrestled and contended with Jacob, than he who spake at sundry times and in divers manners unto the Fathers (Heb. 1:1) the holy Word of God who is called Lord and God, who also

blessed Jacob and called him Israel, saying to him 'Thou hast
prevailed with God.' It was thus that the men of those days beheld
the Word of God, like our Lord's apostles did, who said 'That
which was from the beginning, which we have seen with our own
eyes, and looked upon, and our hands have handled, of the Word
of Life (St. John 1.1) which Word of Life Jacob also saw and
added 'I have seen God face to face.' "

From thence Jacob ascended into Bethel, there to build an
altar where he dedicated his life to God. Many who pass through
this exalting experience are conscious of the presence of the
Christ, and of His pouring out a tender blessing upon their endeavors. Bethel means *the House of God*, and it is in Bethel that a
victorious candidate makes a complete dedication.

Hyppolytus, an ecclesiastical writer of the third century and a
pupil of Irenaeus, made the following statement with reference to
Christ as described in Jacob's prophecy (Gen. 49:9) and in Revelation (5:5); "Now since the Lord Jesus Christ, who is God, on
account of his kingly and glorious state, was spoken of before as a
lion."

Four of the most distinguished Church Fathers—Justin Martyr, Clement of Alexandria, Irenaeus and Tertullian — assert that
it was none other than the Christ who appeared to Moses in the
burning bush. This phenomenon was a reflection of the Cosmic
Christ as He drew closer and closer to the earth prior to His human
incarnation. Christ is the Lord of the Sun and Chief among the Fire
Spirits, the Archangels. The Christian Dispensation is intimately
guided by the Hierarchy of Leo, the Lords of Flame. Hence, the
Fire Initiation is directly connected with the Christ Mysteries. This
Fire is not a flame that burns but a light that purifies and trans-
mutes. The bush that "burned," in that it became ablaze with
light, was not consumed. This experience of Moses is a veiled
account of the exaltation engendered by the Fire Initiation.

In agreement with many Church Fathers, Justin Martyr believed that it was Christ who talked with Moses out of the bush,
and he condemned those who confounded God the Father with His
Son. "Those who think that it was always God the Father who
spoke to Moses, (whereas He who spoke to him was the Son of

God, who is also called an Angel, and an Apostle), are justly convinced both by the prophetical spirit, and by Christ himself, for knowing neither the Father nor the Son. For they who say that the Son is the Father, are convinced of neither knowing the Father nor of understanding that the God, is also God. And formerly He appeared to Moses and to the other prophets in the form of fire as an incorporeal image.''

Clement of Alexandria is another authority for the claim that it was Christ who said to Moses: "I am the Lord thy God which have brought thee out of the land of Egypt." It is this Christ power which always delivers an aspirant out of Egypt, the land symbolical of bondage to the senses and to the darkness of mortal mind.

Moses was permitted to view the Promised Land, the land flowing with milk and honey (the Christ Dispensation of the Aquarian-Leo cycle). The saintly Origen tells us that it was the Christ who gave Moses on the holy mountain the Tables of the Law, when Moses was being taught to read the Akashic Records. He saw that the civilization of the Fifth Root Race was to have its foundation in the laws that became known as the Ten Commandments. He saw further that the Christ Himself would bring an extension of these laws, which He did by the precepts enunciated in the Sermon on the Mount. Humanity of the Fifth Root Race is still far from the development scheduled for it in the devine plan. Only a few of its members have reached the evolutionary status where they live in full accord with the Ten Commandments; and fewer still have any conception of the spiritual import of the Sermon on the Mount.

As stated throughout the *New Age Bible Interpretation* series, polarity is the keyword of mystic Christianity. The two columns of polarity are formed by the Ten Commandments (the masculine column) and the Sermon on the Mount (the feminine column). For the Christed man of the coming Aquarian-Leo Race, the Ten Commandments will be the foundation on which he establishes his daily life, while the Sermon on the Mount will be its superstructure as he rises into higher dimensions of unfoldment.

Dr. Rudolf Steiner, in the volume *The Gospel of St. John,* asserts that "When he heard the voice calling unto him saying,

'When thou wouldst proclaim my name, say that I AM hath said it unto thee,' here for the first time sounds forth the knowledge and manifestation of the Logos, of the Christ . . . Isaiah spake with him.' With whom did Isaiah speak? Reference is made here to the passage in Isaiah 6: 1 which reads: 'In the year that King Uzziah died I saw also the Lord sitting upon a throne, high and lifted up, and His train filled the temple.'

"Whom did Isaiah see? This is clearly told here in the Gospel of St. John. He saw the Christ. . . the Logos of which the Gospel of St. John speaks. The writer of this Gospel means nothing more nor less than that the One who could always be perceived in the Spirit became flesh and dwelt among us."

The question is sometimes asked why Jesus is not mentioned in the Old Testament. His name is there but in another form. The Hebrew equivalent for the Greek name Jesus is Joshua. In Numbers 13:16 Joshua was called Jehoshua, which means *Jehovah is the Saviour*.

This is exactly the meaning of the word Jesus as given in Matthew 1:21: "And thou shalt call his name Jesus: for he shall save his people from their sins." The fact that Joshua bore a name of such high vibratory power is in itself an evidence of this high spiritual attainment.

On the road to Jericho Joshua was met by a shining Being bearing a flaming sword. So impressed was he by its splendor that he prostrated himself on the ground before this Being. The celestial visitor, according to Joshua, was "captain of the host of the Lord," who bade him remove his shoes from off his feet for the place whereon he stood was holy ground. Joshua did so. This record states that Joshua lifted up his eyes and looked, he beheld "a man over against him with his sword drawn in his hand: and Joshua went up to him, and said unto him, Art thou for us, or for our adversaries? And he said, Nay, but as captain of the host of the Lord am I now come. What saith my lord unto his servant?"— Joshua 5:13-15.

Commenting on the above passage, Origen says: "Joshua, therefore, not only knew he was of God, but that he was God; for he would not have worshipped if he had not known him to be God.

For who else is captain of the host of the Lord except our Lord Jesus Christ?'' This agrees with the judgment of other Church Fathers that the One who appeared either in human form or in that of an Angel to any of the patriarchs was the Christ.

Having attained perfect equilibrium within himself, which is an evidence of high Initiateship, Joshua is said to have caused the Sun and Moon to stand still. He was the most advanced disciple of Moses, his successor as teacher and leader of Israel, and an emissary of the coming Christ Dispensation.

Elijah's ascent into heaven in a chariot of fire is the description of another illuminated spirit who was being prepared through the Fire Initiation to work on both inner and outer planes in anticipation of the coming of Christ. This was likewise the Initiation of the three holy men who were cast into a fiery furnace yet remained unharmed, as recorded in the Book of Daniel. In its entirety this Book contains much information relative to Initiation of Fire. (See Vol III, *New Age Bible Interpretation.*)

The Book of Daniel correlates closely with the work of the Hierarchy of Leo. It was the Initiation by Fire, as it guards the threshold of the Christ Mysteries, that the Supreme Teacher referred to when He told Nicodemus ''Except a man be born of water and of the spirit, he cannot enter the kingdom of God,'' the new Christed order.

Concerning the three holy men (Initiates) who were thrown into the fiery furnace, the following observation was made by Tertullian: ''Jesus was seen by the king of Babylon in the furance with his martyrs, being the fourth person like the Son of man; the same was expressly revealed to Daniel himself as the Son of man, coming as a judge with the clouds of heaven, as the scripture showed beforehand that the Gentiles were afterwards to know him in the flesh, whom Nebuchadnezzer had long before seen without flesh, and recognized in the furance, and acknowledged him to be the Son of God.''

# CHAPTER XXXIII

## PSALMS AND PROVERBS

Hippolytus affirms that David "wrote prophetic psalms upon the true Christ, our God, and evidently declared all the things which happened to him in his suffering. . . and how that Christ humbled himself and put on the form of the servant Adam."

Justin Martyr quotes the whole 72nd psalm to prove that Christ was the King of glory, and declares that this entire psalm was written in honor of Him and none other. In his *Apologies* he asserts that in many instances the King referred to in the psalm was not David or Solomon, but the Lord Christ Himself. As another example, he quotes the 24th psalm: "Lift up your heads, O ye gates . . . and the King of glory shall come in. Who is this King of glory? The Lord of Hosts, he is the King of glory." This is a reference to Christ and the host of His ministering Angels and Archangels who always accompany Him.

In the 72nd psalm the Initiate singer was reading in the Mystic Scrolls of the glad day when Christ would be proclaimed Regent of earth and Saviour of the world. In that time of rejoicing every knee shall bow before Him and every voice proclaim Him Lord of Lords and King of Kings.

The scope of this volume does not permit a detailed study of Pslams, but it may be seen that throughout the Book, and in accordance with the teachings of the Church Fathers, the sorrow and the joy, the pain and the exaltation of the Christ theme echoes and re-echoes like a song within a song.

Cyprian speaks of Christ as the first begotten, the wisdom of God by whom all things were made. In support of this statement, he quotes Proverbs 8:22-31 as follows:

*The Lord possessed me in the beginning of his way, before his works of old.*

*I was up from everlasting, from the beginning, or ever the earth was.*

*When there were no depths, I was brought forth; when there were no fountains abounding with water.*

*Before the mountains were settled, before the hills was I brought forth: While as yet he had not made the earth, nor the fields, nor the highest part of the dust of the world.*

*When he prepared the heavens, I was there: when he set a compass upon the face of the depths:*

*When he established the clouds above: when he strengthened the fountains of the deep:*

*When he gave to the sea his decree, that the waters should not pass his commandment: when he appointed the fountains of the earth:*

*Then was I by him, as one brought up with him: and I was daily his delight, rejoicing always before him:*

*Rejoicing in the habitable part of his earth; and my delights were with the sons of men.*

Many of the Fathers were of the same opinion regarding the Christ as was Cypri Cyprian.

It has been interpreted by some that the builder in Proverbs 9:1 refers to the Cosmic Christ, by whom all things were made: "Wisdom hath builded her house, she hath hewn out her seven pillars." Spiritual science would interpret the seven pillars as the seven planes of substance and of consciousness, the seven Creative Days (Periods) embracing a complete evolutionary cycle.

King Solomon the Wise was the highest Initiate of the Old Testament Dispensation. The exquisite Song of Solomon is the spiritual insignia, as it were, of his profound wisdom. This song of songs reveals perfect equilibrium; the rhythmic cadence of absolute balance has never been more beautifully expressed in any language: "My beloved is mine, and I am his: he feedeth among the lilies.'' Esoteric Christianity teaches that there exists an intimate bond between this highest Initiate of the Old Dispensation and the Master Jesus, highest Initiate of the New Testament Dispensation. The mission of the latter was to surrender his perfect human body for the Christ's use during the three years of His ministry—for, as various Christian Fathers have asserted, it was essential for the Christ to veil His celestial radiance by a human form else no man could have borne the power and splendor of His presence.

# CHAPTER XXXIV

## THE PROPHETS

The God who appeared either in human form, or that of an Angel to any of the patriarchs was Jesus Christ.

—Origen

The Prophets occupied a unique position in Old Testament history. They were messengers and channels between the inner and outer realms. Every religion has an inner and an outer teaching, the latter for the masses and the former for the few. The Prophets were interpreters of the inner meanings. Their messages centered largely in the Messiah theme and the preparation for His coming.

Among the most illustrious of these Prophets was Isaiah. The pages of his subline Book are replete with predictions of the Christ and the glorious dispensation He will establish upon a new earth. Furthermore, Isaiah's seership encompassed not only the coming of the Christ but also that of John, the forerunner of the Lord, and the Virgin Mother of Jesus, as the following passages make clear.

*The voice of him that crieth in the wilderness, Prepare ye the way of the Lord, make straight in the desert a highway for our God.*

*Every valley shall be exalted, and every mountain and hill shall be made low: and the crooked shall be made straight, and the rough places plain: And the glory of the Lord shall be revealed, and all flesh shall see it together: for the mouth of the Lord hath spoken it.*
*—Isaiah 40:3-5*

> *Therefore the Lord himself shall give you a sign;
> Behold, a virgin will conceive, and bear a son, and
> shall call his name Immanuel.*
> —Isaiah 7:14

> *For unto us a child is born, unto us a son is given:
> and his name shall be called Wonderful, Counsellor, the
> mighty God, The everlasting Father, The Prince of
> Peace.*
> —Isaiah 9:6

> *And there shall come forth a root out of the stem of
> Jesse, and a Branch shall grow out of his roots.*
> *And the spirit of the Lord shall rest upon him, the
> spirit of wisdom and understanding, the spirit of counsel
> and might, the spirit of knowledge and of the fear of the
> Lord . . . But with righteousness shall he judge the
> poor, and reprove with equity for the meek of the
> earth. . . The wolf also shall dwell with the lamb, and
> the leopard shall lie down with the kid; and the calf and
> the young lion and the fatling together; and a little child
> shall lead them . . . They shall not hurt or destroy in all
> my holy mountain: for the earth shall be full of the
> knowledge of the Lord, as the waters cover the sea.*
> —Isaiah 11:1,2,4,6,9

Ezekiel's wondrous vision is a most significant utterance regarding the Christ who was yet to come:

> *Now as I beheld the living creatures, behold one
> wheel upon the earth by the living creatures, with his
> four faces.*
> *The appearance of the wheels and their work was
> like unto the colour of a beryl: and they four had one
> likeness: and their appearance and their work was as it
> were a wheel in the middle of a wheel.*
> —Ezekiel 1:15,16

Here Ezekiel was studying the work of the four Recording Angels, Taurus, Scorpio, Aquarius and Leo. Taurus and Scorpio

are the Hierarchies under which planetary karma is being liquidated. This is described in the Books of the Prophets as the travail,
sorrow and desolation which they predict will come upon earth.
Many of these prophecies are strangely familiar at the present
time, for planetary karma is being liquidated now; and this purging
will continue until earth's karmic sheet is clean.

Aquarius is depicted as the Son of Man, a sign symbolic of
the Christed Age to come. Leo is the home of the Hierarchy of
Flame: that is, of love and light. These two signs proclaim that
when the Son of Man comes He will be the supreme light of the
world, and love will be the motivating power of all mankind.

The following passages taken from several Old Testament
Prophets have been understood by biblical interpreters down
through the centuries as referring to the Christ:

> *And he shall judge many people, and rebuke strong
> nations afar off and they sall beat their swords into
> plowshares, and their spears into pruninghooks; nation
> shall not lift up sword against nation, neither shall they
> learn war any more.*
>
> *But they shall sit every man under his vine and
> under his fig tree; and none shall make them afraid; for
> the mouth of the Lord of hosts hath spoken it.*
>
> *—Micah, 4:3,4*
>
> *Behold, I will send my messenger, and he shall
> prepare the way before me: and the Lord, whom ye
> seek, shall suddenly come to his temple, even the mes-
> senger of the covenant, whom ye delight in.*
>
> *—Mal. 3:1*
>
> *Behold, the days come, saith the Lord, that I will
> raise unto David a righteous Branch, and a King shall
> reign and prosper, and shall execute, judgement and
> justice in the earth.*
>
> *—Jer. 23:5*
>
> *I saw in the night visions, and, behold, one like the
> Son of man came with the clouds of heaven, and came
> to the Ancient of days, and they brought him near
> before him.*

*And there was given him dominion, and glory, and*
*a kingdom, that all people, nations, and languages,*
*should serve him: his dominion is an everlasting domin-*
*ion which shall not pass away, and his kingdom that*
*which shall not be destroyed.*
—Dan, 7:13,14

The Prophet Joel, reading in the Akashic Record and noting
therein the wonder of things which are to be in the coming age,
predicts the Great Day of the coming of the Lord (the fulfillment
of spiritual law) in the following inspired words:

*I will pour out my spirit upon all flesh; and your*
*sons and your daughters shall prophesy, and your old*
*men shall dream dreams, your young men shall see*
*visions:*
*And also upon the servant and upon the handmaids*
*. . . will I pour out my spirit.*

A careful survey of the Prophets will furnish numerous references of like nature. The pattern of these prophetical Books is
largely the same. They deal with the three principal themes: the
sorrow and desolation engendered by planetary karma; the dawning hope of the coming Messiah; the establishment of a new Christ
Dispensation.

The Old Testament School of the Prophets was succeeded by
the Order of the Essenes, members of which are mentioned in the
New Testament. Again, the work of this holy Order was to prepare
for the coming of the Lord Christ. The parents of Initiate Mary and
of John the Baptist were members of this Order. With the completion of Christ's earthly ministry their mission ended and they disappeared, as far as history is concerned, by being absorbed into the
first Christian communities. Their important role as custodians of
the ageless Mysteries, along with initiatory teachings of the early
Christians, was lost sight of by the Church relatively soon after its
founding.

Esoteric Christians, however, always recognized the Essenes

as possessors and transmitters of the Temple Wisdom and prophetic powers that came down through their immediate predecessors, the Hebrew Prophets. This fact is now coming to light, and is being brought to the attention of the general public by the recent discovery of Essenian writings known as the *Dead Sea Scrolls.*

Hippolytus asserts that the Lord Christ was the inspiration of all the Prophets. The Book of Zechariah, one of the most mystical of the prophetic Books, foretells the coming of Christ, who is termed "the BRANCH," and also the establishment of His kingdom on earth, His death, and His second coming.

We have referred to the Aquarian-Leo cycle during which definite preparation will be inaugurated for His coming. Some mystic Christians predict that Christ will return during the following Capricorn-Cancer cycle. Zechariah describes the holy "remnant," those pioneers who will be prepared to receive the Lord Christ and to work for Him. These pioneers will have awakened within themselves the Christ principle—that latent divinity within each individual which is awakened by a sincere endeavor to emulate Him. This awakening brings a transformation of consciousness that affects the life and, finally, the body of an aspirant. Zechariah describes this process as two olive trees, a lighted candle between them, which stand before an anointed One. The transforming action effects a great change in the cerebro-spinal and the sympathetic nervous systems, which have a direct connection with man's desire and vital bodies, respectively. When they are in balance spiritual development is greatly facilitated. (This subject is considered in detail in the third volume of the Old Testament series.) The lighted candle between the two olive trees is the spinal spirit fire which, when lifted to the head, awakens powerful spiritual organs located therein. Zechariah likens the head of an awakened one to a golden bowl, for these organs then shed a golden luminosity that appears like a radiant aura around the whole body. The Prophet describes such pioneers as holy ones who come from the north, east, south and west in the New Jerusalem.

As previously observed, the second coming of Christ may occur during the next Capricorn-Cancer cycle. Thus the Christ would return under His own sign Capricorn, while pioneers under

Cancer would ascend with Him to His own world of Life Spirit or Christ consciousness, the world of the great *oneness*. Here full recognition is attained that all things are part of God, and that God is part of all things. Here it is the New Age pioneers will be able to proclaim with Christ. "The Father and I are one!"

Malachi is the last Book of the Old Testament. Words of its concluding chapter contain the promise of all promises: "But unto you that hear my name shall the Sun of righteousness arise with healing in his wings." These inspiring words are as a bridge of light between the preparatory work of the Old Testament and its sublime culmination in the New.

# CHAPTER XXXV

## THE COSMIC CHRIST

*The unutterable knowledge of the Mysteries concerning Christ, the true God, is secret.*

*—Origen*

*And this is life eternal, that they might know thee the one true God, and Jesus Christ whom thou hast sent.*

*I have glorified thee on earth: I have finished the work which thou gavest me to do.*

*And now, O Father, glorify me with thine own self with the glory which I had with thee before the world was.*

*John 17:3-5*

*Christ the power of God, and the wisdom of God.*

*—I Cor. 1:24*

*The Word of God, showing the greatness of the knowledge of the Father that it is comprehended and known in its full extent and primarily by Him only, but in a secondary sense by those who have their reason enlightened by Him who is Word and God, says, No one knoweth the Son, etc. (Matt. 11:27) for no one can know him who is uncreated, and begotten before every created nature in its full extent, so well as the Father who begot him; nor can anyone know the Father so well as the animate Word, who is His Wisdom and Truth.*

*—Origen*

As we approach the several aspects of the Christ Mystery, we seem to hear again the angelic voice that spoke to Joshua: "Loose thy shoe from off thy foot; for the place whereon thou standest is holy." The Christ Mystery is so sublime and so far-reaching in its import that it transcends any human definition. So profound are its meanings that they can never be plumbed or expressed by mere words; they can be sensed only in the silence of spiritual contemplation.

All great religions give recognition to the triune nature of the Godhead. In Christianity it consists of Father, Son and Holy Ghost. To this Trinity Rosicrucians assign the following attributes: *power* to the Father; the *Word* to the Son, the Cosmic Christ; *motion* to the Holy Ghost. In connection with his vision on the Isle of Patmos, John and Revelator declares: "I saw heaven opened . . . his eyes were as a flame of fire . . . and his name is called The Word of God" (Rev. 19:11-13). In the opening verses of his Gospel, John describes the Word in phrases that carry living creative potency scarcely suspected by the average reader or hearer of his words: "In the beginning was the Word, and the Word was with God, and the Word was God. The same was in the beginning with God. All things were made by him; and without him was not anything made that was made."

St. Paul expresses the same thought in Colossians 1:15-19, wherein he speaks of Christ as being "the image of the invisible God, the firstborn of every creature: For by him were all things created, that are in heaven, and that are in earth, visible and invisible, whether they be thrones, or dominions, or principalities, or powers: all things were created by him, and for him: And he is before all things, and by him all things consist. And he is the head of the body, the church: who is the beginning, the first-born from the dead; that in all things he might have the pre-eminence. For it pleased the Father that in him should all fulness dwell."

In Revelation 21:6 John also repeats the Christ's statement that He was at the very beginning of manifestation: "I am Alpha and Omega, the beginning and the end." In the Old Testament Isaiah makes a similar statement that is applicable only to the Christ. In Chapter 44, Verse 6 we read: "Thus saith the Lord the

King of Israel, and his redeemer the Lord of hosts. I am the first, and I am the last; and beside me there is no God.''

Origen calls Christ ''the vapor of the power of God, and pure efflux of the glory of the Almighty, the effulgence of eternal light, and unspotted mirror of the energy of God.''

In the *Rosicrucian Cosmo-Conception*, Max Heindel states that: ''In the first chapter of John this Great Being is called God. From this Supreme Being emanates The Word, the Creative Fiat 'without whom was not anything made,' and this Word is the alone-begotten Son, born of His Father (the Supreme Being) before all worlds—but positively not Christ.'' Here Max Heindel is making a distinction between the Cosmic Christ and the Christ in His planetary and historical aspects. ''Grand and glorious as is Christ,'' he continues, ''towering high above mere human nature, He is not this Exalted Being. Truly, 'the Word was made flesh,' but not in the limited sense of the flesh of one body, but the flesh of all that is, in this and millions of other solar systems.''

The Word is a signature of tremendous power. It is composed of four letters, two feminine and two masculine. All creation is composed of four basic elements, namely, Fire, Air, Earth and Water. The twelve creative Hierarchies which surround this universe and are engaged in the continuous process of creation, work through these four elements. Fire and Air are masculine or positive elements; Water and Earth are negative or feminine. The Hierarchies of Taurus, Virgo and Capricorn, working through the Earth element, are centered in the Word, the Son aspect or the feminine potency of God. The Hierarchies of Aries, Leo and Sagittarius, working through the Fire element, are centered in the power or masculine aspect of God. So it is that spirit works upon matter to create. The Hierarchies of Gemini, Libra and Aquarius are centered in motion or the third aspect of God. Pythagoras states: ''That which ceases to move ceases to live.''

This motion means devine harmony or tone. The combined tones of the twelve zodiacal Hierarchies produce the music of the spheres. Thus, all things are created by the Word (tone or music). ''By the word of the Lord, were the heavens made; and all the hosts of them by the breath of His mouth,'' declares the psalmist.

Every created thing possesses its own individual keynote. The human archetype, the pattern of the physical body, is formed by the devine Hierarchies in high spiritual realms; and each human archetype has its own individual keynote which sounds as long as physical expression continues. In the present state of human development only those who have attained initiate consciousness hear this musical keynote. As man develops spiritual hearing he will be able to listen to his own soul-song.

The three Hierarchies of Cancer, Scorpio and Pisces, working through the elements of Water, are teaching mankind the law of equilibrium. This law expresses the secret of perfect balance, and is known in its fullness by earth's Masters only. Not having attained balance, mankind in general, while he can observe its operation in nature, is not able to see its workings within himself. The most perfect example of balance is best seen, perhaps, in the incoming and outgoing tides of the sea. When man eventually manifests perfect polarity within himself he will overcome disease, old age and death.

Rosicrucian students are admonished to take into meditation the opening verses of St. John's Gospel, which will help them to realize that the Word is the focusing center through which the twelve creative Hierarchies pour their creative forces.

There is a specific power in every name, so no person should bear a name with which he is not physically congenial. Each time one's name is sounded its forces register upon his personality, harmoniously or inharmoniously. The noun *name* has four letters: "m" and "e" that are feminine; "n" and "a" that are masculine. *Amen* is composed of the same four letters transposed. The chanting in early Christian churches was really an invocation calling down the protection and blessing of the stellar forces. Disciples were commanded to heal in the *name* of the Lord Christ; and the word *Amen* was used to surround servitors with devine protection. Hence, the Word is the divine creative center for disseminating the love and light of the Cosmic Christ.

In the complete Christ cycle, which is elucidated in this volume, we note the work of the Holy Trinity in connection with the Christ activity during the three summer months while the Sun is passing through the zodiacal signs of Gemini, Cancer and Leo.

This work is incorporated in the Church calendar as the Feast of Trinity Sunday. We have observed how the activities of the Seraphim (Hierarchy of Gemini) are stepped down to earth during the month of June under the guidance of the Holy Spirit. During the month of July the transmutation forces of the Cherubim (Hierarchy of Cancer) are stepped down under the guidance of the Lord Christ. During the month of August the love power of the Lord of Light (Hierarchy of Leo) is stepped down to earth through the powers of the Father. The three work together in such harmony and unity that they are literally three in one or one in three. As man awakens to the higher life he gradually spiritualizes his will, acquires wisdom, and sublimates the life force within his own being.

The Father channels the will principle; the Christ, the wisdom principle; the Holy Spirit, the activity principle. The last literally infuses forms with life. He works with the life principle which is present in all creation; and is the guardian of the sacred force, the creative principle of God. Therefore, every living thing is under his guardianship. God creates and Christ formulates, while Holy Spirit activates form.

Hence, we see how the one unforgivable sin is the sin against Holy Spirit. This sin is the misuse of the creative life force as it manifests in the individual. Yet it is not God who metes out punishment for its commission. Instead, the individual brings upon himself pain, sorrow, disease and death as the reaction to his failure to observe the sacredness of the creative fire within himself. Such dire consequences will continue to plague man until he learns to live true to the divine nature of the Holy Spirit by conserving the life force within his own body.

As we approach the Aquarian Age the work of the Holy Spirit will become more apparent and better understood. One of his paramount activities is to enlighten humanity regarding the purpose and mission of the Lord relative to the earth planet and all creatures living upon it. It was to the Holy Spirit that the Christ referred when He said, "If I go not away, the Comforter will not come unto you; but if I depart, I will send him unto you . . . and he will shew you things to come."

When man reaches that high development where he is prepared to receive the four Christ Initiations, brought to earth by the Lord Christ Himself, he will be able to see these three divine beings engaged in their cosmic activities. This state, however, belongs to a far-off evolutionary day. Even Christ's Disciples received only the first of these Christed Initiations on the Day of Pentecost. Meditation upon this glorious prospect will inspire an aspirant to dedicate himself anew to loving, selfless service, and will shorten the time before he can join that company of consecrated souls to whom these Initiations are given in advance of the race as a whole.

The subject of the Cosmic Christ is so profound that to grasp even faintly the nature of this exalted Being it is not only helpful but necessary to consider it from various points of view. Here with is an extended quotation of most illuminating elucidation by Max Hiendel:

It is from visible sun that every particle of physical energy comes. And it is from the spiritual invisible sun that all of the spiritual energy comes. Man could not stand the direct spiritual impulse that comes from the sun and, therefore, it had to be sent by way of the Moon. That is the origin of race religions. Later when man could take spiritual impulse more directly, Christ, the present Earth Spirit, came to prepare this. The difference between the Christ of the Earth and the Cosmic Christ is best seen by an illustration. Imagine a lamp in the center of a hollow sphere of polished metal. The lamp will send rays from itself to all points of the sphere, and will reflect lamps in all different places. So the Cosmic Christ, —the highest initiate of the Sun period—, sends out rays. He is the spiritual sun. The sun is threefold. We see the outside,—the physical sun. Behind that, or hiding in that, is the spiritual sun whence comes the impulse of the Cosmic Christ Spirit. Outside the other two is something we call Vulcan,— that can be seen only as a half globe. In occultism we say that is the body of the Father. When we had risen so far that the Christ Spirit could be entertained on earth, then a ray of the Cosmic Christ came here and incarnated in the body of our Elder Brother Jesus. After the sacrifice on Golgotha he drew himself into the earth, and became its Indwelling Planetary Spirit.

## EARTH'S INDWELLING SPIRIT

*Ray of the Sun God, by whose mighty power*
*The earth is borne through space, we come to Thee,*
*That we may learn the secret of a love*
*Which chooses suffering, when it might be free.*

*O great Sun Spirit, cramped within the earth,*
*Thou suff'rest,—its strait bounds imprison Thee!*
*Thou seekest human channels for Thy love;*
*Thou askest human hands to set Thee free.*

*Thou pourest out Thy life and love for man,*
*That man may learn to give himself to Thee,*
*To be a human channel for Thy love,*
*Through which the power shall flow to set Thee free.*

*O Christ, Thy love finds echo in our hearts!*
*Our hands would lift the burden borne by Thee.*
*Ourselves we offer, channels for Thy love;*
*Ourselves we offer, that Thou may'st be free.*

         —Author Unidentified.

# CHAPTER XXXVI

## THE PLANETARY CHRIST

*The all-prevading Cosmic Love which had pre-
viously been present everywhere outside and around the
earth, had, with the death of Jesus, been born into the
earth . . . When Jesus of Nazareth died on the Cross, at
that moment there was born for the earth something that
was previously to be found only in the Cosmos. The
death of Jesus of Nazareth was the birth of the Cosmic
Love within the sphere of the earth.*
                                          —Rudolf Steiner

*Who I am thou shalt know when I depart.*
*What I now seem to be, that I am not.*
*But what I am thou shalt see when thou comest.*
    —Echoes from the Gnosis, The Hymn of Jesus

The planetary Christ is a glorious Archangel, supreme among
the archanglic Host. The Hierarchy of Capricorn is the home of the
Archangels; but during the period of His mission to this planet,
Christ and His ministering Hosts makes their home in the spiritual
sheath of the Sun—for each heavenly body has a spiritual sheath
extending far into space beyond its visible form. In the same way
every human being has a spiritual extension beyond his physical
vehicle.

From the very beginning of civilization the most primitive
religions paid homage to this great Being Who dwells in the Sun.
High priests of Mystery Temples taught their most advanced disciples the truth relative to this glorious Sun Being, and they looked
forward to a time when He would descend to earth and become the
world's Redeemer. Those who were clairvoyant could see the
Solar Lord to whom they paid homage. But there came a day when

they could no longer see Him, and then they knew that His human embodiment was imminent. From country to country, from prophet to master, from master to teacher, from teacher to disciple passed the glad tidings that the Blessed Lord, He who was to be the Saviour of the world, was close to earth.

In pre-Christian time Zoroastrians worshiped the Sun. However, theirs was not obeisance to the visible orb in the heavens but to the Sun Spirit, the Solar Logos, Whom they called Ahura Mazda, the Golden Aura or light — to be known later as the Christ. In the words of Dr. Rudolf Steiner: "Through great cosmic processes this exalted Being drew ever nearer to the earthsphere and His approach could be clairvoyantly traced ever more clearly. A clear recognition," he continues, "of Christ was forthcoming when His great forerunner Moses received His revelation in the fire of lightning on Mt. Sinai."

### The Baptism

At last the great day came. An intense silence pervaded all things. The very heartbeat of nature seemed stilled by the peace that passeth all understanding. The high exaltation of the celestial Hosts seemed very near. Then the heavens opened and the pure white dove of the Holy Ghost rested upon the head of the Master Jesus, as the voice of God was heard proclaiming: "This is my beloved Son, in whom I am well pleased." The most wondrous of all events had come to pass, for the Lord Christ had taken possession of the body which had been so lovingly and painstakingly prepared to receive Him. The vehicle of the Master Jesus, the fairest and most perfect this earth could produce, now became the abode of the Lord Christ for the three years of His earthly ministry. Wonder of wonders, the most exalted arch-angelic Being had incarnated to walk and talk with men! Three wondrous years they were, years which left their ineffable impress upon the entire human race and upon this planet for all time to come.

To again quote Dr. Rudolf Steiner, "Before the Baptism in the Jordan, the Christ Being did not belong to the earthly sphere. From worlds beyond the earth, from super-earthly spheres He had come down to earth. And the experiences between the Baptism in the Jordan and Pentecost were necessary in order that Christ, the heavenly Being, might be transformed into Christ, the earthly Being. . . A higher, non-earthly Being comes down into the earth-sphere—until, under the influence of this Being, the earth-sphere shall have been duly transformed. Since the days of Palestine the Christ Being has therefore been a power in the earth itself.''

After the Baptism and the Crucifixion, the most important event in Christ's earthly sojourn was the Transfiguration. To briefly recapitulate the status of the Lord Christ in relation to the divine Trinity: The God of our solar system, which includes the earth, operates through the triune powers of the Father, Son and Holy Ghost, the three aspects of which are Will, Wisdom and Activity.

At the time of the Transfiguration the Christ, operating through Wisdom, the second principle of the solar Godhead, was lifted into at-one-ment with the Word, the second principle of the Supreme Being. This divine attunement caused His countenance to shine with a radiance brighter than the Sun, while His raiment became whiter than snow.

A number of World Teachers have attained on the glory of transfiguration. This was the climax of their earthly lives, after which they passed into other spheres. Not so in the case of Christ Jesus. With Him the Transfiguration took place early in His ministry. Not until after this sublime occurrence did the most important phase of His ministry take place.

## Golgotha

As previously observed, there are some who assert that the Curcifixion of Christ is to be understood as a symbolical presentation of a major step in the initiatory process. It is that. But it is also an historical enactment. It cannot be stressed too often or too emphatically that the uniqueness of Christ's redemptive mission was the manifestation in a human embodiment and in the physical realm of something that had hitherto been enacted only in initiatory rituals held in Mystery Temple—rituals correspondingly experienced in the life of every disciple upon the Path leading to Illumination. The full significance of Christ's incarnation is lost if its historical aspect is not accepted. The Golgotha event was the most momentous the earth has ever known, for it marked the turning point in evolution for both man and the planet.

This planet, in common with man, is composed of a physical core with sheaths of increasingly finer texture: etheric, astral, mental and spiritual. These sheaths permeate the physical body and they also extend beyond its surface. Man must create his own vehicles from the substance of these auras. The name Adam means *red earth*. "Dust thou art, and unto dust thou return" is the biblical edict regarding the physical body. Literally, the planet we live on is our Mother Earth.

Just prior to the coming of Christ mankind had reached the nadir in evolution. History will bear out this statement. Evil, lust, selfishness and general wickedness had so charged the psychic atmosphere that there was available to man no suitable substance wherewith to build clean desire (emotional) bodies. Christ's mission was to transmute this condition; otherwise it would have rendered humanity incapable of spiritual progression. During the interval between His Crucifixion and Resurrection, the Lord Christ labored at cleansing and purifying the astral (desire) envelope of earth, and He has continued this cosmic work ever since. When His spirit left the body it entered into the heart of earth, at which time the light of His aura was so brilliant that, as the biblical record states, "the earth was darkened." This golden Christ light spread throughout the whole planetary orb, raising its vibratory tone.

The historical event that occurred at Golgotha has never been repeated, but His sacrifice for the redemption of humanity did not, we repeat, begin or end with that immolation. The sacrifice continues on a planetary scale and is repeated annually in His recurring cyclic ministry. In the fall of each year the Cosmic Christ, the Sun Spirit, descends from on high—whereto He ascends at the Summer Solstice—and initiates His re-entry into the earthly sphere. Starting from its outer sheath, He descends by degrees until He reaches the very heart of the planet at the Winter Solstice. Between the Autumn Equinox and the Spring Equinox He operates within the body of earth, recharging it with a life-giving impulse that aides humanity on its upward course. During the other half of the year, from the Spring Equinox to the Autumn Equinox, He ministers from beyond the confines of earth, meanwhile replenishing His spent energy at the throne of the Father preparatory to another release of redemptive force into the life stream of man and planet.

Each time the Lord Christ enters the earthly sphere He increases quantitatively its two higher spiritual ethers. One of these is the beautiful golden ether of the heavenly realm. St. Paul states that on the Christ's return man is to meet Him in the air—which means in the etheric realm, the lowest realm to which He will descend at His second coming. By virtue of the spiritual assistance received by humanity since the Lord's descent to the physical plane, it is now possible for "all who will" to meet Him part way up the "ladder"; but to do this it is necessary for man to incorporate into his very being the higher ethers that compose his soul-body. The shortest, safest and quickest way to develop these higher ethers is through living a life of loving, self-forgetting service to others. Thus man fashions his soul-body out of the two higher blue and golden ethers. It is now possible for all to prepare such a vehicle to meet the Christ at His second coming.

Each year, as the Christ infuses earth with the energies of life, light and love, the rhythm of the entire planet is accelerated. Gradually it is being attuned to its own musical keynote as sung by Angels each Christmastime: "On earth peace, good will toward men." Someday men will learn to "beat their swords into plowshares: and their spears into pruninghooks," and there will be no more war. The mystic Christian is not dismayed by the chaos and dissolution appearing to take place throughout the world, for he realizes that the darkest hour is always just before the dawn. Across the horizon is seen the bright bow of promise. Thus he knows that each year, as the Christ spirit permeates the earth, lines of demarkation between race and race, nation and nation, are being obliterated. The glad day will yet dawn when the planet will domicile a unified humanity, and the ideals of the Fatherhood of God and the brotherhood of man will be a reality.

Adam and Eve of the biblical record represent early humanity, which lived in the Garden of Eden situated in etheric realms. When its members came under the spell of the sense life through the influence of the Lucifer Spirits, their vibratory rate was lowered to the condition of dense physical matter. In this way infant humanity lost Paradise. It was not driven out of the etheric Garden by an avenging Deity; rather, it forfeited that abode by yielding to an influence that aligned it with the desire realm. The Fall and its dire consequences resulted from the operation of a fixed law, not by any arbitrary decree of the Creator.

Unrestrained indulgence in animal propensities that followed upon Lucifer's injection of his impulse into the desire nature of man had the effect of hardening his etheric body and externalizing its material counterpart—taking on "coats of skin," as the Bible phrases it. The descent into physical existence brought sorrow and suffering, disease and death. Humanity's harkening to Lucifer's temptations and departing from the disciplined way of life ordained by Jehovah for its stage of development is recorded in the biblical statement that Adam and Eve ate of the tree "of the knowledge of good and evil." Prior to this the children of earth knew *good* only. Afterwards they were fated to work their way back to this *good* which, when attained, will be on a higher level of manifestation because of lessons learned through painful experiences.

The etheric body is composed of four ethers of varying density. The two lower ethers take care of bodily functions while the two higher ones build soul qualities. As a result of man's descent into materiality the two higher ethers are largely latent, thus preventing him from immortalizing his imperfect physical vehicle. For this reason it is much easier for him to live a worldly existence than a spiritual life. This preponderance of lower ethers attune his etheric body to worldly vibrations, so it requires intensive effort for him to develop such soul qualities as discrimination and will power.

In His annual descent to earth, the Lord Christ brings rein-
forcements of the two higher spiritual ethers. Also, during the
course of His re-entry into the planet He cleanses its entire desire
envelope, so desire substance of ever-increasing purity is available
to man for incorporation into his astral body.

The Lord Christ is building in the etheric realms the New
Jerusalem, which is to be the home of humanity in the Christ
Dispensation. Many persons possessing extended (etheric) vision
are able to contact Him therein, and to observe the wonderful
preparations being made. As already said, the physical body cannot function in the etheric world; so those who would meet Him
"in the air" must build their soul-bodies from the two higher
ethers. Nor do disease, sorrow, old age or death have any place in
the etheric world, that realm of light wherein mankind will be
reunited with its Lord. It is known that He is even now making His
appearance to those who are able to contact Him at that level, a
fact which marks the beginning of His second coming.

# CHAPTER XXXVII

## THE HISTORICAL CHRIST

*For this reason also, our Lord in the latter times, having summoned up everything in himself, comes unto us, not as he might have come, but as we were able to behold him, for he might have come to us in his incorruptible glory, but we could never have borne the greatness of his glory.*

*—Iranaeus* (A.D. 185)

*Jesus was born of the seed of David, according to the flesh (Romans 1:3) and son of God on account of his first born essense.*

*—Origen*

*He took the form of a servant and though He was of an invisible nature as being equal to the Father, He yet took a visible appearance and was found in the appearance of a man.*

*—Ibid*

*The only begotten Word of God, who is God of Gods, divested himself according to the scriptures, lowering himself voluntarily to what he was not and clothed himself with his glorious flesh. He is afterwards said to be highly exalted and received the name which is above every name as if on account of his human nature he had it not, and almost like a favor. But in real truth it was not a gift as of things which originally did not belong to him; very far from it. It should rather be considered a returning and recurrence to what belonged to him originally and substantially, and so as much to be lost. Therefore he says when he had incarnately submitted to the means of the human nature, Father, glorify me with the glory which I had, etc. (John 17:5) for he was always in divine glory existing together with his own Father before all age and time and the foundation of the world.*

*—Hippolytus*

*Wait for Him who is beyond all times, eternal, invisible; who for our sake became visible; who was not tangible; who was incapable of suffering, and for our sake suffered; who endured in various ways for us.*
*—Ignatius in his Epistle to Polycarp*

*He is in all respects also a man the creature of God; and therefore summing up mankind in Himself, the invisible became visible, the incomprehensible became comprehensible, the impossible became possible, and the World became man.*

*—Ibid*

*Christ is man and God, formed of each nature, that He might be mediator between us and the Father.*
*—Cyprian*

### The Nativity

In the beginning of man's evolution, recounted biblically in the story of Adam and Eve, the human race came under the impress of the Lucifer spirits. It was no longer able to live in the etheric realms, the Garden of Eden. A lowering of its vibratory rate projected it into the dense material condition still prevailing, under which man came under the domination of the senses and their attendant limitation and sorrow. There were some human beings, however, who did not succumb to the temptation of the Lucifers but remained as pure Angels. Among these were those sublime egos whom we know as the Master Jesus and his perfected mother, the Blessed Mary. Therefore, at the Assumption Mary could be easily translated from the physical to the etheric plane. Angels have no concept of human passion; so Mary, bearing no earthly stain, was at home with Angels.

Upon that holy night when the great ego whom we know as Jesus came to live upon earth, the spiritual forces which accompanied him were so powerful that despite the passage of thousands of years they continue to echo and re-echo in commemoration of his birth. The high spiritual force that enfolded the planet on that wonderful occasion is the basis for many beautiful legends. It is said that roses suddenly blossomed amid the snow; that strange, fair flowers bearing the imprint of angelic faces sprang up in barren wastes; that in stalls and fields across the world cattle knelt as though in prayer, while Angels sang an anthem of peace and good will among men.

### *The Presentation in the Temple*

To repeat, each event in the life of the Master correlates with a step on the Path of Discipleship. The presentation in the Temple represents a time of dedication. An aspirant rededicates himself many times, each time gaining deeper understanding and receiving higher spiritual compensation.

Anna and Simeon were both Temple Initiates. They possessed the ability to read the Akashic Records. There they learned of the sublime mission of the Master Jesus and of Mary's part in its fulfillment. Mary was able to read further in these Records. She had previously understood something of the Master's mission, but now she fully realized the sacrifice it involved, and the suffering and sorrow it would bring to her. This was the *sword* that pierced her heart. The seven sorrowful mysteries of the Blessed Virgin as taught in the Church begin with the *Presentation in the Temple*.

## The Flight Into Egypt

The Bible is the most beautiful Book of Angelology. Joseph was warned by an Angel to take the Holy Child and his mother into Egypt, and Angels guarded their journey. When the danger was past, Angels accompanied them back to their home in Nazareth. Annunciation of the birth of both Jesus and Mary was proclaimed by Angels. During the infancy of Mary her home was an angelic shrine. Angels were her companions and teachers during her Temple years. The time of her translation from this earthly sphere was announced by Angels; and in her Assumption she rose to live in the realm of these bright Spirits.

Not only was the nativity of Jesus announced by joyous angelic proclamations, but his childhood was guarded by their holy presence. They poured out their blessing upon the Baptism, and gave their strength to Christ Jesus at the time of the *Temptation*. They hovered among the glories of the *Transfiguration* and appeared in the shadows of *Gethsemane*. Angels poured their blessings upon *Golgotha;* their joys upon the *Resurrection;* and at the *Ascension* proclaimed the glad tidings that He would come again.

The angelic ministry to the world is both beautiful and varied. Angels lift and strengthen and bless in so many different ways. Unfortunately, however, few humans have any awareness of their nearness or their ministry. The tides of the sense world have risen so high they have blinded the eyes of the masses to even the existence of the angelic world. Young children are often conscious of the presence of Angels and delight in their loving ministrations; but as the years pass and their minds become more centered in things of the earth earthy, the lovely visions are likely to fade or be looked upon lightly as vagaries of the imagination. Only chastity and purity can restore their clear seeing. If everyone were as pure as the Holy Jesus and his blessed mother, Angels and men would commingle in one vast and glorious brotherhood. "Only the pure in heart shall see God" is a biblical dictum. It is equally certain that only the pure in heart shall see and commune with the angelic world.

### The Boy Jesus in the Temple

The Holy Family remained for three years in Egypt. Many and wonderful are the legends concerning the life and works of the young Jesus during this time. He was in such complete attunement with the One Mind, the immanent Power of God which is latent in all created things, that whatever he looked upon or touched was imbued with new and vibrant life. Legend says that he made birds of clay which came to life and flew away when he laid his hands upon them. He healed lepers and caused the lame to walk, the blind to see, and he cast out obsessing entities. At all times and in all places his presence was a benediction to those he contacted.

At the expiration of three years the Holy Family returned to its home in Nazareth.

Later, as was their custom, Mary and Joseph went to Jerusalem for the Passover. By then Jesus had reached the age of twelve so, for the first time, they took the boy with them. When the feast days were ended they began their journey homeward. Noting Jesus' absence, they concluded that he was with the other children of their party; but when nightfall came and he was not to be found, they returned to Jerusalem to look for him. "After three days they found him in the temple, sitting in the midst of the doctors." How much these words conceal, and how much they reveal! In the ancient Mysteries the Initiation ceremonies extended over a period of three years, and Initiation is always connected with the Temple. Jesus had attained to the age which marks the birth of the desire or astral body. Since his desire was purity itself, it emanated a golden glory that caused even the learned ones to marvel at its brilliance.

Jesus returned to Nazareth with his parents and was obedient to them. "The child grew, and waxed strong in spirit, filled with wisdom: and the grace of God was upon him."

From his eighteenth to thirtieth year he taught and served. In many countries stories are still told of the fair young Master who came performing wonder-workings and "expounding such wisdom as had never before been accessible to the minds of men." From

China, Egypt, Babylon, India, Greece, Persia and other countries where Temple Mysteries had been inaugurated came these wondrous accounts. "And Jesus increased in wisdom and stature, and in favor with God and man."

## The Baptism

One of the predominant numerical patterns found in the Bible is that of *twelve and one*. In the heavens there are twelve zodiacal signs surrounding the central Sun. In the esoteric government of the world there are twelve great Teachers surrounding the Cosmic Christ. To each of these Teachers the Christ rays out His infinite love and wisdom, which are then given expression in a manner appropriate to the age and to the people they are to serve. Once this universal source of all religious systems is recognized, separateness will yield to unity among those of varying persuasions. The Christ is, in deed and in truth, what He proclaimed Himself to be when He said, "I am the light of the world" and "no man cometh unto the Father but by me." This liberating truth is the dominant theme of the third volume of *New Age Bible Interpretation* which, perhaps, makes it the most significant volume of the series.

The principal theme of the Old Testament is the life of Jacob surrounded by his twelve songs. Their influence extends through every Book of the Old Testament. The central theme of the New Testament is the Lord Christ and His twelve Disciples. Their influence extends through every Book of the New Testament.

That sublime event termed the Baptism marks the beginning of the Christ Era upon earth. Long and careful was the preparation for this portentious occurrence. As already said, two high Temple Initiates, Joachim and Anna, were chosen by angelic annunciation to become the parents of the highest Master who ever came to earth in a feminine body, the Blessed Mary. By her assistance, together with that of Angels, the Master Jesus built the purest, most perfect body it was possible to fashion out of physical substance, and this perfect body he relinquished to the glorious archangelic Christ at the Baptism, when the heavens opened and the voice of God was heard in blessing that exalted Being who henceforth ministered to earth as Christ Jesus. Even the most perfect physical vehicle, however, could not long withstand the tremendous radiation of an archangelic Spirit. It was necessary, therefore, that Christ Jesus frequently retire for a period of physical restoration. Among those who ministered to His needs at such times were the Essenes, a holy sect which, over a period of several centuries, had made preparations for the coming of the Lord.

The Master Jesus, by reason of his supreme sacrifice, became the "first fruits" of humanity. He has been active ever since, working from spiritual realms, particularly with every organization, every group and every individual that accepts the Lord Christ as the Saviour of the world. He will be with the Christ again when the latter sets up the new Christian Dispensation, as will the disciples Mary and Joseph, the saints, and the followers of the early Christian Church.

"Whosoever will" may come. This promise by the Christ was not spoken to the people of His time only; it applies equally to persons of every age and clime, race and nation. Whosoever will may come and prepare himself through pure and spiritual living to be numbered among those pioneers who will be found worthy to return with the Lord Christ and to aid Him in establishing the new Christian Dispensation, the building of the new heaven and new earth.

# CHAPTER XXXVIII

### THE MYSTICAL CHRIST

*Let the Christ be formed in you.*
*Christ in you, the hope of glory.*
*—St. Paul*

*Jesus, the Syrian Avatara . . . told his followers*
*how and what they might achieve by following this*
*Pathway, so that ultimately they can become such as He*
*was—such as He was so far as wisdom and power*
*went; for in the heart of every human being there is a*
*divinity, his own inner god, which the Christians of a*
*mystical turn of mind call the immanent Christ.*
*Our doctrines tell us of a long line of such*
*Teachers, each of whom became one with his inner*
*divinity, with the god within, the immanent Christos, the*
*inner Buddha; and having become so at one with inner*
*divinity, they knew all necessary knowledge because*
*they saw it, and therefore could they teach the truth.*
*—Dr. G. de Purucker in* THE STORY OF JESUS

*God's spirit falls on me, as dewdrops on a rose,*
*If I but, like a rose, my heart to Him unclose;*
*The soul wherein God dwells,—what church could*
*holier be?—*
*Becomes a walking tent of heavenly majesty.*

*In all eternity no tone could be so sweet,*
*As where man's heart with God in unison doth beat.*

*Hold, there! Where runnest thou? Know heaven is in
thee;
Look thou for God elsewhere, His face thou'llt never
see.*

*Lo! in the silent night a child to God is born,
And all is brought again that e'er was lost or lorn.*

*Could but thy soul, O man, become a silent night,
God would be born in thee and set all things aright.*

*Though Christ a thousand times in Bethlehem be born
And not within thyself, thy soul will be forlorn.
The cross on Golgotha thou lookest to in vain
Unless within thyself it be set up again.*
                                        *—Angelus Silesius*

The Christ Mystery is fourfold. First, there is the Christ in the
Sun who has been the Lord and Director of all great world
religions. Second, there is the Christ who incarnated on earth at
the time of Jesus' Baptism and who, on the momentous day of His
sacrifice on Golgotha, became its indwelling Planetary Spirit.
Third, there is the Christ to be born in man himself. Then there is
the historical Christ. It was to this fourfold Christ Mystery that
Paul referred when he said, "Behold, I show you a mystery."

This fourfold Mystery is under the guidance of the Holy
Trinity. The Christ in the Sun is under the supervision of the Lord
God. The Christ that took embodiment at the Baptism is under the
direction of the Son, the Cosmic Christ. The Christ to be born in
man is under the guidance of the Holy Spirit. The Holy Spirit has
always been the great mystery of the Trinity. Humanity in the
coming New Age will understand increasingly something of the
scope of its nature and work.

The next important step in human evolution is the birth of
Christ in man. The travail attendant upon the birth is causing much
of the current inharmony, unrest and turmoil. No man can be a

pioneer of the new race until the Christ has been born within himself. The call set forth by the Holy Spirit to all who are ready and willing to listen is for complete dedication in the service of the Lord Christ. It is the mission of the Holy Spirit relative to the Christian of the new race which led the Lord to declare, "If I go not away, the Comforter will not come unto you; but if I depart, I will send him unto you . . . and he will shew you things to come."

When the Holy Spirit activated the Christ principle within the Disciples they thought only Christed thoughts, they spoke only Christed words, they performed only Christed deeds. These men, who had been timid and fearful, now stepped forth unafraid. Thomas was no longer doubtful; Peter was no longer fearful; John no longer followed from afar off. No threats of persecution, imprisonment or even death could deter them. Their sole objective in life was to serve the Lord Christ and to walk in His ways.

One day, as Peter and John repaired to the Temple for prayer, at the "Beautiful gate" they came upon a man who had been lame from birth. Peter said to him, "Silver and gold have I none; but such as I have I give thee." Immediately strength returned to the man's ankles and feet and, arising, he entered with them into the Temple, greatly rejoicing. Peter and John recalled the words of Christ during their final days together when He declared of the Holy Spirit, "He shall glorify me: for he shall receive of mine, and shall shew it unto you"--John 16:14.

The glory of the awakened Christ within them shone about their heads as a halo of golden light. In the high state of the consciousness which was now theirs there were no differences, no inharmonies, for they abode in the realization of everlasting oneness. Hence they understood all languages and could speak in every tongue. Also, they understood the deeper meaning of the Christ's words to them: "When he, the Spirit of truth, is come, he will guide you into all truth"—John 16:13. The Disciples had become literally supermen or God-men.

Such is the meaning of the Mystical Christ within, that high attainment envisioned by St. Paul as he wrote to the Galatians "of whom I travail in birth again until the Christ be formed in you."

This Mystical Christ is the divinty that is latent in every human being. The Word, the Cosmic Christ, became flesh and dwells within all creation. This realization of the oneness of all life gives new meaning to the Fatherhood of God and the brotherhood of man. The well known American author and poet, Henry Van Dyke, expressed the reality of Christ's immanence in these beautiful lines:

> *Never more thou needst seek Me—*
> *I am with thee everywhere;*
>
> *Raise the stone and thou shalt find Me,*
> *Cleave the wood and I am there.*

This immanence of Christ will be the fundamental teaching of the New Age. It is significant to note that liberal churches and universal truth groups, keyed to the New Age, stress above all else the awakening of the Christ principle within each individual. How is this to be accomplished?

The perfection of the physical body is based upon the survival of the fittest. The growth of the soul body is based upon the law of sacrifice. In bygone days men were taught to sacrifice their material possessions. There is instruction after instruction throughout the Old Testament for bringing the firstlings of the flocks and laying them upon the altar of sacrifice. And today many churches teach their parishioners the law of tithing. However, mystic Christians understand that this law must be carried further; they must learn to place *themselves* at the altar as a sacrificial offering.

The awakening of Christ within oneself, like all processes of birth, is slow and gradual. First, the aspirant must make his dedication to the Christ ideal. If he is earnest and sincere in this dedication he will find himself coming into closer attunement with this ideal. It will be easier for him to think Christed thoughts, to speak words and perform deeds in accord with a Christed life. He will be conscious of a sense of well-being he has never before known—the same sense reached by the early Christians even while living in the gloomy Catacombs and when faced with forbidding forms of persecution and death. However, awakening the Christ within has compensation that no worldly circumstance or condition can destroy. Nor can they be over-balanced by material possessions.

In preparation for His second coming, the Lord Christ is drawing closer and closer to earth. At certain times he is in etheric realms just above the physical plane, and many advanced souls are becoming conscious of the benediction shed by His nearness. Some there are who have been caught up to kneel in adoration and homage before Him and to hear the intoning of His blessed voice. This sometimes happens during hours when the physical body is in repose or asleep. Again, a person may be caught up in an exaltation of consciousness during the hours of a busy day. It may be to strengthen him for meeting a crisis, or to mitigate some deep and agonizing sorrow. Whatever the reason, and whenever it may occur, one's life can never be quite the same after a moment in His sublime presence. Whatever he does, he will bear the impress of divinity and be motivated by a desire for increased opportunities to serve "in His name."

The activities of such a fortunate person will continue until death completely loses its sting in the realization that it is merely a transition from the physical to the etheric plane. He will discover that while dwelling in the physical realm he is free to serve in the higher realm and that after passing through the change called death, he will abide in the etheric yet be free to serve in the physical world. He learns that this life and the life "beyond" are two aspects of a grand and glorious whole, whereof the Lord Christ is both the center and the circumference.

> *The gate of another age flies open—the age of soul;*
> *the kingdom of God in man.*
> —*Aquarian Gospel*

> *The way of search leads from that which lies with-*
> *out to that which dwells within. It reveals step by step*
> *the hidden life which every form and symbol veils. It*

*assigns to the aspirant certain tasks which lead to his understanding and produce a wisdom that meets his deep need.*

—*Alice Bailey*

Throughout the pages of *New Age Bible Interpretation* frequent mention is made of the Path of Initiation as outlining the principal events in the life of the Lord Christ from His birth to His Resurrection and Ascension. The same interpretation has been used extensively in this volume relative to the four Christ aspects: the Cosmic, the Planetary, the Historical and the Mystical. The latter is the most important in regard to human development as it relates to the Christ within.

The Holy Birth refers to the Christ principle awakened within man. When this new birth takes place in an individual, a tremendous new power emanates from his mind and a greater love radiates from his heart. Human values are largely reversed. Interests of the average person are centered in the objective side of life. Upon awakening the Christ within, interests become focused primarily in the subjective side. Then one better understands the true significance of Paul's words: "The things which are seen are temporal; but the things which are not seen are eternal."

Upon a neophyte's *Presentation in the Temple,* an occasion of dedication and consecration, the Christ force within him is vivified, strengthened and augmented. This attainment is followed by a *Flight into Egypt,* for the Path of Discipleship is always checkered by alternate sunshine and clouds. As Longfellow, the beloved American poet, so aptly expresses the idea:

> *Into each life some rain must fall,*
> *Some days must be dark and dreary.*

It is thus that man is able to meet sorrow with as much fortitude as he faces joy; and he learns the lesson St. Paul had mastered, as indicated by his statement that "None of these things move me." If a person is honest and sincere in his self-examination and self-analysis, he will admit that his most valuable lessons have been learned in life's shadow rather than in its sunshine.

Once the tests in Egypt have been passed, the next step is the *Return to Nazareth*. The aspirant, accompanied by Angels, is brought up into Nazareth to grow in strength and understanding.

Through the *Teaching in the Temple* the Christ within becomes the dominant power of his life. "Out of the abundance of the heart the mouth speaketh." Then his paramount desire is to share his priceless inner realization with all who are willing to receive it. As soon as he has proven himself worthy, opportunities and ability to communicate his spiritual knowledge will be available.

By the *Rite of Baptism* the spiritualized force of mind and the radiant love of heart are united in divine at-one-ment. Birth of the Christ within is now complete, and the aspirant comes forth a Christed individual. Baptism heralds the beginning of a new life, a life in which the personality is secondary because the Christ consciousness reigns supreme. The head of the now illumined One is crowned by a halo of light as the white dove of Holy Spirit rests thereon in blessing, and the Voice of God declares, "This is my beloved son in whom I am well pleased." St. Paul, who followed this path, came to know that "God tempers the wind to the shorn lamb." Whoever analyzes its steps is well aware that this is true.

After the *Holy Birth* and the *Presentation in the Temple* comes a testing by the *Flight into Egypt*. Then follows the *Return to Nazareth* which, in turn, leads to the more advanced steps of the *Teaching in the Temple* and the *Rite of Baptism*. The greater the attainment, the more subtle the temptation. The narrower the Path, the steeper the ascent. The *Rite of Baptism* is succeeded by the most difficult test yet encountered, a test known as the *Great Temptation*.

When the energies of head and heart are united in harmonious blending, a dynamic force of attraction is released in the aspirant. This force is operative on the physical, mental and spiritual planes, and he is made fully aware of the meaning of Christ's promise that

"Whatsoever ye shall ask in my name, that will I do." Recognizing that this power is now his, he is faced by an alternative fraught with dire possibilities: shall he use it to attract to himself the pleasures and comforts, the affluence, adulation and prominence that it places within his reach; or shall he turn his back upon these allurements and abide by his dedication to a selfless life, using his power for the redemption of man and the perfection of God's kingdom on earth? It is at this point that the Path narrows exceedingly. Unfortunately, many who have tried seriously to ascend thereon turn back and walk no more with Christ. Even those brave souls who are victorious are compelled to repeat over and over again—as did the Christ—"Get thee behind me, Satan."

Having demonstrated courage sufficient to overcome the *Great Temptation,* the aspirant is now ready for a Rite referred to as *The Transfiguration,* an attainment followed by the high exaltation of the *Love Feast.* Through this Rite he passes into life eternal. His mind is so spiritualized and his heart so illumined that he literally thinks with his heart and loves with his mind. He is thus worthy to partake of the *Love Feast.* The essences of his exalted mind and heart, the bread and wine of the Feast, transcend time and space; they may be sent to the farthest ends of earth for the purpose of blessing and healing. Through these essences developed within themselves, the Disciples were taught by the Lord Christ to so spiritualize and consecrate these elements that they could be used to uplift their fellow man. This makes clear the significance of His saying "I am the bread of life" "my blood is the water of eternal life," or words to that effect.

By passing through the experience of *The Transfiguration* an aspirant approaches the summit of human attainment. He can now radiate the dynamic spiritual power engendered within himself as a great light, whether he be working in the physical, mental or spiritual realm. His light is no longer "hidden under a bushel." Having reached this high degree of unfoldment, he is—or should be—prepared for the formidable test of *Gethsemane.*

Certain it is that the Path of Discipleship is long and arduous. Many years, even many earth lives are required to reach its ultimate goal. This done, *all* has to be renounced. Any fame, prestige, adulation of power that a disciple has acquired must be put behind him. He must be willing to descend into obscurity and declare with the Christ, "I can of myself do nothing." When the Lord permitted Himself to be taken at Gethsemane and, later, to be nailed upon the cross, both He and His mission were failures in the estimation of worldly men. In fact, they were so considered among His intimate followers. Comparatively few individuals are called upon to meet such a test, for few ever reach the place on the Path where it is necessary. Abraham's Gethsemane was the demand that he sacrifice his son Isaac. Not until he was willing to make this supreme renunciation was he able to walk and talk consciously with angelic Beings.

Complete renunciation and entire selflessness are inevitably demanded of those traveling the Path of Discipleship, whether in ancient or modern times. Frequently during the ordeals experienced thereon does a disciple repeat the prayer of the Christ: "O my Father, if it be possible, let this cup pass from me." If he is victorious he will add, "Nevertheless not as I will, but as thou wilt."

After *Gethsemane* come *The Crucifixion*. While this is a Rite of pain and sorrow, it is also a Rite of glorification. The disciple who has renounced all finds that he has gained all. The powers of heaven and earth do his bidding. A fundamental law of occult unfoldment, a law that the Christ taught to His Disciples, is expressed in His statement: "For whosoever hath, to him shall be given . . . but whosoever hath not, from him shall be taken away even that he hath."

The *Resurrection* and the *Ascension* are final steps in ascending into the Great Light. One who qualifies for them is Christed indeed. He will meet the Lord in the ethers at the time of His second coming, and serve with Him to the end of the age in an exalted state of *conscious immortality*.

*Spirit of undying Beauty, Sun of unfading love,*
*teach this humanity to know Thee in Thy worlds, and*

*knowing Thee to see Thy handiwork in flower-petal, scented bough, and singing voice, and in the marking intricate and delicate, of beetle, serpent, bird; to find Thee finally within himself, transcendent glory of the man, made God.*

*—Mary Gary*

*New Age Bible Interpretation* is centered in the fundamental teaching that the Lord Christ came to earth as the Supreme Wayshower for all mankind. His purpose was to teach man how to awaken the Christ divinity within himself; for, as St. Paul asserts, we are all Christs in the making. The principal events during the Lord's earthly sojourn outline the important soul-lessons each individual must learn in order to awaken this latent divinity. It was not necessary that Christ Himself pass through all these experiences; but He chose so to do that He might demonstrate how man could meet and rise victorious over the various trials. The perfect pattern has been given us. Paul said of the Lord, "He was in all points tempted like as we are, yet without sin."

The Path of Discipleship is rough and precipitous. However, when an awakening seeker becomes conscious of the Christ within himself, nothing in this life that is not connected with his quest retains any value. Once he has partaken of celestial food, all the delicacies of the world heaped together are utterly tasteless, for he at last comprehends the full meaning of the words spoken by our Blessed Lord: "I have meat to eat that ye know not of" and "Whosoever drinketh of the water that I shall give him shall never thirst."

St. John, the highest Initiate of the New Testament Dispensation, also referred to such Christed attainment.

*Beloved, now we are the sons of God, and it doth not yet appear what we shall be.*

*—I John 3:2*

The Lord Christ has dedicated Himself to the transcendent service of guiding humanity to this supernal estate. Hence, mystic Christians read a deep meaning into the most comforting of His promises:

> *Lo, I am with you alway, even unto the end of the world.*

# CHAPTER XXXIX

## SEVEN KEYS TO THE CHRIST MYSTERY

Herein is given a brief summation of the keys, seven in number, to what may be the most important elucidation of the Christ Mysteries. Earnest students are admonished to study these seven keys carefully, together with their description as given in the Bible; and then, by long and prayerful meditation, make them active and vital factors in their daily lives.

### Key Number One
### *The Immaculate Conception*

The Immaculate Conception is the Holy Rite whereby the fire that burns in man's personality is transmuted into the light of pure spirit. In the process of transmutation the red fire of Mars, the desire force generated by the Lucifers, is displaced by the golden Sun force, the pure love-power of the Christ. This will be the paramount transformation to take place in the whole race during the coming age.

Late in human evolution certain centers were developed in the currents of man's desire body. These centers are largely latent in the majority of people, for they can be awakened only through spiritual development. As yet they have come into their full splendor only in those who have received the higher Degrees of Initiation. However, these centers, all twelve of them, are latent in the body of every individual. When awakened and functioning, they become twelve glorious lights.

The centers are variously located in the physical vehicle. Two are in the feet; two at the knees; one at the base of the spine; one each in the solar plexus, the heart and the throat; two in the cranium. In oriental Mystery Schools these centers are referred to as "lotus blossoms"; by mystic Christians they are described as "the roses that bloom upon the cross of the body." They do not come into their full luminosity until after the first of the Greater or Christ Initiations has been reached. Centers below the diaphragm are not fully awakened until a disciple passes all four of these Christ Initiations; therefore humankind is not very familiar with their functioning or the processes involved in their activation. All centers located above the diaphragm are awakened during the course of the nine Lesser Initiations, so more is known about the means and manner of their functioning. There are other centers to be activated through further spiritual unfoldment, but the ones treated here are the most important at man's present stage of evolution.

When the center at the base of the spine bestirs itself, its deep red color gradually lightens to a clear, pure radiance that is tinged with deep orange-gold as one's nature is increasingly purified and spiritualized. The forces of this center aid the transmutation and purification process throughout the entire body.

With vitalization of the center located at the solar plexus there comes a greater sense of reverence toward the physical vehicle as a fitting temple for the indwelling spirit. As this realization is born, all the activities of the physical vehicle are strengthened and harmonized with the higher principles. Radiations from this center are a vivid green, the color of verdant nature, and they serve to stimulate all the life processes.

The rose can bloom in the heart only as compassion reaches out to include all living creatures, for the heart center can never become a translucent light until love is its motivating power. The golden blossom at a disciple's heart can never reach full unfold-ment so long as he nourishes his body upon the flesh of his younger brothers, or uses their hide, fur or feathers to gratify his vanity. He must hold sacred, and give loving care to all lesser creatures before this rose unfolds its radiant petals. When finally awakened, this center resembles a miniature sunburst of golden splendor.

The rose at the throat center, where resides the power of speech, will not come into full bloom so long as hasty, unkind or destructive words are spoken through it. The neophyte must make supreme dedication of his voice in service to the Christ. He must be able to say "For myself I ask nothing; and from myself I give all unto others." Such dedication unfolds the petals of this rose so that it gives off a soft blue radiance, to which inspiration adds silvery tones.

In other writings we have referred to the two lights in the head. The pituitary gland will become someday a perfect image-building center, while the pineal gland will be the sanctuary wherein abides the power of will as servant of the spirit. These centers are bathed in exquisite shades of violet, to which aspiration adds the luster of shining gold. In these centers may be found the mystery relative to the origin of the rosary.

When all twelve of the body centers are alight, a disciple is clothed in the "golden wedding garment," ready to meet the Bride-groom and go in with Him to the Marriage Feast.

KEY NUMBER TWO
*The Holy Birth*

The Virgin Mary and her husband Joseph were Temple Initiates. Having learned all lessons belonging to the objective life, they had committed themselves permanently to Temple service. To further the divine plan, however, they renounced Temple life and returned to the lay world to become householders. Thus they sought to secure a proper environment during the formative years of the child who was to be known as the Master Jesus.

On that first magic Christmas Night a golden light suffused the entire world. Hosts of Angels and Archangels, singing exultant hosannas, descended to earth and mingled with men, becoming visible to many of them. On this glorious golden Ray, Mary was swept heavenward where, amidst joyous acclamations, the Holy Babe was given into her keeping.

## KEY NUMBER THREE
### *The Baptism*

When the Master Jesus stepped into the waters of the River Jordan he made the great sacrifice of surrendering the body he had built that the archangelic Christ might use it during the three years of His ministry. Once more, as on Holy Night, the heavens were filled with the resounding hosannas of Angels; and the voice of God was heard proclaiming "This is my beloved Son, in whom I am well pleased."

The Gospel of St. Mark opens with the Rite of Baptism. The Gospel of St. John opens with the Rite of the Mystic Marriage, wherein water is turned into wine. There is an intimate relation between these two events. The Rite of Baptism was observed by the Disciples on Holy Saturday preceding the Resurrection. By it each one was learning to disassociate *at will* his ego from its physical vehicle. In the Rite of the Mystic Marriage the Christ taught His Disciples how to bring the forces of mind and heart into equilibrium; in other words, how to manifest polarity, through which it is possible to perform such miracles as turning water into wine. This Rite is a preparation for the wonders of Pentecost.

## KEY NUMBER FOUR
### *The Transfiguration*

During the course of His ministry the Lord Christ endeavored to help His most advanced Disciples—Peter, James and John—to understand something of the deep mystery of His mission. To them He gave evidence of His supernatural powers and His celestial glory. He taught them how to so lift their consciousness as to behold the dazzling radiance of His archangelic body. Almost overcome by His transfigured Being, they knelt before Him in reverence and adoration.

Origen has this to say concerning the exaltation experienced by the privileged Disciples upon beholding the glory of the Christ on the mount: "You will ask whether when He was transfigured before those who were taken by Him to the high mountain, He was seen by them in the form of God in which He existed before; since to those who were below He had the form of a servant, but to those who followed Him after six days He had not that but the form of God.''

As given at length in the chapter on Christ is the Old Testament, many of the most advanced teachers and prophets of that Dispensation prepared their disciples for the coming of the Christ. As Peter, James and John gazed in awe upon the sublime spectacle of the transfigured Christ, they saw standing beside Him Moses and Elijah, two of the highest Initiates of Old Testament days who had worked to prepare their followers for the Lord Christ's coming.

KEY NUMBER FIVE
*Gethsemane*

It was the mission of Christ to identify Himself with the destiny of earth and its humanity. It was the final work He had to accomplish before His Crucifixion. It was in this agonizing trial that He entered into complete identification with the destiny of the human race.

The Christ has shared the most transcendent experience of His ministry, the Transfiguration, with the same three advanced Disciples, Peter, James and John. Now he asked them to share with Him the darkest and most agonizing hour of His earthly sojourn. He had hoped they might assist Him during this period of travail. But it was for the Christ, our glorious type-pattern, as it has been for every aspirant on the ascending Path: there was no one but the Father to share with Him His darkest hour. So the Gospel records that His three most enlightened Disciples *slept.* They were not equal to the exacting watch for which they had been called.

Their inability to measure up to the demands of this tragic occasion, and thus lose an opportunity for unsurpassed service, is a warning to all who dedicate themselves to the Christ. Unless adequate preparation is made they will not be alert to what is taking place, and so they will not give heed to the call of their Lord and Master.

### Key Number Six
#### *The Crucifixion*

The Baptism heralded the beginning of the Lord Christ's ministry to earth and man while the Crucifixion marked the high point of that ministry. At the Crucifixion, He who came as a mediator between heaven and this plane entered into the heart of the planet and became its indwelling Spirit. Since then His ministry has been both from within the sphere itself. The heart of earth is His planetary center. Each year the Christ force enters therein with added intensity and volume, making it easier for that force to find a dwelling place in the heart of man. This was the wonderful revelation that came to St. Paul on the road to Damascus that he later incorporated into instruction given to his disciples.

Those who claim that Christ as a personality never lived, that His life was but a symbolic rendering of the initiatory Path, and that the Crucifixion is also symbolic, miss the very crux of esoteric or mystic Christianity.

A thousand years with the Lord are but as a day. In the Second Creative Day recorded in Genesis (Sun Period), Archangels were passing through a stage of development corresponding to our present human evolution. Their densest vehicles were formed from desire or astral substance. (The etheric body did not become manifest until the succeeding Moon Period nor the physical body until the present Earth Period). The Christ was chief of this archangelic life wave, and He then dedicated Himself to serve as guardian of earth-in-the-making. Eons passed before the planet was ready to receive Him into its innermost center.

When the Sun was passing by precession through the sign Aries, the Lamb, He came as the Good Shepherd to the sheep that had lost their way. Preparations for His coming were begun when the Sun passed by precession through Libra, the sign opposite Aries, approximately ten thousand years earlier. Initiate Teachers were sent to different parts of the world, each with a similar message, to make ready an inner circle of disciples for that glorious event: the coming of the Light of the Sun Who was to be the Light of the world. As time passed the preparation was more and more clearly defined. To China came Lao Tse and the worship of Kwan Yin, she who represents the Divine Feminine. In Egypt worship centered in Osiris and Isis; in Babylon it was Izdubar and Ishtar; in Greece, Apollo and Minerva; in India, Buddha and his mother Maya; in Persia, Zoroaster and Ainyahita; and finally, in Palestine, Jesus and the Virgin Mary. Down through the ages those disciples who were aware of the incarnation-to-come were making ready for it, and not least among them were the Three Wise Men of the East.

St. Augustine recognized this age-after-age preparation for the coming of the Christ. Said he: "That which today is called Christian religion existed among the ancients and has never ceased to exist from the origin of the human race until the time when the Christ Himself came and men began to call Christianity the true religion which already existed beforehand." Christianity carried on from where previous revelations left off.

There was an intimate relationship between the early Christian Mysteries and the Mithraic Mysteries of Persia. Tertullian was reported to have been an Initiate of the Persian School before he contacted Christianity. Jerome writes of these Mysteries with so much understanding that he probably belonged to their inner circle. As in all esoteric Schools, the Mithraic Mysteries were in seven Degrees. These Degrees bore symbolic names representative of specific attainments. The First Degree, which always deals with man's overcoming his lower nature, was known as *The Raven.* The Second was *The Occultist;* the Third, *The Warrior;* the Fourth, *The Lion.* The Fifth was the most important and the most far-reaching in its effect. At this point an Initiate had attained complete self mastery and was given the name of the country to which he belonged. Hence, in the Mithraic School an Initiate of the Fifth Degree was called *The Persian.*

Rudolf Steiner has the following to say about this Fifth Degree: "In the Fifth Degree he was ready for an extension of consciousness giving him the power to become the spiritual guardian of his people, whose name was therefore conferred upon him. An Initiate of the Fifth Degree was lifted into the sphere where he participated in the life of the Archangeloi. To enable the Archangeloi to lead the people aright, there must be Initiates of the Fifth Degree on earth. These Initiates are the intermediaries between those who are the actual leaders of the people and the people themselves.''

With the coming of Christ the Mysteries assumed a more exalted form than ever before, for in the Christian Mystery School the sublime teachings of the Christ are united with those of the Ancient Mysteries. These augmented Mysteries will become the cornerstone of the new Aquarian religion. As previously noted, St. John's initiatory name was Lazarus, and he was the first to be initiated into these sublime Mysteries. Through them he overcame death and opened the portals of immortality that all who followed in his footsteps might enter thereby into the glorious privilege of being one of those disciples whom the Christ holds closest to His heart.

During the interval between the Crucifixion and the Resurrection the Lord Christ worked to purify the desire (astral) realm of the planet—a realm which mankind had so infused with evil that human evolution was being greatly retarded. No longer was there available any suitable desire substance out of which to form clean, pure astral bodies. The dark miasmic envelope surrounding the earth created a condition that rendered many persons easy prey to earth-bound obsessing entities—referred to in the Bible as ''evil spirits'' to be cast out.

At the time of the Crucifixion Christ rent the veil before the Temple of Initiation, making it possible for ''whosoever will to come'' and partake of the waters of eternal life. This is beautifully symbolized in the biblical statement that ''the veil of the temple was rent in twain.'' As said before, in the light of esoteric Christianity it is clear that the mission of Christ was not concluded with the Crucifixion. Then it was that He truly became the Planetary Christ.

At the Autumn Equinox of each year He reincarnates within the physical earth-sphere and works therein during the six months that the Sun is passing through the zodiacal signs below the equator. He is then cleansing and purifying the astral envelope of the planet, in which labor He is assisted by Michael and Hosts of

Archangels. Thus, year by year, men are able to draw into their physical vehicles finer and finer desire material. From Eastertime to the Autumn Equinox, while the Sun is transiting signs north of the equator, the Lord Christ is working on the spiritual envelope of earth, infusing it with higher spiritual forces drawn from the zodiacal Hierarchies encircling our solar system. Such is the cosmic process by which earth's "golden wedding garment" is being fashioned.

Never again will the Lord Christ descend in a physical body to walk among men. Henceforth His activity will be centered in the etheric realm, biblically known as the Garden of Eden. Those who serve with Him in this Edenic abode will have woven their own golden "wedding garments"; in other words, they will have built etheric bodies capable of functioning on the etheric plane. Such a vehicle can be fashioned in one way only; that way is through the dedication of self in service to others.

As humanity becomes Christed, the physical elements of earth will be progressively refined until the whole race will literally "live, move and have its being" in the etheric realm. Then will the purpose of this planet as now constituted be fulfilled. The Christ will have completed His sublime mission, and a Christed race will live amidst the glories of "a new heaven and a new earth."

Golgotha was the most momentous of all world events. It stands at a point between the nine lesser pre-Christian Mysteries and the four Greater Mysteries established by the Lord Himself. When the pre-Christian Mystery Schools taught their disciples to prepare for "the Great One Who was to come," the teaching was accompanied by a vision of a man nailed upon a cross. When Christ's blood flowed on Golgotha He became the indwelling Lord of earth as well as the Lord of heaven. As its indwelling Spirit He comes into more intimate contact with all mankind. This makes it easier for human beings to awaken the Christ principle within themselves. To the extent that men learn to activate this principle do they take on the character of world saviours and share in the redemptive work of the Christ. Thus they become forerunners of His second coming.

It is the mission of the Archangel Michael, chief messenger of the Blessed Lord, to bring to New Age pioneers a deeper understanding of the Cosmic Christ in relation to both humanity and the planet, and to the role of the Planetary Christ in the evolution of all mankind. Such understanding will be basic to New age religion.

Perhaps the most important phase of the Golgotha event was Christ's giving to man an initial realization of love as a power. Men had long looked upon love as a passion, a sentiment or an ideal; but Christ demonstrated how the power of love can perform miracles. It is the power that causes the planet to rotate on its axis and to describe an orbit around the Sun. The "law of attraction" spoken of by astronomers is but another name for the love-power.

The Lord Christ exercised this power when He left the realm of the Archangels to become Regent of earth; and again when He made the sacrifice on Golgotha in service to man. He continues so to do when His bright presence is imprisoned within the planet during six months of every year that He may renew its forces and bring redemption to the race. Doubtless the most comprehensive definition of the power of love is found in His own words: "Greater love hath no man than this, that a man lay down his life for his friends."

Those who would become pioneers in the Lord's work of establishing the New Galilee must incorporate the love-power within themselves by living lives of such purity and selfless service that they will be qualified to take over the direction of the earth and to further the redemption of humankind. Only by such service can the Christ be released from his voluntary bondage to mortality, that He may re-ascend unto His archangelic home-world whereof He is the supreme Initiate.

### KEY NUMBER SEVEN
*The Resurrection*

Throughout the ages disciples have been taught that the Resurrection Degree marks the culmination of the initiatory Path. This Degree also signals the ultimate triumph of life over death. The Ancients said that man alone knows death, for the gods know only metamorphosis. The transmutation of death into eternal life is accomplished in the Degree of Resurrection. The Lord Christ, the sublime Way-shower upon the Path of Initiation, left His grave clothes within the empty tomb to symbolize spirit's supremacy and authority over a limited personality associated only with physical incarnation.

Advanced disciples of the Ancient Mysteries—and true of those in the modern day—were taught to *consciously* bridge the seeming chasm between waking and sleeping, between life and death. St. Paul referred to this attainment when he stated that the last enemy to be overcome by man is death, a consciousness which identifies those advanced ones who walk the way of illumination. It will be the common heritage of the race at the end of the present Earth Period, for in the final conquest of death the spirit is set free from bondage to mortality.

Mystic Christians recognize that the Golgotha sacrifice is both an historical and an annual event, and will continue to be the latter until a sufficient number of persons have become Christed to carry forward the redemptive work. As the Lord Christ continues His cyclic service, innumerable celestial Beings bestow upon Him reverence and adoration in gladsome hosannas. In response He intones the majestic words "All power is given unto me in heaven and in earth."

The Lesser Mysteries reach a climax in the Resurrection Degree. The Greater (Christ) Mysteries introduce a higher Degree in the Rite of the Ascension. Those who attain to this Degree are able to follow the Christ to His own home-world of Life Spirit, the realm of that exalted unity signified thus by Christ Jesus: "I and my Father are one." This realization was reached by the Disciples on the Day of Pentecost. Someday it will be reached by all mankind through the first of the Greater Mysteries established by the Christ while on earth. To repeat, humanity's attainment by the end of the present Earth Period may be referred to as the work of the first of the Greater or Christ Initiations. When the disciples manifested its power at Pentecost, they became god-men.

The work of the second of the Greater Initiations will be manifested by humanity during the following Jupiter Period, when both man and the planet will transcend the state of physical matter. They will then function in etheric vehicles, and earth conditions will be similar to those which existed in the Garden of Eden. Disease, old age and death will be no more. The essences of man's physical body having been incorporated into a higher etheric vehicle, it will be an extremely sensitive instrument with capacities far beyond present comprehension. His mind will be so spiritualized as to manifest innate God-power, enabling him to work with life as expressed through the plant kingdom. This power is now used by Angels to create and develop growing things in nature. Man will also be able to transit images from his own mind to the consciousness of others. If he is describing a particular scene, his hearer will be seeing an exact picture of it. Those who receive instructions from angelic Beings already know that the development of picture-consciousness is an essential part of their teaching.

With the Rite of Assumption the Virgin Mary was lifted up to dwell with Angels. In the wonder and beauty of her etheric home she beheld conditions as they would prevail during the Jupiter Period. She is, therefore, the perfect type-pattern for the disciple of the second Christ Initiation, and for all humanity in the succeeding Period.

Through the third of the Greater Initiations an exalted soul attains powers and abilities that will not be known to mankind in general until what is termed the Venus Period. In this advanced stage of development man's desire body will be perfected. Spiritual essences of both his physical and etheric bodies will be incorporated into a still finer vehicle, while desire itself will become as *light*. Literally, he will live, move and have his being in a body of light. During the Jupiter Period man will evolve a picture-consciousness. In the Venus Period he will be able to imbue such images with sentient life.

St. John the Beloved is the perfect type-pattern of humanity in the Venus Period, also that of an Initiate passing through the third Christ Initiation. Hence John, the Venus type-pattern, is the Disciple who came closest to the loving heart of the Christ. His magnificent Gospel is an unmatched utterance relative to the far-reaching power of love.

In the Vulcan Period, which will correspond to the fourth of the Greater (Christ) Initiations, man will attain unto divine perfection. The spiritual essences of his physical, etheric and desire bodies will be incorporated into a mental vehicle so he will then possess "this mind . . . which was also in Christ Jesus." This creative life force will be focused in his heart, the love center. His larynx will become an organ of creation through the power of the spoken word. Thus generation will be exalted into regeneration. The Lord Christ Himself is the type-pattern of perfected man in the Vulcan Period. He is also the first Initiate to pass into the glories of the fourth and last of the Greater Initiations. It was in reference to man's eventual exalted estate that David, a high Initiate of the Old Testament Dispensation, gave forth the following inspired utterance:

> *What is man, that thou art mindful of him? and the son of man that thou visitest him?*
> *For thou hast made him a little lower than the angels, and hast crowned him with honor and glory.*
> —Psalms 8:4,5

An ancient mural in the Church of the Campo Santo in Pisa, Italy. A remarkable representation of the conception of early Christians of the Christ in His cosmic aspect.

An ancient mural in the Church of the Campo Santo in Pisa, Italy.
A remarkable representation of the conception of early Christians
of the Christ in His cosmic aspect.

# PART V

# The Cycle of the Year with Christ

# CHAPTER XL

At the present time few persons have any conception of the spiritual significance of commonly observed ecclesiastical feasts. While the Church of Rome and the Church of England observe many of these festivals, their inner meaning has been largely lost. As has been stated before in the *New Age Bible Interpretation* series, the Christian Mystery Temple is located in the ethers above the City of Jerusalem. It was in this high and holy area that these feasts had their origin, and there they continue to be observed in their full splendor and majesty. During the observances a dynamic spiritual power is poured out upon earth. This is one of the many channels used by the Lord Christ for the spiritualization of the planet.

*October — November — December*

When the Sun enters Libra, which heralds the coming of October, the golden Christ force passes into earthly realms as this sublime Being begins anew His annual sacrifice, an event termed *the cosmic crucifixion*. To it St. Paul referred in Romans 8:22: "For we know that the whole creation groaneth and travaileth together until now." At this season of the Autumn Equinox a disciple should renew his dedication to walk in the way of the Lord despite any vicissitudes and hindrances that may beset his path.

During November the Christ force permeates the desire realm of earth. Then a disciple should strive to purify his lower nature in order to aid the Great Ones in their work of cleansing earth's astral envelope. He must especially seek to become a more efficient channel for service, both as a visible and an invisible helper.

In the early days of human manifestation a part of the work performed by the Scorpio Hierarchy, which presides over the zodiacal month of November, was to awaken man's ego, thus assisting him in achieving individualization. During the present stage of human evolution a disciple, working under the jurisdiction of the Lords of Individuality (Libra) and the Lords of Form (Scorpio), is learning to translate assertiveness into humility and to sacrifice the personal "I" for the impersonal "we"; in other words, to actually live the ideal of *the greatest good for the greatest number*.

Advent Season extends through the month of December and is heralded as a Feast of Light. The spiritual impulses of the season prepare mankind for a downpouring of the heavenly forces accompanying the annual rebirth of the Cosmic Christ into our earthly sphere. Advent is followed by the Winter Solstice, occurring between December 21st and 24th, and culminating in the Christian Feast on December 25th. Christmas must always remain an external observance for an aspirant until the Christ is born within himself. To the degree that he has an awakening will he be able to participate in the high spiritual ecstasy of this most holy season.

### January — February

The twelve Holy Days begin on December 26th and come to a climax on January 6th, with the Feast of Epiphany. This feast commemorates the arrival of the three Wise Men and their rich gifts for the Babe in the manger. On the Path of Discipleship the Feast of Epiphany signifies a disciple's threefold dedication of spirit, soul and body, and their accompanying gifts of love, life and service, to the Christ Child. The spiritual influence of this feast extends through the month of January. During this time the disciple endeavors to cultivate these spiritual attributes and to evidence them by a deeper consecration of the Lord Christ.

In February begins a special preparation for the Lenten Season, when an aspirant undergoes specific disciplines for making spirit paramount in his every thought, word and act. The noun February comes from the Latin Februarius, the name given to the Roman Feast of Purification that was held on the fifteenth day of the second month of the year. During the early days of February the Church likewise celebrates a Feast of Purification as the initial work of the Lenten Season. A mystic Christian disciple observes it as a time of threefold purification, endeavoring to cleanse his physical body by the purest of food; his desire body by virtuous deeds; his mental body by chaste thoughts and truthful words.

These disciplines are by way of preparation for the great transmutation that is the highlight of each yearly observance. Both the mind and body of an aspirant must be sensitized if he is to participate in the ecstatic inpouring of this cosmic feast. Then it is that the Church blesses the candles that are to be used during the ensuing year. To a mystic Christian a candle symbolizes the "light of the world," the Blessed Lord Christ. At the Lenten Season he dedicates himself anew in service to the Christ and endeavors to become a bearer of the light which, according to St. Paul, is also in Christ Jesus.

### March — April — May

The cosmic resurrection occurs in March, when the Christ Spirit is liberated from the earthly sphere and passes into high spiritual realms. The Hierarchies of both Aries and Pisces join with Angels and Archangels in triumphant jubilation over this event. The rhythm of this cosmic hymn was inscribed by Handel in his *Hallelujah Chorus*. Pre-Christian ceremonials celebrating the return of spring and the victory of light over darkness were attuned to these same rhythms.

The Spring Equinox is one of the high points of the year for a disciple. Its keynotes are the freedom and emancipation that lead to a larger life. It is also the time when the Cosmic Christ is freed from the terrestrial fetters that have held Him in bondage during the winter months. Hence, it is the most propitiuous time for an advanced disciple to break the bonds that bind him and to enter the joyous freedom of the spirit.

The Chruch observes the ecclesiastical Feast of the Annunciation in March when nature commemorates the cosmic Feast of the Annunciation, for there is an intimate relationship between man and nature. Therefore one reflects the other. The most sacred rituals observed by man are in attunement with the seasonal transitions. Poets sing in praise of the holy spirit of spring, while nature's green-and-gold splendor gives evidence that returning life forces are responding in triumph to the cosmic resurrection impulse.

An advanced follower of the Path understands that the time has come to merge the sorrow and tears of his personal life (Pisces) with the transforming fires of Aries. As he accomplishes this he joins the mighty chorusing which is echoed and re-echoed by Angels and Archangels: "The Christ is risen, for Christ has now risen within me."

April has been designated the resurrection month. Then it is that the resurgent forces reach their culmination and nature becomes a glorious symphony of color and beauty.

Good Friday is the year's holiest day for the mystic Christian. Orthodox Christians observe it with penitence and mourning because their thoughts are focused upon the suffering and the Crucifixion of the Saviour. Mystic Christians, however, observe it with a profound inner rejoicing and thanksgiving because it brings to a close the Lord's half-year period of incarceration within the physical limits of earth that He may now rise in triumph to higher realms. They understand that His sacrifice and Resurrection are a redemptive service to mankind, a service that will never cease until humanity as a whole stands spiritually free.

When the Lord Christ ascends on his holy day, inner realms take on the appearance of a molten mass of shining gold. In the Holy Grail legend the Knights are told that on Good Friday a dove descends from heaven to replenish the water of life in the sacred Cup, and that they will be able to draw spiritual nourishment therefrom throughout the following year. So it is that the Risen Lord pours out His love and very Spirit to nourish every living thing upon the earth plane. Were it not for this annual replenishment wheat would not produce grain nor would vines bear fruit. In the light of this fact it can be seen that the Lord Christ uttered a profound and literal truth when he said to His Disciples at the Last Supper, "This (bread) is my body which is given for you: . . . This cup is the new testament in my blood, which is shed for you."

In partaking of the sacred Rite of the Eucharist on Good Friday one is partaking of the spiritual body and blood of the Blessed Lord, for the rite channels potent spiritual energies. After having partaken, an aspirant should endeavor to awaken more fully the processes of transmutation within himself. He should strive to put off the old and put on the new, his ideal being to submerge the terrestrial in the celestial man. From this point on he must seek to demonstrate that, literally, he is made in the image and likeness of God.

### June — July — August

One of the most beautiful feasts of the year is that of the Ascension, occurring about the time the Sun passes from Taurus (May) into Gemini (June). It is then that phalanx after phalanx of celestial Beings kneel in adoration in the Christ's exalted presence, and the very stars unite in a symphony proclaiming His majesty and glory. During this holy feast His radiation permeates the earth with an effulgence past all describing, making bright both the physical and the spiritual realms. As nature is in perfect accord with the up-winging Christ currents during the forty days between the Resurrection and the Ascension, the period is of such spiritual significance that it is an auspicious time for a disciple to awaken within himself the powers of clairvoyance, clairaudience and other gifts of the spirit belonging to true discipleship.

The octave Sunday of the Ascension commemorates the Feast of Pentecost, which synthesizes experiences of early disciples who lived in close communion with the Lord Christ during the period already mentioned. On the Day of Pentecost they stepped forth Christed men and women, adequately equipped for the work of establishing His kingdom on earth. The holy day commemorating this event is, in deed and in truth, the year's Whitsun, the white Sunday of the soul; and it marks the highest attainment possible upon this planet.

In the esoteric Church the octave Sunday of Pentecost commemorates the threefold activity of Father, Son and Holy Ghost. It is known as Trinity Sunday and marks the end of spiritual feasts for the year. Other feasts are not observed until the beginning of Advent Season. Although the esoteric meaning of Trinity Sunday has been largely forgotten, so important is it still regarded by the Church that all Sundays from Trinity to Advent are counted as the first, second, third Sunday, and so on, "after Trinity."

Esoteric Christians, however, understand something of the significance of the Trinity observance. They know that Trinity Sunday symbolizes, as it were, the supreme work of the Lord Christ in the cycle of the year. It is during the three midsummer months—June, July and August—that the Christ works in unison with the threefold Godhead and with the three Hierarchies of Gemini (Seraphim), Cancer (Cherubim) and Leo (Lords of Love) in replenishing, energizing and spiritualizing the earth and everything upon it.

When the Sun enters Gemini in the month of June the Lord Christ passes into the third heaven which, in Rosicrucian terminology, is the World of Abstract Thought. This is the highest sphere in the reincarnational cycle attained by humanity at its present stage of development. The first heaven is the World of Color; the second in the World of Tone; the third in the World of Abstract Ideas. The last is a world of pure white light where an illumined soul learns to listen to the Voice of the Silence.

During the month of June the Christ becomes a channel for radiations sent forth by the Seraphim, the Hierarchy of Gemini. He contacts them by means of the Holy Spirit, the third aspect of the Trinity. One of the keynotes of Gemini is *activity;* it is also a keynote of the Holy Spirit. By means of this activity the Seraphim step down the mysteries of Holy Spirit to Gemini's opposite sign, Sagittarius, the Lords of Mind. Here they await man's development and illumination to the point where he is able to understand

and apply the tremendous power of Holy Spirit in his daily life. As
yet humanity in general is able to grasp but faintly the mysteries
connected with the principle and powers of this third aspect of the
Trinity.

During the season that the Sun is transiting the sign Gemini a
disciple will do well to spend as much time as possible in meditation upon the principle of polarity, for it is the most opportune
month of the year for receiving esoteric revelation on this profound
subject. If available, the *Zohar—the Book of Light,* as it was
formerly known—is recommended for study in this connection.

As the Sun enters Cancer in the month of July, the Lord
Christ ascends to His own home world, the World of Life Spirit.
This is the realm where unity and harmony reign supreme; also,
the sphere of consciousness contacted by the disciples on the Day
of Pentecost. It will be the attainment of advanced humanity at the
end of the present Earth Period. It is here that through the operation of the Cosmic Christ, the Son or Word principle and the
second aspect of the Trinity, our Blessed Lord contacts the Hierarchy of Cancer, the Cherubim. These celestial Beings are guardians
of all holy places of heaven and earth, and they hold the great
mystery of life itself. Under the guidance of the Lord Christ this
sacred mystery is stepped down from Cancer to its opposite sign,
Capricorn and given in charge to the Archangels. For this reason
World Saviours who come to earth proclaiming the mystery of the
Holy Birth are born under the sign Capricorn. The observance
known ecclesiastically as the Feast of St. John, he who was the
forerunner of the Christ, occurs during the Summer Solstice season.

In July the soul of earth is steeped in sheer ecstasy. Heaven
bends low while earth is lifted up. In the divine interchange of
spiritual forces the Mystic Marriage between heaven and earth is
consummated. For a four-day interval all desire currents are stilled
so the spiritual forces can reign supreme, and the earth is filled
with the pure white light of spirit. Every disciple who learns how
to place himself in attunement with this mighty inflow will receive
an undreamed-of accession of spiritual awareness. If the disciple
spends much time in meditation during this season he will also

discover a depth of new and profound meaning on the fundamental formula of creation as given by St. John:

> *In the beginning was the Word, and the Word was*
> *with God, and the Word was God.*
> *The same was in the beginning with God.*
> *All things were made by him; and without him was*
> *not any thing made that was made.*
> *                                        —John 1:1-3*

As the Sun reaches the highest point in its northernmost ascension, the Christ likewise ascends into the spiritual realm described biblically as the throne of the Father. This is known in Rosicrucian terminology as the World of Divine Spirit, the abode of the God of this solar system. God is Love and God is Light. *Love* and *Light* are keynotes of the Hierarchy of Leo, the Lords of Flame (Love). Under the supervision of the Lords of Flame, and united with the powers of the Father, the first aspect of the Trinity, the Lord Christ, works with the supreme power of love, the stabilizing force of the earth. Here He becomes the channel for that power whereby He rotates the earth on its axis and revolves it in its orbit around the Sun. This love power is stepped down by the Hierarchy of Leo to its opposite sign, Aquarius; hence, it will be the power animating the new Aquarian Age.

In this season a disciple should endeavor to make love the dominant motivating force of his life. He should aspire to embellish his every word, thought and deed with its magic. The thirteenth chapter of II Corinthians, one of the soul's greatest love songs, is the perfect mantram for both meditation and emulation during the period that the Sun is transiting the royal sign Leo.

### September

In September the Blessed Lord turns from the glory of the highest heavens and begins His descent toward physical realms. Throughout this month the tender, yearning beauty of nature is like that of no other reason, for the Christ is brooding over the earth with the same gentle sorrow He felt as He wept over Jerusalem long ago. His tears were shed because He knew the long ages of pain and suffering through which humanity must pass, in having chosen darkness rather than light. His great heart grieved over the dark clouds that would encompass Jerusalem, the very heart of the planet to which He had dedicated Himself in service and upon which He was pouring out His great love.

September is another month of preparation for a disciple. One of the keywords of Virgo is *sacrifice*. An earnest disciple, preparing himself by means of sacrifice and self-renunciation to take part in the coming winter feasts, meditates often upon the spiritual keynote of Virgo: "If any man desire to be first, the same shall be last of all, and the servant of all." Mark 9:35.

With the Sun entering Libra, and the forces of October permeating the earth, comes the Feast of the Autumn Equinox. On the road to Damascus St. Paul was privileged to view, in the Memory of Nature, this Christ Cycle. As he came to understand the full import of this annual sacrifice of the Sun Spirit, he was transformed from an arch-persecutor of the Christ into one of His most illustrious messengers. In the light of this understanding of Christ's mission to earth, Paul made his supreme dedication in the words "For I determined not to know anything among you, save Jesus Christ, and him crucified." These words should become the very crux of a disciple's dedication as he meditates ever more deeply upon the annual sacrifice of the Blessed Lord.

An aspirant upon the Path of Attainment is sometimes lifted to the mountain top of exaltation that he may be renewed in strength for serving in the valleys below. One who faithfully follows this annual Christ Cycle each year learns to attune himself with the high glory of the three midsummer Feasts of the Holy Trinity, from which he is led to make a deeper dedication and acquires greater spiritual force wherewith to fulfill his tasks and responsibilities during the winter months that lie ahead. As he progresses spiritually in all that this period of preparation makes available, he will become conscious of a downpouring of blessings emanating from the Cosmic Madonna, the highest Initiate of the Hierarchy of Virgo, the Lords of Wisdom. During the course of the preparatory month a disciple so faithful will gain clearer insight into the significance of the beautiful prayer of St. Francis of Assisi, and this will make him more useful as a channel for the descending Christ force in the months to come:

> *Divine Master, grant that I may seek not so much to be consoled as to console, to be understood as to understand, to be loved as to love. For it is by giving that we receive, by forgiving that we are pardoned, and by dying to self that we are born into eternal life.*

As one considers the cycle of the year in the light of the Lord Christ and His mission, he realizes that each month is a blessed sanctuary for him. Then, if month by month he endeavors to find the deep meanings of the Christ's life and work, the aspirant enters into such complete at-one-ment with his Lord that he can sing with Solomon, the illumined seer of the Old Testament, "My beloved is mine, and I am his." Eventually his dedication nears completion in that the Christ becomes so much a part of his personal life that his every thought, word and deed is a reflection of Him. Finally, he will reach a glorious consummation in that oneness with the Lord which St. Paul, seer of the New Testament, voiced in his exultant song, "In him we live, move, and have our being."

# INDEX

# D